A Manual of Hadith

by

Maulana Muhammad Ali

ISBN: 978-1-63923-039-6

A Manual of Hadith

All Rights reserved. No part of this book may be reproduced without written permission from the publishers, except by a reviewer who may quote brief passages in a review to be printed in a newspaper or magazine.

Printed June, 2014

Published and Distributed By:

Lushena Books, Inc
607 Country Club Drive,
Unit E
Bensenville, IL 60106

www.lushenabks.com

ISBN : 978-1-63923-039-6

Printed in the United States of America

A Manual of Hadith

By

Maulana Muhammad Ali

PUBLISHER'S PREFACE

About the Book

"Hadith are oral traditions relating to the words and deeds of the Islamic prophet Muhammad. Hadith collections are regarded as important tools for determining the Sunnah, or Muslim way of life, by all traditional schools of jurisprudence. The Arabic plural is ahī£adith. In English academic usage hadith is often both singular and plural."

(Quote from wikipedia.org)

About the Author

Maulana Muhammad Ali (1874 - 1951)

"Maulana Muhammad Ali (1874-1951) Amir (1914-1951) Muhammad Ali was born in 1874 in Punjab, India.

Muhammad Ali obtained an (M.A.) English and (Ll. B.) Law in 1899. He joined the Ahmadiyya Movement in 1897 and devoted his life to the service of this movement in 1900. Although he considered his movement to be part of Islam, others considered it outside the fold of Islam.

In 1902 Maulana Muhammad Ali became the editor of the Review of Religions, one of the first Islamic journals in English. When Mirza Ghulam Ahmad established the Sadr Anjuman Ahmadiyya (a body to govern the Ahmadiyya Movement) in 1905, he appointed Maulana Muhammad Ali as the Secretary of its executive council. (The successor to this body was Ahmadiyya Anjuman Ishaat-i-Islam of Lahore.) At the time of Mirza Ghulam Ahmad's death in 1908, he was succeeded by Maulana Hakeem Noor-ud-Din, Khalifatul Masih I., who became Head of the Ahmadiyya Movement.

In March 1914, when Maulana Hakeem Noor-ud-Din died, there was a split in the movement, which led to a section of Sadr Anjuman Ahmadiyya including Maulana Muhammad Ali and other senior members of the Ahmadiyya Movement relocating from Qadian to Lahore. They became known as Ahmadiyya Anjuman Ishaat-i-Islam (Ahmadiyya Association for the Propagation of Islam) or in short as the 'Lahori Party'.

Maulana Muhammad Ali led this movement after its foundation in 1914, organising its world-wide missionary activities, and produced a vast amount of literature in English and Urdu. He translated the Qur'an with a commentary in both English and Urdu. His writings in English include: The Religion of Islam, Muhammad The Prophet, A Manual of Hadith, The New World Order and Living Thoughts of the Prophet Muhammad. He died in 1951.

He was succeeded by Maulana Sadr-ud-Din."

(Quote from wikipedia.org)

CONTENTS

PUBLISHER'S PREFACE ....
PREFACE ....
ABBREVIATIONS ....
HOW DIVINE REVELATION CAME TO THE HOLY PROPHET ....
ĪMĀN (FAITH) AND ISLĀM (SUBMISSION) ....
KNOWLEDGE ....
PURIFICATION ....
THE MOSQUE ....
ADHĀN AND IQĀMAH ....
JAMĀ'AH OR CONGREGATION ....
THE IMĀM ....
INSTITUTION OF PRAYER ....
PRAYER-SERVICE ....
FRIDAY SERVICE ....
'ĪD SERVICE ....
SUPEREROGATORY PRAYERS (TAHAJJUD, WITR AND TARĀWĪH) .....
MISCELLANEOUS PRAYERS (ISTIKHĀRAH. SALĀT AL-KUSŪF, ISTISQĀ') ......
BURIAL SERVICE ....
CHARITY AND ZAKĀT ....
FASTING ....
PILGRIMAGE (HAJJ AND 'UMRAH) ....
JIHĀD ....
MARRIAGE ....
DIVORCE ....
BUYING AND SELLING (BUYŪ') ....
CULTIVATION OF LAND (AL-HARTH WA-L-MUZĀRA'AH) ....
MATTERS RELATING TO SERVICE (IJĀRĀT) ....
DEBTS AND MORTGAGE ....
GIFTS (HIBAH AND WAQF) ....
WILLS AND INHERITANCE ....
FOODS AND DRINKS ....
TOILET ....
ETHICS (ADAB) ....
THE STATE (AL-IMĀRAH) ....
ENDNOTES ....

PREFACE

IT is now about forty-five years since, having finished my studies in Arts and Law, I was enlisted, at about the age of 25, as a soldier for the literary service of Islām, by the great Muslim reformer of this age, Hadzrat Mirzā Ghulām Ahmad of Qādiān, the Founder of the Ahmadiyyah Movement. Thank God that during this period He has granted me to contribute to Islamic religious literature more than six thousand pages in English and ten thousand pages in Urdu, in spite of other multifarious duties, first as Secretary of the Sadr Anjuman Ahmadiyyah at Qādiān, and then as President of the Ahmadiyyah Anjuman Ishā'at Islām, Lahore. I am thankful to God again that He has vouchsafed me at this advanced age to do yet another service to the literary cause of Islām.

The present work was undertaken to fulfil, primarily, the need of English converts to Islām, but it is really a work the need of which is felt throughout the English-speaking Muslim world. It is a faithful picture of the culture of Islām at its source, free from foreign influence and independent of later growth. It shows what the Holy Prophet Muhammad, peace and blessings of Allāh be on him, said and did, and what lives his companions led. This is technically known as the Sunnah (lit., a manner of acting or a mode of life) of the Holy Prophet, and is popularly known as Hadīth (lit., a saying), being a record of what he said, did or approved.

Hadīth literature is vast, there being several collections, the most important of which are known as the Sīhāh Sittah or the Six Reliable Works. Among these the Bukhārī, (more fully, the Jāmi' of Muhammad Ismā'īl al-Bukhārī), undoubtedly holds the first place. It is not only the first comprehensive collection of Hadīth but also the most authentic one. As a recent European writer rightly observes, Bukhārī undertook a research into the then prevalent Hadīth "with all the painstaking accuracy of a modern writer." In addition to this in his faqāhah or acumen, Bukhārī surpasses all other collectors of Hadīth.

A translation of the Sahīh Bukhārī was undertaken about eight years ago by Mr. Muhammad Asad, an Austrian convert to Islām; but at first, owing perhaps to the lack of means as compared with the difficulties of the undertaking and, later, to his internment owing to the war, only a fractional part of the work has been published. Even if completed, the work, at a price of about Rs. 120, could decorate only the shelves of big libraries and would not be accessible to the man in the street. But really the Bukhārī is every Muslim's need, and it is this need that I have tried to fulfil by publishing the present work.

In A Manual of Hadīth I have tried to give a compendium of the Sahīh Bukhārī, so far as subjects relating to the practical side of a Muslim's life are concerned. I have not touched the historical or prophetical portions of this great work, as I considered this beyond the scope of a handy treatise. In the arrangement of chapters too, I have mainly followed Bukhārī. But as my object was to make this short treatise complete so far as the requirements of an ordinary Muslim are concerned, I have freely drawn upon other collections of Hadīth, particularly that well-known work called the Mishkāt, rendered into English by Matthews about the year 1870.

I have been compelled, owing to the shortage of paper due to war conditions, to omit many of the details which I originally intended to include in this work. As a matter of fact, I had to cut about a third of the manuscript when I found that sufficient paper could not be had in the market, and the work has suffered on that account. In its present form it contains 690 hadīth, out of which 513 or about three fourths have been taken from the Bukhārī.

I may further draw the reader's attention to two special features of this work. In the first place, every chapter of this work commences with verses of the Holy Qur'ān dealing with the particular subject of that chapter. In this again I have followed Bukhārī, who heads the more important of his chapters with a text from the Holy Qur'ān, and thus shows that Hadīth is only an explanation of the Holy Qur'ān and a secondary source of the teachings of Islām. In fact, a manual of the Holy Qur'ān is an even greater need than this book, and I have long cherished the idea of supplying this desideratum, though I do not know if I shall be spared for its fulfilment.

The second feature of this book, which is quite a novelty . so far as Hadīth literature is concerned, is a brief head-note, following the quotations from the Holy Qur'ān, in which is given a brief summary of the teachings of the Holy Qur'ān and Hadīth on that subject p. vi This head-note will be found useful as it contains a summary of every hadīth given in the chapter, and thus enables the reader to lay his finger on the exact point which is of particular interest to him. By referring to this head-note, he will be able to find the Holy Prophet's guidance on a particular point without going through the whole chapter. I have thus tried my best to facilitate the task of the reader, who in these days of preoccupation with subjects of material interest cannot devote much time to what pertains to his higher moral interests.

As an introduction to this work, I would recommend to the reader to go through the chapter on "Sunnah or Hadīth", in my book The Religion of Islām.

In conclusion, I must give expression to my thanks to Mr. F. W. Bustin, Editor of the The Civil & Military Gazette, Lahore, for having gone through the manuscript, and to Malak Sher Muhammad Khan, B.A. for having gone through a part of the proofs.

MUHAMMAD 'ALI

SECOND EDITION

The second edition of the Manual of Hadīth is being brought out without any material change.

ABBREVIATIONS

ALL references given without an indication of the name are to the Holy Qur'ān, the first figure representing the number of the chapter and the second the number of the verse.

Words uttered by the Holy Prophet are throughout given within inverted commas.

In the references to Hadīth collections, the first number represents the number of the book and the second the number of the chapter, except in the case of the Musnad of Ahmad ibn Hanbal where the first figure stands for the volume and the second for the page. In all references to the Mishkāt, the name of the collection from which the Mishkāt has taken the particular hadīth is also indicated.

AD	stands for	Abū Dāwūd
Ah	"	Musnad of Ahmad
B	"	Bukhārī
DQ	"	Dāra Qutnī
Fr	"	al-Farā id al-Durriyyah
H	"	A Manual of Hadīth
h	"	hadīth
IM	"	Ibn Mājah
LL	"	Lane's Arabic-English Lexicon
M	"	Muslim
Msh	"	Mishkāt
Mt	"	Muwatta'
N	"	Nihāyah

HOW DIVINE REVELATION CAME TO THE HOLY PROPHET

1. "And it is not for any mortal that Allāh should speak to him except by inspiration or from behind a veil or by sending a messenger and revealing by His permission what He pleases" (42:51).

2. "And surely this is a revelation from the Lord of the worlds--the Faithful Spirit has come down with it upon thy heart that thou mayest be of the warners--in plain Arabic language" (26:192-195).

3. "And thus have We revealed to thee an Arabic Qur'ān" (42:7).

4. "The Holy Spirit has brought it down from thy Lord with truth" (16:102).

5. "Whoever is the enemy of Gabriel, surely he revealed it to thy heart by Allāh's command" (2:97).

6. "We have revealed it, revealing portion by portion" (17:106).

Revelation according to the Holy Qur'ān is a universal fact. It speaks of revelation to inanimate objects--heaven and earth (41:11, 12; 99:5)--and of revelation to lower animals (16:68, 69). Revelation to man is undoubtedly of a different nature from these revelations, and it is with this that we are at present concerned. In the first verse quoted above it is stated that Allāh speaks to man--i.e.. revelation to man is granted--in three ways: (1) by infusing an idea into the mind--the word wahy used here carries its original significance of a sudden suggestion; (2) from behind a veil, which includes ru'yā (dream), its higher form kashf (vision) and the still higher form ilhām, when voices are heard or uttered in a state of trance; (3) when a messenger, the angel Gabriel, is sent with the Divine message in clear words to the recipient of the revelation. The third is the highest form of revelation: the Divine message is sent not in the form of a n idea as in the first case or in the form of a vision as in the second but in words through the angel; and it is peculiar to the prophets.[1] The Holy Qur'ān was revealed to the Prophet in words in the Arabic language (vv. 2, 3) through Gabriel, who is also called

Ns	"	Nasā'ī
R	"	Mufradāt of Rāghib
Tr	"	Tirmidhī
v	"	verse (of the Holy Qur'ān)

the Faithful Spirit and the Holy Spirit (vv. 2. 4, 5) the angel descending upon the heart of the Prophet (vv. 2, 5). The last verse shows that the Holy Qur'ān was revealed in portions.

The hadīth narrated in this chapter bear out what has been so clearly established in the Holy Qur'ān. We are told that before the higher revelation, the Prophet received revelation in the form of dreams; that the Prophet's first experience of higher revelation was marked by the appearance of the Angel, who communicated to him the first Divine message in words, contained in the first five verses of ch. 96, and that the Prophet related his existence to Waraqah who believed in him, saying that it was the angel Gabriel who brought the Divine message to Moses (h. 2). The prophet's second experience of the higher revelation was similar to the first (h. 3). It is further shown that the higher revelation of the Holy Qur'ān came in words through Gabriel (hh. 4, 5). He felt a great strain when this revelation came to him: he perspired even on cold days and grew heavier and a change came over him. (hh. 5-8). It appears that to receive this spiritual experience he was translated to another sphere, and his detachment from the material environment was so real that it brought about a physical change as well.

1. [2]'Umar ibn al-Khattāb said, I heard the Messenger of Allāh, peace and blessings of Allāh be on him, say:

"Actions shall be judged only by intention[3], and a man shall have wha he intends; so whoever flies from his home[4] for the sake of Allāh and His Messenger, his flight shall be accounted for the sake of Allāh and His Messenger, and whoever flies from his home for the sake of worldly gain which he aims to attain or a woman whom he wants to marry, his flight shall be accounted for that for which he flies."

(B. 83:23; 1:1).

2. 'Ā'ishah said: The first revelation that was granted to the Messenger of Allāh, peace and blessings of Allāh be on him, was the true dream in a state of sleep,[5] so that he never dreamed a dream but the truth of it shone forth like the dawn of the morning. Then solitude became dear to him and he used to seclude himself in the cave of Hirā',[6] and therein he devoted himself to Divine worship for several nights before he came back to his family and took provisions for this (retirement); then he would return to

Khadījah[7] and take (more) provisions for a similar (period), until the Truth[8] came to him while he was in the cave of Hirā'; so the ange (Gabriel) came to him and said, Read. He (the Prophet) said, "I said I am not one who can read." And he continued: "Then he (the angel) took hold of me and he pressed me so hard that I could not bear it any more, and then he let me go and said, Read. I said, I am not one who can read. Then he took hold of me and pressed me a second time so hard that I could not bear it any more, then he let me go again and said, Read. I said, "I am not one who can read." (The Prophet) continued: "Then he took hold of me and pressed me hard for a third time, then he let me go and said, 'Read in the name of thy Lord Wh created--He created man from a clot--Read and thy Lord is most Honourable.'"[9] The Messenger of Allāh, peace and blessings of Allāh be on him, returned with this (message) while his heart trembled and he came to Khadījah, daughter of Khuwailid, and said, "Wrap me up, wrap me up," and she wrapped him up until the awe left him.[10] Then he said to Khadījah, while he related to her what had happened: "I fear for myself."[11] Khadījah said, Nay, By Allāh, Allāh will never bring thee to disgrace, for thou unitest the ties of relationship and bearest the burden of the weak and earnest for the destitute an honourest the guest and helpest in real distress.

Then Khadījah went with him until she brought him to Waraqah ibn Naufal ibn Asad ibn 'Abd al-'Uzzā, Khadījah's uncle's son, and he was a man who had become a Christian in the time of Ignorance,[12] and he used to write the Hebrew script, and he wrote from the Gospel in Hebrew what it pleased Allāh that he should write, and he was a very old man who had turned blind. Khadījah said to him, O uncle's son Listen to thy brother's son. Waraqah said to him, My brother's son! What hast thou seen? So the Messenger of Allāh, peace and blessings of Allāh be on him, related to him what he had seen. Waraqah said to him, This is the angel Gabriel whom Allāh sent to Moses;[13] would that I were a young man at this time-would that I were alive when thy people would expel thee! The Messenger of Allāh, peace and blessings of Allāh be on him, said, Would they expel me? He said, Yes; never has a man appeared with the like of that which thou hast brought but he has been held in enmity; and if thy time finds me (alive) I shall help thee with the fullest help. After tha not much time had passed that Waraqah died, and the revelation broke off temporarily.[14]

(B. 1:1.)

3. Jābir said, speaking of the temporary break in the revelation, (The Holy Prophet) said in his narrative:

"Whilst I was walking along, I heard a voice from heaven and I raised up my eyes, and lo! the Angel that had appeared to me in Hirā' was sitting on a throne between heaven and earth and I was struck with awe on account of him and returned (home) and said, Wrap me up, wrap me up.

Then Allāh revealed: 'O thou who art clothed! Arise and warn, And thy Lord do magnify, And thy garments do purify, And uncleanness do shun'."[15]

Then revelation became brisk and came in succession.[16]

(B. 1:1.)

4. Ibn 'Abbās ... said,

The Messenger of Allāh, peace and blessings of Allāh be on him, used to exert himself hard in receiving Divine revelation and would on this account move his lips. ... so Allāh revealed:

"Move not thy tongue with it to make haste with it. Surely on Us devolves the collecting of it and the reciting of it." (75:16, 17.)

.... So after this when Gabriel came to him the Messenger of Allāh, peace and blessings of Allāh be on him, would listen attentively, and when Gabriel departed, the Prophet, peace and blessings of Allāh be on him, recited as he (Gabriel) recited it.[17]

(B. 1:1.)

5. 'Ā'ishah reported that Hārith ibn Hishām asked the Messenger of Allāh, peace and blessings of Allāh be on him, O Messenger of Allāh! How does revelation come to thee? The Messenger of Allāh, peace and blessings of Allāh be on him, said:

"Sometimes it comes to me like the ringing of a bell and that is the hardest on me, then he departs from me and I retain in memory from him what he says; and sometimes the Angel comes to me in the likeness of a man and speaks to me and I retain in memory what he says."[18] Ā'ishah said, And I saw him when revelation came down upon him on a severely cold day, then it departed from him and his forehead dripped with sweat.[19]

(B. 1:1.)

6. Zaid ibn Thābit said, Allāh sent down revelation on His Messenger, peace and blessings of Allāh be on him, and his thigh was upon my thigh and it began to make its weight felt to me so much so that I feared that my thigh might be crushed.

(B. 8:12)

7. Safwān ibn Ya'lā reported tha Ya'lā said to 'Umar, Show me the Prophet, peace and blessings of Allāh be on him, when revelation is sent down to him. So when the Prophet, peace and blessings of Allāh be on him, was in Ji'rānah[20] and with him a number of his companions. . . . revelation came to him. Thereupon 'Umar made a sign to Ya'lā; so Ya'lā came and over the Messenger of Allāh, peace and blessings of Allāh be on him, was a garment with which he was covered and he entered his head under the garment), when (he saw that) the face of the Messenger of Allāh, peace and blessings of Allāh be on him, was red and he was snoring;[21] then that condition departed from him.(B. 25:17.)

8. 'Ubādah ibn al-Sāmit said, The Prophet, peace and blessings of Allāh be on him, felt, when the revelation was sent down upo him, like one in grief and a change came over his face.

And according to one report:

He hung down his head, and his companions also hung down their heads,[22] and when that state was over, he raised his head.

(M-Msh. 27:5.)

ĪMĀN (FAITH) AND ISLĀM (SUBMISSION)

1. "The Messenger has faith in what has been revealed to him from his Lord and so have the believers; they all believe in Allāh and His angels and His books and His messengers: we make no difference between any of His messengers" (2:285).

2. "And those who believe in that which has been revealed to thee and that which was revealed before thee and of the Hereafter they are sure" (2:4).

3. "O you who believe! Believe in Allāh and His Messenger and the Book which He has revealed to His Messenger" (4:136).

4. "The dwellers of the desert say, We believe, Say, You believe not; rather say, We submit; and faith has not yet entered into your hearts" (49:14).

5. "The faithful are only those who believe in Allāh and His Messenger, then they doubt not and struggle hard with their wealth and their lives in the way of Allāh" (49:15).

6. "And to Him submits whoever is in the heavens and the earth" (3:82).

7. "Whoever submits himself entirely to Allāh while doing good (to others)--he has his reward from his Lord" (2:112).

8. "And remember the favour of Allāh to you when you were enemies. Then He united your hearts, so by His favour you became brethren" (3:102).

9. "And say not to any one who offers you salutation, Thou art not a believer" (4:94).

The basis of all higher religions is a faith in Divine revelation, because God is known to man, and personal contact with Him is established, only through revelation. Man can make all discoveries in the sphere of the finite but he cannot discover the Infinite God; it is God Who reveals Himself to man, and it is therefore only through Divine revelation that man can know God. Bukhārī, who was gifted with special insight into matters religious, begins his Jāmi' with the book of Revelation and follows it with the book of Faith. But the conception of faith in Islām is widened in two ways. In the first place, faith here stands not for faith in revelation to one person or one generation but a faith in revelation to all people in all ages (v. 1). It is a faith in the books of Allāh, and in the messengers of Allāh, in all the books and messengers that preceded the Holy Prophet (v. 2). And secondly, faith here combines both belief and actions; in v. 3, believers are asked to believe, which means that they should bring their faith to its full development by good deeds and sacrifices; v. 4 shows that the first step is that of mere acceptance of Islām and the second is that when faith has taken root in-- entered--the heart. When this stage is reached, a man becomes capable of the highest deeds of sacrifice (v. 5). Islām or submission to Divine laws is the rule of nature (v. 6) and man attains perfection only when he submits himself to the revealed laws of God (v. 7). Islām, however, does not aim only at individual perfection it also establishes a vast brotherhood of humanity, membership or which cannot be denied even to the man who simply offers the Islamic salutation (vv. 8, 9).

Hadīth related in this chapter begin with the basic fact that religion does not consist in hard religious exercise, but in living a good life in which due regard is paid to the rights of others (hh. 1-3). Good actions, it is further stated, spring from a good heart and hence the need of faith which rules the heart (h. 4). Īmān (faith) and Islām, (submission to Divine law) are often used but Īmān strictly indicates the acceptance of a principle which is the basis of action--the theoretical side--, and Islām the action itself--the practical side of man's life (hh. 5. 6). But theory and practice here go hand in hand, and the actions which spring from faith are also called faith. One's faith is therefore greater or less as one's actions are more or less beneficial to humanity. Faith is spoken of as love: the man who has faith in Allāh does not spare the doing of good to the nearest passer-by, so broad is his love for humanity (b. 7); he loves the whole of humanity and most of all the Holy Prophet, because he is the greatest benefactor of humanity (h. 8); his love for his brother is not mere word of mouth, but he is guided by that love in his everyday relations with him (h. 9); he loves Allāh most of all and loves humanity for the sake of Allāh and thus his love for humanity is based on the purest of motives (h. 10).

The next three hadīth show what Islām is. It does not simply mean a certain declaration; the declaration of Divine Unity and prophethood of Muhammad brings a man into the fold of Islām, but to be a Muslim he must live the life of a Muslim, the life of a man who lives in perfect peace with others. The first condition of that life is that he shall not cause injury to any man, either with his tongue or with his hand (h. 11). Such injury, is said to be an act of transgression, even disbelief (hh. 12, 13), It is not permissible however, to go to the other extreme and call a Muslim a disbeliever or turn him out of the pale of Islām because he has committed an act of disbelief. So long as a man declares his faith in the Unity of Allāh and the prophethood of Muhammad, he is a Muslim (hh. 16. 17f). Nay, a man who offers prayers like Muslims with his face to the Qiblah has the covenant of Allāh and His Messenger that he shall be dealt with as a member of the Muslim brotherhood (b. 15). p. 18 And the Holy Qur'ān goes even further and accepts the Islamic salutation as sufficient proof that such a man is a Muslim, whatever his differences with others (v. 9). H. 18 gives another description of what Islām in practice is.

1. Abū Hurairah reported that The Prophet, peace and blessings of Allāh be on him, said:

"Religion is easy, and no one exerts himself too much in religion but it overpowers him; so act aright and keep to the mean and be of good cheer and ask for (Divine) help at morning and at evening and during a part of the night."[23]

(B. 2:29.)

2. Ā'ishah reported that The Prophet, peace and blessings of Allāh be on him, entered upon her and with her was a woman. He asked, "Who is this?

('Ā'ishah) said, She is such and such a one; and began to speak (highly) of her prayers. He said:

"Enough; only that is binding on you which you are able to do; by Allāh, Allāh does not get tired but you get tired, and the devotions dearest to Him are those in which the devotee perseveres.[24]

(B. 2:31.)

3. 'Abd Allāh ibn 'Amr reported,

The Messenger of Allāh, peace and blessings of Allāh be on him, said to me, "O 'Abd Allāh! Am I not told that thou fastest in the day time and standest up in devotion during the night?" I said, Yes, O Messenger of Allāh. He said:

"Do not do so; keep fast and break it and stand up in devotion (in the night) and have sleep, for thy body has a right over thee, and thine eye has a right over thee, and thy wife has a right over thee, and the person who pays thee a visit has a right over thee."[25]

(B. 30:55)

4. Nu'mān ibn Bashīr said,

I heard the Messenger of Allāh, peace and blessings of Allāh be on him, say:

What is lawful is manifest and what is unlawful is manifest and between these two are doubtful things which many people do not know. So whoever guards himself against the doubtful things, he keeps his religion and his honour unsullied, and whoever falls into doubtful things is like the herdsman who grazes his cattle on the borders of a reserve--he is likely to enter it. Know that every king has a reserve (and) know that the reserve of Allāh in His land is what He has forbidden. Know that in the body there is a bit of flesh; when it is sound the whole body is sound, and when it is corrupt the whole body is corrupt. Know, it is the heart."[26]

(B. 2:38.)

5. Abū Hurairah said,

The Prophet, peace and blessings of Allāh be on him, was one day sitting outside among the people when a man came to him and asked, What is faith (Īmān)? He said:

"Faith is that thou believe in Allāh and His angels and in meeting with Him and (in) His messengers and that thou believe in being raised to life (after death)."

He asked, What is Islām? (The Prophet) said:

"Islām is that thou shalt worship Allāh and not associate aught with Him and (that) thou keep up prayer and pay the zakāt as ordained and fast in Ramadzān."

He asked, What is ihsān (goodness)? (The Prophet) said:

"That thou worship Allāh as if thou seest Him; for if thou see Him not, surely He sees thee."[27]

(B. 2:36.)

6. Ibn 'Umar said, The Messenger of Allāh, peace and blessings of Allāh be on him, said:

"Islām is built on five (things), the bearing of witness that there is no god but Allāh and that Muhammad is the Messenger of Allāh and the keeping up of prayer and the payment of zakāt and the pilgrimage and fasting in Ramadzān."[28]

(B. 2:1.)

7. Abū Hurairah said, The Messenger of Allāh, peace and blessings of Allāh be on him, said:

"Īmān (Faith) has over seventy, or over sixty, branches; the most excellent of these is the saying, There is no god but Allāh, and the lowest of them is the removal from the way of that which is harmful and modesty (hayā') is a branch of faith."[29]

(M. 1:58.)

8. Anas said, The Messenger of Allāh, peace and blessings of Allāh be on him, said:

"None of you has faith unless I am dearer to him than his father and his son and all mankind."[30]

(B. 2:7.)

"Whoever dies while he knows that there is no god but Allāh enters paradise."[38]

(M-Msh. I.)

18. "Religion is faithfulness to Allāh and His Messenger and to the leaders of Muslims and Muslims in general."[39]

(B. 2:42.)

KNOWLEDGE

1. "Read in the name of thy Lord Who created; He created man from a clot. Read and thy Lord is most Honourable, Who taught to write with the pen. taught man what he knew not" (96:1-5).

2. "Allâh will exalt those of you who believe and those who are given knowledge to high degrees" (58:11).

3. "And say, O my Lord! increase me in knowledge" (20:114).

4. "And whoever is given knowledge is given indeed abundant wealth" (2:269).

While faith brings about the spiritual and moral development of man, knowledge brings about his intellectual development, and therefore stands next in importance to faith. In Bukhârî's arrangement therefore "knowledge follows faith." The first revelation that came to the Holy Prophet is admittedly the first quotation given above. These verses not only lay stress on both reading and writing but also speak of the Lord of Honour in this connection, showing that man can attain to honour only through knowledge. This is expressly stated in v. 2. The Holy Qur'ân even directs the Holy Prophet to seek more and more knowledge (v. 3). It is in fact full of praise for knowledge: the words ya'lamûn (they ponder), yatafakkarûn (they reflect), yatadhakkarûn (they meditate) and other similar expressions occur on almost every page of the Holy Qur'ân. V. 4 speaks of knowledge as great wealth. Such is also the import of the very first hadîth quoted in this chapter, which speaks of both wealth and knowledge as things which man desires naturally to seek and in which all men should try to emulate each other (h. 1). The Holy Prophet made it incumbent on those who came to him to seek knowledge to impart the same to others (hh. 2. 3), and desired even those who were considered to be in the lowest strata of society to be uplifted to the highest level through education (h. 4). Islâm, in fact, lays the basis of mass education, education of men as well as women, of children as well as adults. The Holy Prophet himself made arrangements for the education of women (h. 5). Writing was encouraged (hh. 5-9), and acquisition of knowledge was made the standard of excellence (h. 10). It is spoken of in the highest terms of praise (hh, 11-14), and this explains the unsatiable thirst for knowledge of the Muslims of earlier days. H. 15 makes it incumbent upon every Muslim, man or woman, old or young. that he should acquire knowledge, and thus introduces the principle of compulsory education. A warning is given that when a nation gives up the acquisition of knowledge, its downfall is sure (h. 16).

1. 'Abd Allâh ibn Mas'ûd said,

The Prophet, peace and blessings of Allâh be on him, said:

"There shall be no envy but (emulate) two[40]: the person whom Allâh has given wealth and the power to spend it in the service of Truth, and the person whom Allâh has granted knowledge[41] of things and he judges by it and teaches it (to others)."[42]

(B. 3:15.)

2. Mâlik ibn al-Huwairith said, The Prophet, peace and blessings of Allâh be on him, said to us:

"Go back to your people and teach them."[43]

(B. 3:25.)

3. Ibn 'Abbâs reported on the authority of the Prophet, peace and blessings of Allâh be on him:

"Let him who is present impart knowledge to him who is absent."

(B. 3:37.)

4. Abû Mûsâ said, The Messenger of Allâh, peace and blessings of Allâh be on him, said:

"There are three persons for whom there is a double reward: . . . the person who has a slave-girl, and he brings her up and trains her in the best manner and he educates her and gives her the best education, then sets her free and marries her, he has a double reward."[44]

(B. 3:31.)

5. Abû Sa'îd Khudrî said,

The women said to the Prophet, peace and blessings of Allâh be on him, The men have got an advantage over us in approaching thee therefore appoint for us a day from thyself; so he promised them a day in which he met them and he exhorted them and gave them commandments.[45]

(B. 3:35)

6. Abû Hurairah reported that The Khuzâ'ah murdered a man of the Banû Laith in the year of the conquest of Makkah, as a retaliation for the murder of one of them whom they had murdered. The Prophet, peace and blessings of Allâh be on him, was informed of this, so he mounted his riding camel and delivered an address . . . Arid there came a man from among the people of Yaman and said, Write it down for me, O Messenger of Allâh! So he said: "Write down for such and such a one."[46]

(B. 3:39.)

7. Abû Hurairah said, There was no one from among the companions of the Prophet, peace and blessings of Allâh be on him, who reported more hadîth from him than myself, but

'Abd Allâh ibn 'Amr used to write while I did not write.

(B. 3:39)

8. Zaid ibn Thâbit reported that,

The Prophet, peace and blessings of Allâh be on him, commanded him to learn the writing of the Jews (in Syriac[47]) so that I wrote for the Prophet, peace and blessings of Allâh be on him, his letters and read out to him their letters when they wrote to him.

(B. 93:40.)

9. Abû Hurairah reported,

A man from among the Ansâr said . . ., O Messenger of Allâh! I hear from thee a hadîth which pleases me very much but I cannot retain it in memory. The Messenger of Allâh, peace and blessings of Allâh be on him, said "Seek the help of thy right hand."[48]

And he made a sign with his hand for writing.

(Tr. 39:12.)

10. Abû Hurairah said, The Messenger of Allâh, peace and blessings of Allâh be on him, said:

People are mines, like mines of gold and silver; the more excellent of them in the days of Ignorance are the more excellent of them in Islâm when they attain knowledge."[49]

(M-Msh. 2:I.)

11. Abû Hurairah said, The Messenger of Allâh, peace and blessings of Allâh be on him, said:

"The word of wisdom is the lost property of the believer, so wherever he finds it he has a better right to it."[50]

(Tr. 39:19.)

12. Anas said,

The Messenger of Allâh, peace and blessings of Allâh be on him, said:

"He who goes forth in search of knowledge is in the way of Allâh till he returns."

(Tr. 39:2.)

13. The Prophet, peace and blessings of Allâh be on him, said:

Whomsoever Allâh intends to do good, He gives right understanding of religion." And

"Knowledge is maintained only through teaching."[51]

(B. 3:10.)

14. "The learned ones are the heirs of the prophets--they leave knowledge as their inheritance; he who inherits it inherits a great fortune."[52]

(B. 3:10.)

15. Anas said,

The Messenger of Allâh, peace and blessings of Allâh be on him, said:

"The seeking of knowledge is obligatory upon every Muslim."[53]

(Bhq-Msh. 2.)

16. Anas said, The Messenger of Allâh, peace and blessings of Allâh be on him, said "Of the signs of the Hour is that knowledge shall be taken away and ignorance shall reign supreme."[54]

(B. 3:21.)

PURIFICATION

1. "And thy Lord do magnify, And thy garments do purify, And uncleanness do shun" (74:3-5).

2. "Surely Allāh loves those who turn to Him again and again, and He loves those who purify themselves" (2:222).

3. "Attend to your adornment at every time of prayer." (7:31).

4. "O you who believe! When you rise up to prayers, wash your faces and your hands as far as the elbows and wipe our hands and (wash) your feet to the ankles; and if you are under an obligation to perform a total ablution, have a bath; and if you are sick or on a journey, or one of you come from the privy, or you have had contact with women, and you cannot find water, betake yourselves to pure earth and wipe your faces and your hands therewith; Allāh does not desire to put on you any difficulty but He wishes to purify you and that He may complete His favour to you, so that you may be thankful" (5:6).

Purification, though a necessary preliminary to prayer, is an independent subject and is dealt with as such in Hadīth collections. The first three quotations from the Holy Qur'ān given above require in general terms that the man who would turn to his Lord should be pure in body and garments. The Purification of the body is thus made a preliminary to prayer so that by external purification a man's attention may be directed to the purification of the soul which is aimed at in prayer. V. 4 gives the details of ablutions which are necessary before prayer. Purity of the body is thus required as a preliminary to the purity of mind, and the Muslim who is required to say prayers five times a day must needs keep himself and his clothes always clean.

It is true that an intelligent man should know for himself what cleanliness is, but religion aims at giving directions to men in all stages of civilization, in early states as well as in the more developed ones. Moreover. the masses among all people stand in need of minute details, and hence while the Holy Qur'ān simply gives the general direction to keep oneself in a state of cleanliness, Ḥadīth gives the necessary details. As a matter of fact Islām directs attention to many details of personal cleanliness of which even the more civilized people are ignorant.

I have divided the chapter into five sections. The first deals with natural evacuations. Purification is called half the faith (h. 1) and the key to prayer (hh. 2. 3), It must not be forgotten that purity of the body is a prelude to the purity of the soul (h. 4). Full regard must be paid to personal cleanliness as well as public hygiene (hh. 5-13). Spitting in public places is forbidden (hh. 16, 17).

The second section deals with tooth-brushing which occupies a very prominent place in the Muslim's cleanliness. It is spoken of as a means of purifying the mouth and seeking the pleasure of the Lord (h. 18), which is to show that God loves even bodily cleanliness. Great stress is laid upon its use (hh. 19, 20), and the minimum requirement is that the tooth-brush should be used after getting up from sleep (hh. 21, 22), A clean mouth is in fact the greatest help for the preservation of health. Its importance is further emphasized in h. 23, The third section gives the details of ablution (hh. 25 36) and shows when a fresh ablution becomes necessary (hh. 37-41). A prayer directing attention to purity of the spirit must be offered when the ablution has been performed (h. 43).

The fourth section deals with total ablution or bath, which is made compulsory once a week (hh. 44-46). Particular occasions on which bath must be taken are mentioned in hh. 47-50, A person under an obligation to have a bath on account of janābah and a menstruating woman are not impure (hh. 51, 52). Some details are given in hh. 53, 54, and taking a bath naked in an open place is strictly forbidden (1.1. 55).

The fifth section deals with tayammum or wiping the face and hands with pure dust when water is not available for ablution or bath, though it may be available for drinking or domestic purposes, or when the use of water is likely to be harmful (hh. 56-58). This act is as it were a reminder that purification before prayer is an essential thing.

SECTION I.--NATURAL EVACUATIONS

1. 'Abū Mālik said,

The Messenger of Allāh, peace and blessings of Allāh be on him,

"Purification is half the faith."[55]

(M-Msh. 3.)

2. Jābir said, The Messenger of Allāh, peace and blessings of Allāh be on him, said:

"The key to paradise is prayer and the key to prayer is purification."

(Ah-Msh. 1)

3. Ibn 'Umar said,

The Messenger of Allāh, peace and blessings of Allāh be on him, said:

"Prayer is not accepted without purification, nor (is) charity (accepted) out of what is acquired by unlawful means."[56]

(M-Msh. 3:l.)

4. Anas said,

When the Prophet, peace and blessings of Allāh be on him, went to privy, he used to say:

"O Allāh! I seek refug in Thee from impure deeds and evil habits."[57]

(B. 4:9.)

5. Anas reported,

When the Prophet, peace and blessings of Allāh be on him, went out for natural evacuation, I and a boy used to go and with us there used to be a bucket of water.[58]

(B. 4:15.)

6. 'Abd Allāh said,

The Prophet, peace and blessings of Allāh be on him, went to ease himself and he asked me to bring him three pebbles.[59]

(B. 4:21.)

7. 'Ā'ishah said,

The Messenger of Allāh, peace and blessings of Allāh be on him, said:

"When one of you goes to ease himself, let him take with him three pebbles with which to clean himself, for these will suffice him."

(AD-Msh 3:2.)

8. Jābir said,

When the Prophet, peace and blessings of Allāh be on him, wanted to ease himself he went (to a distant place) until no one could see him.[60]

(AD-Msh 3:2.)

9. Abū Mūsā reported,

The Prophet, peace and blessings of Allāh be on him, said:

When one of you wishes to pass urine, let him seek the proper place for urinating."[61]

(AD-Msh. 3:2.)

10. 'Ā'ishah said,

'The right hand of the Messenger of Allāh, peace and blessings of Allāh be on him, was for his ablution and his food, and his left hand for cleaning after easing himself and for removing noxious things.

(AD-Msh. 3:2.)

11. Mu'ādh said,

The Messenger of Allāh, peace and blessings of Allāh be on him, said:

"Abstain from three objects of curse, easing near springs of water and on roads and under (a tree where men sit for) shade."[62]

(AD-Msh. 3:2.)

12. Hudhaifah said,

I saw myself and the Prophet, peace and blessings of Allāh be on him, going together and he came to a heap of sweepings of a people behind a wall and he was standing as one of you stands, then he passed the urine.[63]

(B. 4:61.)

13. Abū Hurairah said,

When the Prophet, peace and blessings of Allāh be on him, went to the privy, I brought to him water in a small vessel or in a leather bag and he used water for cleaning, then rubbed his hand on the ground,[64] then I brought to him another vessel of water and he made ablution.

(AD-Msh. 3:2.)

14. 'Ā'ishah said,

When the Prophet, peace and blessings of Allāh be on him, came out of the privy, he used to say:

'I seek Thy protection."

(Tr-Msh. 3:2.)

15. Anas said,

When the Prophet, peace and blessings of Allāh be on him, came out of the privy, he used to say:

"Praise be to Allāh Who has removed from me noxiousness and given me health."

(IM-Msh. 3:2.)

16. Anas said,

The Prophet, peace and blessings of Allāh be on him, spat in a cloth of his.[65]

(B. 4:70.)

17. Anas reported that The Prophet, peace and blessings of Allāh be on him, saw phlegm on the front (wall of the mosque) and it was painful to him to such a degree that (signs of) it could be seen in his face...

Then he took hold of a corner of his sheet and spat in it then turned one part of it over the other and said:

"Rather let one do like this."[66]

(B. 8:31)

SECTION 2.--THE TOOTH-BRUSH

18. 'Ā'ishah said on the authority of the Prophet, peace and blessings of Allāh be on him,

"The tooth-brush purifies the mouth and is a means of seeking the pleasure of the Lord."[67]

(B. 30:27.)

19. Abū Hurairah said, on the authority of the Prophet, peace and blessings of Allāh be on him, "Were it not that I would place too heavy a burden on my community, I would have commanded them to use the tooth-brush at every ablution."

(B. 30:27.)

20. Anas said,

The Messenger of Allāh, peace and blessings of Allāh be on him, said:

'I have spoken to you about the tooth-brush too often."

(B. 11:8.)

21. Hudhaifah said,

When the Prophet, peace and blessings of Allāh be on him, got up during the night (for tahajjud), he used to clean his mouth with the tooth-brush.

(B. 4:73)

22. 'Ā'ishah said,

'Never did the Prophet, peace and blessings of Allāh be on him, wake up after sleeping at night or in the day, but he used the tooth-brush before he performed ablution."[68]

(AD-Msh. 3:1)

23. Shuraih ibn Hānī said,

asked 'Ā'ishah, What was the first thing the Messenger of Allāh, peace and blessings of Allāh be on him, did when he entered his house?

She said, Tooth-brushing.

(M-Msh. 3:3.)

SECTION 3.--ABLUTION OR WUDZŪ'

24. Sa'īd ibn Zaid said,

The Messenger of Allāh, peace and blessings of Allāh be on him, said:

"That man has not performed ablution who does not remember Allāh in doing it."⁶⁹

(Tr-Msh. 3:4.)

25. Yahyā al-Māzinī reported that

A man said to 'Abd Allāh ibn Zaid, Canst thou show me how the Messenger of Allāh, peace and blessings of Allāh be on him, performed ablution? 'Abd Allāh ibn Zaid said, Yes.

So he sent for water and poured it over his hands and washed his hands twice, then he rinsed his mouth and sniffed water into his nose thrice, then he washed his face thrice, then he washed his hands up to the elbow twice, then he wiped his head with both his hands so that he carried them from the front and brought them back he began with his forehead until he carried them to his neck, then he brought them back to the place from which he had started then he washed his two feet.

(B. 4:38.)

26. Ibn 'Abbās said,

The Prophet, peace and blessings of Allāh be on him, performed ablution (washing each part) once only.

(B. 4:22.)

27. 'Abd Allāh ibn Zaid reported that

The Prophet, peace and blessings of Allāh be on him, performed ablution (washing each part) twice.

(B. 4:21)

28. It is reported about 'Uthmān that

He performed ablution at Maqā'id, and said, May I not show you the ablution of the Messenger of Allāh, peace and blessings of Allāh be on him? Then he performed ablution (washing each part) thrice.[70]

(M-Msh. 3:44)

29. 'Ā'ishah said,

The Prophet, peace and blessings of Allāh be on him, was fond of beginning on the right side, in putting on his shoes and in combing his hair and in performing his ablution, (in fact) in all his actions.

(B. 4:31.)

30. Abn Hurairah said,

The Messenger of Allāh, peace and blessings of Allāh be on him, said:

When you put on clothes and when you perform ablution, begin with the right side."[71]

(AD-Msh. 3:4.)

31. Ibn 'Abbās reported that The Prophet, peace and blessings of Allāh be on him, wiped his head and also his two ears, the internal parts of them with his two forefingers and the back parts of them with his two thumbs.[72]

(Ns-Msh. 3:4.)

32. 'Amr ibn Umayyah said,

I saw the Prophet, peace and blessings of Allāh be on him, passing his hands over his turban and his boots.

(B. 4:48.)

33. Mughīrah said,

I was with the Prophet, peace and blessings of Allāh be on him, in a journey, and I bent down to take off his boots but he said, "Leave them alone, for I put them on in a state of cleanness;"[73] then he passed his hands over them both.

(B. 4:49.)

34. Mughīrah said,

The Prophet, peace and blessings of Allāh be on him, performed ablution and passed his hands over the socks and the shoes.

(A D-Msh. 3:9.)

35. Abū Bakrah reported on the authority of the Prophet, peace and blessings of Allāh be on him, that

He allowed one who is journeying three days and nights and one who is not on a journey one day and night to wipe his boots (instead of washing his feet) when he had put them on in a state of cleanness.

(DQ-Msh. 3:9.)

36. Abū Hurairah said,

The Messenger of Allāh, peace and blessings of Allāh be on him, said:

"Prayer is not accepted of a man who voids himself[74] until he performs ablution."

(B. 4:2.)

37. Anas said,

The Prophet, peace and blessings of Allāh be on him, used to perform ablution at every prayer. I (his disciple) said, How did you act? He said, Ablution sufficed one of us until he voided himself.

(B. 4:55.)

38. Anas said,

The companions of the Prophet, peace and blessings of Allāh be on him, used to wait for the night ('Ishā') prayer until their heads nodded (in drowsiness), then they said their prayers and did not perform ablution.

(AD-Msh. 3:l.)

39. Ibn 'Abbās said,

The Messenger of Allāh, peace and blessings of Allāh be on him, said:

"Ablution is necessary for him who sleeps reclining, for when he reclines his joints are relaxed."

(Tr-Msh. 3:l.)

40. Abu-l-Dardā' reported that

The Messenger of Allāh, peace and blessings of Allāh be on him, vomited, then performed ablution.

(Tr. 1:64.)

41. It is related about Ibn 'Umar that

He washed his feet after the water, with which he had washed (other parts), had dried up.[75]

(B. 5:10.)

42. Umar said,

'The Messenger of Allāh, peace and blessings of Allāh be on him, said:

Anyone who performs ablution and does it thoroughly, then says I bear witness that there is no god but Allāh, He is One. there is no associate with Him, and that Muhammad is His servant and His Messenger; O Allāh! make me of those who turn to Thee again and again and make me of

those who purify themselves'--the eight doors of paradise are opened to him; he enters it by whichever of them he pleases."

(Tr. 1:42.)

SECTION 4.--BATH

43. 'Abd Allāh ibn 'Umar reported that The Messenger of Allāh, peace and blessings of Allāh be on him, said:

"When one of you comes to the Friday gathering, he should take a bath."

(B. 11:2.)

44. 'Amr ibn Sulaim said, The Messenger of Allāh, peace and blessings of Allāh be on him, said:

"Taking a bath on Friday is incumbent on every one who has attained to puberty and he should use the tooth-brush and use scent if he can find it."

(B. 11:3.)

45. Abū Hurairah said, The Messenger of Allāh, peace and blessings of Allāh be on him, said

"It is incumbent upon every Muslim that he should take a bath (at least) once in every seven days and wash his head and his whole body."[76]

(B. & M.-Msh 3:10)

46. Abū Hurairah said,

The Messenger of Allāh, peace and blessings of Allāh be on him, said:

"The person who washes a dead body should take a bath."

(IM-Msh. 3:11.)

47. Qais ibn 'Āsim reported that

He was initiated into Islām, and the Prophet, peace and blessings of Allāh be on him, commanded him to take a bath with water and (leaves of) the lot tree.[77]

(Tr. Msh. 3:11.)

48. 'Ā'ishah reported that

The Prophet, peace and blessings of Allāh be on him, commanded the taking of a bath on four occasions: on account of janābah,[78] and on Friday, and in case of cupping, and after washing a dead body.

(AD-Msh. 3:11.)

49. 'Ā'ishah reported that

A woman asked the Prophet, peace and blessings of Allāh be on him, as to her bathing after menstruation; so he told (her) how to take a bath.[79]

(B. 6:13.)

50. (It is related) on the authority of Abū Hurairah that The Prophet. peace and blessings of Allāh be on him, met him on a certain road of Madīnah when he (Abu Hurairah) was junub. Considering myself unclean I left him, then I went and took a bath. Then he (Abu Hurairah) came, and (the Prophet) said, "Where wast thou, O Abu Hurairah?" He said, I was junub, so I did not like that I should sit with thee while I was in a state of impurity. He said:

"Allāh be glorified, the believer does not get impure."[80]

(B. 5:21)

51. Anas said,

When a woman among the Jews had her menses, they would not eat with her and would not be with her in the same room; so the companions of the Prophet, peace and blessings of Allāh be on him, asked the Prophet, peace and blessings of Allāh be on him, and Allāh revealed to him, "They ask thee about the menses." (2:222.) The Messenger of Allāh, peace and blessings of Allāh be on him, said:

"Do everything except the sexual intercourse."[81]

(M-Msh 3:12.)

52. Ibn 'Abbās said, Maimūnah said,

I placed water for the Prophet, peace and blessings of Allāh be on him, to bathe with, and he washed his hand twice or thrice, then he poured water on his left hand, then he washed his private parts, then he rubbed his hand on earth, then he rinsed his mouth and sniffed water into his nose and washed his face and his two hands (up to the elbow), then he poured water on his body, then he changed his place and washed his two feet.

(B. 5:5.)

53. 'Ā'ishah said,

The Prophet, peace and blessings of Allāh be on him, did not perform ablution after taking a bath.

(Tr.-Msh. 3:5.)

54. Ya'lā said, The Messenger of

Allāh, peace and blessings of Allāh be on him, saw a man bathing (naked) in an open place; so he ascended the pulpit and praised and glorified Allāh, then said:

"Surely Allāh is the Possessor of modesty, Concealer of faults--He loves modesty and concealing of that in which there is shame; so when one of you takes a bath, let him screen himself from being seen."[82]

(AD-Msh. 3:5.)

SECTION 5.--TAYAMMUM

55. Abu Dharr said,

The Messenger of Allāh, peace and blessings of Allāh be on him, said:

Pure earth serves the purpose of a Muslim's ablution, though he may not find water for ten years. When he finds water, he should wash with it his body, for that is better."[83]

(AD-Msh. 3:10.)

56. 'Ammār said, The Messenger of Allāh, peace and blessings of Allāh be on him, sent me on some business, and (while journeying) I became a junub and did not find water, so I rolled about on earth as an animal rolls, and I mentioned this to the Prophet, peace and blessings of Allāh be on him, He said, "It was sufficient for thee that thou shouldst have done thus;" and he struck his hand on earth once, then he shook off its dust and wiped with it the back of the (right) hand with the left or the back of the left with the (right) hand, then wiped his face with both (hands).[84] (B. 7:8.)

57. It is related that 'Amr ibn al-'Ās became a junub on a cold night, so he resorted to tayammum and recited the verse, "Do not kill yourselves, for Allāh is Merciful to you" (4: 29). This was mentioned to the Prophet, peace and blessings of Allāh be on him, he did not censure (him.) [85]

(B. 7:7.)

58. Jābir said, We went out on a journey, and a stone struck a man from among us and wounded his head, and he bad nocturnal pollution ... . (The Prophet) said:

"........It was sufficient for him to perform tayammum and to have a bandage on the wounded part, then to wipe it and wash the rest of his body."[86]

(AD-Msh. 3:10.)

THE MOSQUE

1. "Surely the first house appointed for men is the one at Bakkah blessed and a guidance for nations" (3:95).

2. "And from whatsoever place thou comest forth, turn thy face towards the Sacred Mosque; and wherever you are, turn your faces towards it" (2:150).

3. "And had there not been Allāh's repelling some people by others, certainly there would have been pulled down cloisters and churches and synagogues and mosques in which Allāh's name is much remembered" (22:40).

4. "And who is more unjust than he who prevents men from the mosques of Allāh that His name should be remembered therein and strives to ruin them" (2:114),

5. "The mosques are Allāh's" (72:18).

6. "The idolaters have no right to visit the mosques of Allāh" (9:17).

The first mosque built on the earth is the Sacred Mosque, the Ka'bah built at Makkah also called Bakkah (v. 1); and all mosques should therefore face towards the Sacred Mosque (v. 2: h. 3). The Prophet's Mosque at Madīnah was a simple structure made of rough material; and though in rebuilding it finer material was used by 'Uthmān, the third Caliph, it still retained its simplicity (b. 4). A mosque should be a simple structure . it should not be decorated (b. 5), and should have no pictures or statues in it (b. 8). It should be kept clean (hh. 9,10) and even perfumed (h. 9). Its only furniture consists of a pulpit, wherefrom the Imām delivers a sermon on Fridays or addresses people on other important occasions. and of mats on which prayers are said (hh. 11, 12), though prayers may be said even on bare ground (h. 13).

The whole earth being a mosque (h. 1), prayers may be offered anywhere, singly or in congregation, and accordingly no consecration of the mosque is necessary. Prayers may be said even in a non-Muslim house of worship, provided it contains no statues or pictures (h. 8). Building of a mosque is an act of great merit (h. 2). No Muslim can be denied the right to enter a mosque and offer prayers therein (v. 4). A mosque is said to be Allāh's (v. 5); it is thus not the property of any person. though 'its management must necessarily be in the hands of someone, the builder of the mosque or any one appointed by him; nor can a mosque when once built be diverted to any other use; once a mosque always a mosque. A place set apart in a house for saying prayers in congregation would, however, retain its private nature (b. 14).

The mosque is meant primarily for Divine worship. To the Muslim, however, the mosque means much more than a mere house of Divine worship which could, in fact, be offered anywhere; it is the real centre for the society of Islām in a certain locality, as the Ka'bah is the centre for the Muslims of the whole world. The mosque is also the cultural centre of Islām. The Prophet's Mosque at Madīnah had a kind of boarding-house, called the Suffah, attached to it, for students, where at one time as many as seventy students were accommodated (hh. 16, 17). In fact, the mosque is plainly stated to be a place, to which one should go to learn or teach some good (h. 18). The Suffah of the Prophet's Mosque has left its legacy in the form of the maktab or madrisah (the school)--considered a necessary adjunct to the mosque to this day--and the library which was generally attached to the more important mosques by Muslims in all ages.

The mosque, being the essential meeting-place of Muslims five times a day, became also a general centre where all important matters relating to the welfare of the Muslim community were transacted and where Muslims gathered together on all important occasions. The Holy Prophet himself (with his wife 'Ā'ishah) witnessed a display with lances given by some Abyssinians in the mosque (b. 19). Hassān ibn Thābit recited in the mosque his poems in defence of the Holy Prophet (h. 20), juridical affairs were also settled ill the mosque (b. 21). A tent was set up for a wounded soldier in the mosque (b. 22). Even a freed handmaid had a tent set up for her in the yard of the Mosque (h. 23). Deputations were received in the mosque and sometimes even lodged there (h. 24). A prisoner who was an idolater was once kept in the mosque (h. 25). On another occasion it served the purpose of the treasury (h. 26). The mosque was thus not only the spiritual centre of

Muslims but also their educational, political and social centre, their national centre in a general sense.

Notwithstanding all that has been said above, the sacredness of the mosque as the house of Divine worship, was fully observed. On the one hand, non-Muslims were received and even lodged there, but, on the other, the Holy Qur'ān plainly laid it, down that they had no right to visit the mosques (v. 6) It was only on sufferance that they were admitted there. While many affairs relating to the welfare of the community were attended to in the mosques, yet all this was to be done with the respect due to the House of God. The raising of voices in the mosque was forbidden (h. 27), and spitting therein is called a sin (h. 29). In all those matters which related to the sanctity of the mosque, Muslims were, however, told to be lenient (h. 31). Carrying on any kind of trade in the mosque is strictly prohibited, as is also the reciting of poems, and even sitting in circles and indulging in talk at the time of prayer (h. 32). The mosque should not be used as a thoroughfare, and the doors of the houses should not open on to it (h. 33). Nothing is to be done in the mosque which may give offence to others; and it is for this reason that the eating of raw onions or garlic when going to the mosque is prohibited (h. 34). Saying prayers with the shoes on is permitted (b. 35), but the general practice now is to take them off before entering the mosque as a mark of respect. It would be improper to take dogs inside the mosque, though if a dog happens to pass through it, the mosque is not thereby defiled (b. 36).

An important question relates to a junub and a menstruating woman entering the mosque. According to hadīth narrated in the previous chapter, neither the junub, nor the menstruating woman, is najs, i.e., defiled or impure (V: 51, 52): and when an idolater (man or woman) can enter the mosque as already shown there could be no prohibition against Muslims. In h. 23, it is clearly stated that a woman was allowed to have a tent pitched in the mosque and she resided in it, and there is nothing to show that she was turned out when she had her monthly courses. And 'Ā'ishah was told by the Holy Prophet that menstruation did not affect her hands in any way (h. 30) and consequently it affected no other part of the body. Therefore Hadīth speaking of the prohibition for the junub and the menstruating woman to enter the mosque must be taken as having a limited application, in the sense that they cannot enter the mosque in order to say prayers.

1. Jābir reported that, The Prophet, peace and blessings of Allāh be on him, said:

"I have been granted five things which were not granted to any one before me: and for me the earth has been made a mosque and a means of purification; therefore, if prayer overtakes any person of my community, he should say his prayers (wherever he is)[87]......"

(B. 7:l.)

2. 'Uthmān ... said ... I heard the Messenger of Allāh, peace and blessings of Allāh be on him, say:

"Whoever builds a mosque, desiring thereby Allāh's pleasure, Allāh builds for him the like of it in paradise."

(B. 8:65.)

3. Abd Allāh ibn 'Umar said,

'When the people were saying their morning prayers (in the mosque) at Qubā, a man came to them and said, A portion of the Qur'ān has been revealed to the Messenger of Allāh, peace and blessings of Allāh be on him, during the night and he has been commanded to turn his face towards the Ka'bah; so they turned their faces towards it; and their faces were towards Syria, so they turned round to the Ka'bah.[88]

(B. 8:32)

4. Abd Allāh ibn 'Umar 'reported that

The Mosque was, in the time of the Messenger of Allāh, peace and blessings of Allāh be on him, built of unburnt bricks and its roof was of palm-boughs resting on columns of the stems of palm-trees.

(B. 8:62.)

5. Ibn 'Abbās said, The Messenger of Allāh, peace and blessings of Allāh be on him, said:

"I have not been commanded to decorate the mosques."

(AD-Msh. 4:7.)

6. 'Umar ordered the building of the Mosque and said, I give people shelter from rain; and beware of painting (it) red or yellow, for thou wilt thus cause people to fall into trial.

(B. 8:62.)

7. Anas said,

They will vie with one another (in building mosques), then they will not visit them but a little.

(B. 8:62.)

8. Umar said, 'We do not enter your churches on account of the statues on which are figures.

And Ibn 'Abbās used to say his prayers in the church except a church which had statues in it.

(B. 8:54.)

9. 'Ā'ishah said, The Messenger of Allāh, peace and blessings of Allāh be on him, ordered the building of the mosque in habitations and that it should be kept clean and perfumed.

(AD-Msh. 4:7.)

10. Abū-Hurairah reported that

A black man or a black woman used to clean the mosque and he died. The Prophet, peace and blessings of Allāh be on him, asked about him and they said, He is dead. He said, "Why did you not inform me about him; lead me to his--or, he said, her--grave." So he came to his grave and offered prayers on it.[89]

(B. 8:72.)

11. Sahl said, The Messenger of Allāh, peace and blessings of Allāh be on him, sent message to a woman:

"Tell thy carpenter slave to make for me (a pulpit of) pieces of wood, on which I may sit."[90]

(B. 8:64.)

12. Maimūnah said,

The Prophet, peace and blessings of Allāh be on him, used to pray on the mat.

(B. 8:21.)

13. Anas said,

We used to say our prayers with the Prophet, peace and blessings of Allāh be on him, and one of us put a corner of his cloth at the place (where his forehead touched the ground) in prostration, on account of the severity of heat.[91]

(B. 8:21)

14. Barā' ibn 'Āzib said prayers in congregation in the mosque of his house.[92]

(B. 8:46.)

15. Ibn 'Umar reported (that) the Prophet, peace and blessings of Allāh be on him, "Say a part of your prayers in your houses and do not make them graves."[93]

(B. 8:52.)

16. Abū Hurairah said,

I saw seventy of the dwellers of the Suffah,[94] and not one of them had an over-garment.

(B. 8:58.)

17. Abū Hurairah said,

The dwellers of the Suffah were guests of Muslims. They had neither families to lodge with nor any property.

(Tr. 35:36.)

18. Abū Hurairah said,

I heard the Messenger of Allāh, peace and blessings of Allāh be on him, say:

"Whoever comes to this mosque of mine, and he does not come but for some good which he would learn or teach, he is like one who is engaged in jihād in the way of Allāh; and whoever comes for any purpose other than this, he is like a man who casts looks at the property of another."[95]

(IM-Msh. 4:7)

19. 'Ā'ishah said,

One day I saw the Messenger of Allāh, peace and blessings of Allāh be on him, at the door of my apartment, and the Abyssinians were sporting in the mosque, and the Messenger of Allāh, peace and blessings of Allāh be on him, screened me with his over-garment whilst I saw their sport.[96]

(B. 8:69.)

20. Abū Salmah reported that

He heard Hassān ibn Thābit calling Abū Hurairah to witness, I beseech thee by Allāh, didst thou hear the Prophet, peace and blessings of Allāh be on him, say:

"O Hassān! Reply on behalf of the Messenger of Allāh; O Allāh! help him with the Holy Spirit."

Abu Hurairah said, Yes.[97]

(B. 8:68.)

21. Jābir said,

I came to the Prophet, peace and blessings of Allāh be on him, and he was in the mosque . . . at early forenoon time; he said, "Offer two rak'ahs of prayer"; and he owed me a debt, so he paid it to me and gave me more than was due.

(B. 8:59)

22. 'Ā'ishah said,

Sa'd was wounded in the median vein of the arm in the battle of the Ditch, and the Prophet, ordered a tent to be set up (for him) in the mosque, so that being near he might visit him (frequently.)

(B. 8:77.)

23. 'Ā'ishah reported that

A certain tribe of the Arabs had a black slave-girl whom they set free .... Then she accepted Islām. 'Ā'ishah said, She had a small tent pitched for her in the mosque.[98]

(B. 8:57.)

24. Anas reported that

A party of the 'Ukl came to the Prophet, peace and blessings of Allāh be on him, and they were lodged in the Suffah.

(B. 8:58)

25. Abū Hurairah said,

The Prophet, peace and blessings of Allāh be on him, sent some horsemen towards Najd, and they brought a man of Banī Hanīfah, called Thumāmah ibn Uthāl, and they tied him to one of the columns of the mosque.[99]

(B. 8:76.)

26. Anas said,

The Prophet, peace and blessings of Allāh be on him, had some money brought to him from Bahrain. He said, "Put it in the mosque." And it was the greatest amount of money that was ever brought to the Messenger of Allāh, peace and blessings of Allāh be on him. Then the Messenger of Allāh, peace and blessings of Allāh be on him, came out for prayer and did not pay any heed to it. When he had finished the prayer, he came and sat near it, and he did not see any one but gave him (out of it.)[100]

(B. 8:42.)

27. Sā'ib said,

I was standing in the mosque when some one threw a pebble at me. I looked at him and it was 'Umar ibn al-Khattāb, and he said, Go and bring to me these two (men). So I brought them to him and he said, Who are you or where do you come from? They said, We are of the people of Tāif. He said. If you had been of the residents of the city, I would have punished you. Do you raise your voices in the mosque of the Messenger of Allāh, peace and blessings of Allāh be on him?

(B. 8:81)

28. Mālik said,

'Umar made a courtyard, called the Butaihā', on one side of the mosque, and said, Whoever intends to talk loudly or recite poems or raise his voice, let him go to this courtyard.

(Mt-Msh. 4:7.)

29. Anas said,

The Prophet, peace and blessings of Allāh be on him said:

"To spit in the mosque is a sin and its atonement is to bury it."[101]

(B. 8:37.)

30. 'Ā'ishah said,

'The Prophet, peace and blessings of Allāh be on him, said to me:

"Hand me over the mat from the mosque."

I said, I am menstruating. He said:

"Thy menses are not in thy hand."

(M-Msh. 3:12.)

31. Abū Hurairah said,

An Arab of the desert stood up and began urinating in the mosque. People were about to take hold of him but the Prophet, peace and blessings of Allāh be on him; said to:

"Leave him alone and throw a bucket of water over his urine, for you have been raised to deal with people gently and you have not been raised to deal with them harshly."[102]

(B. 4:58.)

32. The Messenger of Allāh, peace and blessings of Allāh be on him, prohibited the reciting of poems in the mosque and selling and buying in it and that people should sit in circles in the mosque on Friday before prayers.[103]

(AD-Msh. 4:7.)

33. Abū Sa'īd Khudrī said,

The Prophet, peace and blessings of Allāh be on him, delivered a sermon and said,

"Let no door be left that should open into the mosque but it should be closed, except the door of Abu Bakr."[104]

(B. 8:80)

34. Qurrah reported that

The Messenger of Allāh, peace and blessings of Allāh be on him, forbade the eating of these two plants, i.e., raw onions and garlic, and said:

"Whoever eats them let him not approach our mosque."[105]

And he said:

"If you eat them unavoidably, then have their offensive smell destroyed by dressing."

(AD-Msh. 4:7.)

35. Abū Maslamah said,

I asked Anas ibn Mālik, Did the Prophet, peace and blessings of Allāh be on him, say his prayers with his shoes on? He said, Yes.[106]

(13. 8:24.)

36. 'Abd Allah ibn 'Umar said,

The dogs came into and went out of the mosque in the time of the Messenger of Allāh, peace and blessings of Allāh be on him, and they did not wash (the mosque) with water on that account.

(B. 4:34.)

37. Abn Usaid said,

The Messenger of Allāh, peace and blessings of Allāh be on him, said:

When one of you enters the mosque, he should say, 'O Allāh! open for me the doors of Thy mercy'; and when he goes out, he should say, 'O Allāh! I beg of Thy grace of Thee'."

(M-Msh. 4:7.)

ADHĀN AND IQĀMAH

1. "O you who believe! When the call is given out for prayer on Friday, hasten to the remembrance of Allāh and leave off business." (62:9)./}

The adhān (lit. an announcement) is an announcement of the time of prayer in the words of h. 3, on hearing which Muslims flock to the mosque or to a place of prayer. and the iqāmah (lit. setting upright of a thing or establishing an affair) is a similar call in the words of h. 4, at which those gathered in the mosque arrange themselves into ranks and the prayer service is started. Though prayers were said in congregation from the very start when this institution was established very early at Makkah the adhān and the iqāmah were introduced after the flight to Madīnah. But the adhān is not only an announcement to the people to gather together for prayer; it is as well a declaration of the principles of Islām, made with a loud voice, from every locality inhabited by Muslims. It is an announcement to the whole world five times a day as to what Islām is and what it stands for. In the shahādah there is a declaration of the basic principles of Islām that there is no god but Allāh--God is only One--and that Muhammad is the Messenger of Allāh. In the takbīr there is the declaration that Allāh is the greatest of all and that, therefore a Muslim bows before none but Allāh-- Allāhu Akbar the watchword of Islām is repeated no less than six times in the adhān. In hayya 'ala-l-salā (come to prayer) there is the declaration of the real message of religion which is the realization of the divine in man. This can only be attained through prayer, by drinking deep at the Divine source. In hayya 'ala-l-falāh (come to success) we are told that success or full development of the human faculties, can be attained only through prayer or the realization of the divine in man.

The adhān thus serves a double purpose; it is an announcement of the time of prayer and at the same time an announcement of the principles of Islām and the significance underlying them. It replaces the meaningless ringing of a bell or the blowing of a trumpet by the most effective propaganda of religion that can be thought of. To everyone's door, nay, to his very ears. is carried the message every morning, every noon, every afternoon, every evening and at the time of going to bed that the Unity of God and the messengership of Muhammad, peace and blessings of Allāh be on him, are the fundamental principles Islām, and that any one can attain to complete self-development through the realization of the divine in him, which is brought about by prayer.

Muslims must give up all business on hearing the call for prayer (v. 1). How adhān was started is stated in hh. 1, 2, while h. 3 gives the words of the adhān and h. 4 the words of the iqāmah. Hh. 5-8 relate to the mode of delivery of the adhān, while hh. 9, 10 show that the adhān must be delivered from a high place and in the loudest voice so that it may reach the largest number of people, The deliverer of the adhān must be a man who is respected for his virtues and he should take no remuneration for this service (hh. 11, 12). The call must be obeyed (h. 13). The words of the adhān should be repeated when it is being delivered, and a prayer must be offered after it has been delivered (hh. 14-16). The adhān may be called out earlier than the time of prayer if there is some other object in view (h. 17). Hh. 18. 19 relate to the delivery of the iqāmah.

1. It is reported about Ibn 'Umar that he used to say,

The Muslims when they came to Madīnah used to gather together and they made an appointment for prayers; no call was given for it. So they talked about it one day. Some of them said, Have a bell like the bell of the Christians; others said, Rather a bugle like the horn of the Jews; 'Umar said, Would you not appoint a man who should sound a call for the prayer.[107] The Messenger of Allāh, peace and blessings of Allāh be on him, said, "O Bilāl! get up and give a call for prayer."

(B. 10:1.)

2. Anas said,

When the number of people increased, they conversed that they should make known the time of prayers by some means which they may recognize. So they mentioned that they should light the fire or ring a bell. Then Bilāl was commanded to callout the adhān, repeating the words, and to say the iqāmah, uttering the words only once.

(B. 10:2.)

3. Abū Mabdhūrah said,

I said, O Messenger of Allāh! Teach me the way of delivering the adhān. He said, So he touched his forehead (and) said:

"Thou shouldst say:

'Allāh is the Greatest, Allāh is the Greatest, Allāh is the Greatest, Allāh is the Greatest.'

Thou shouldst raise thy voice with it; then thou shouldst say,

'I bear witness that there is no God but Allāh, I bear witness that there is no God but Allāh, I bear witness that Muhammad is the Messenger of Allāh, I bear witness that Muhammad is the Messenger of Allāh.'

Thou shouldst lower thy voice with it; then thou shouldst raise thy voice with the bearing of witness,

'I bear witness that there is no God but Allāh, I bear witness that there is no God but Allāh, I bear witness that Muhammad is the Messenger of Allāh, I bear witness that Muhammad is the Messenger of Allāh. Come to prayer, Come to prayer; Come to success, Come to success'.

Then if it is the morning prayer, thou shouldst say, 'Prayer is better than sleep' 'Prayer is better than sleep';

(Then thou shouldst say),

'Allāh is the Greatest, Allāh is the Greatest, there is no God but Allāh.'"[108]

(AD-Msh. 4:4.)

4. Ibn 'Umar said,

In the time of the Messenger of Allāh, peace and blessings of Allāh be on him, (sentences of) the adhān used to be repeated twice, and (those of) the iqāmah (were uttered) only once, with this exception that he used to say, Prayer is ready, Prayer is ready.[109]

(AD-Msh. 4:4.)

5. Sa'd reported that

The Messenger of Allāh, peace and blessings of Allāh be on him, commanded

Bilāl to put his two forefingers into his ears (when delivering the adhān); this, he said, would help in the raising of thy voice.

(IM-Msh. 4:4.)

6. It is related about Bilāl that he put his two forefingers into his ears (when delivering the adhān), while Ibn 'Umar did not put his fore-fingers into his ears;[110] and Ibrāhīm said, There is no harm in delivering the adhān without performing ablution; and 'Atā' said, Ablution is necessary and it is the (Prophet's) practice.

(B. 10:19.)

7. Abū Juhaifah said,

That he saw Bilāl delivering the adhān. (He said), So I followed him when he turned his face to one side and to the other in the adhān.

(B. 10:19.)

8. Mūsā said,

I saw Bilāl (when) he went forth to the Abtah and delivered the adhān, so when he reached hayya 'ala-l-salā, hayya 'ala-falāh, he turned his neck to the right side and to the left and did not turn round.[111]

(AD. 12:34.)

9. A woman of the Banī Najjār said,

My house was the highest house in the environs of the mosque and Bilāl used to deliver the morning adhān on it.[112]

(AD. 2:31)

10. 'Abd Allāh reported ... that

Abu Sa'īd Khudrī said to him, I see thee living among goats and in the desert, so when thou are among thy goats or in thy desert and deliverest the adhān for prayer, raise thy voice with the adhān, for neither jinn nor man nor anything else hears the voice of the crier within its reach but it shall bear witness for him on the day of Resurrection.[113]

(B. 10:5.)

11. Abū Hurairah said, The Messenger of Allāh, peace and blessings of Allāh be on him, said:

"The Imām is a surety and the deliverer of the adhān is one in whom confidence is placed;[114] O Allāh! direct aright the leaders of prayer and grant protection to the deliverers of the adhān."

(AD. 2:32)

12. Uthmān ibn Abi-l-'Ās said,

O Messenger of Allāh! Make me the imām of a people. He said:

"Thou art their imām and do thou follow the weakest of them[115] and appoint a mu'adhdhin who does not take any remuneration for his adhān."[116]

(AD. 2:39.)

13. Abu Hurairah said,

The Messenger of Allāh, peace and blessings of Allāh be on him, commanded us (saying):

"When you are in the mosque and a call for prayers is sounded, let not one of you go out until he has said his prayers."

(Ah-Msh. 4:23.)

14. Abū Sa'īd Khudrī reported that

The Messenger of Allāh, peace and blessings of Allāh be on him, said:

"When you hear the adhān, say what the mu'dhdhin says."

(B. 10:7)

15. Yahyā said,

Some of our brethren related to me that when he (Mu'āwiyah) heard the words, Come to prayer, he said, There is no strength nor power but in Allāh, and he said, Thus did we hear your Prophet, peace and blessings of Allāh be on him, say.[117]

(B. 10:7.)

16. Jābir reported that The Messenger of Allāh, peace and blessings of Allāh be on him, said:

"Whoever says when he hears the adhān,

'O Allāh! the Lord of this perfect call and everliving prayer, grant to Muhammad nearness and excellence and raise him to the position of glory which Thou hast promised him,'

My intercession will be due to him on the day of Resurrection."

(B. 10:8.)

17. 'Abd Allāh reported on the authority of the Prophet, peace and blessings of Allāh be on him, (who) said:

"Let not the adhān of Bilāl prevent one of you from taking his breakfast,[118] for he delivers the adhān while it is night, so that he may send back the one of you who is saying his prayer or awaken the one who is sleeping."

(B. 10:13.)

18. Abd Allāh reported that The Messenger of Allāh, peace and blessings of Allāh be on him, said:

"Between every two adhāns, there is a prayer for him who likes."[119] (He said this) thrice.

(B. 10:14.)

19. Ziyād said that

He delivered the adhān, and Bilāl desired to call out the iqāmah but the Prophet, peace and blessings of Allāh be on him, said:

"O brother of Sudā'! The one who calls out the adhān shall call out the iqāmah.",[120]

(Ah. IV, 169.)

JAMĀ'AH OR CONGREGATION

1. "And establish prayer and pay the zakāt and bow down with those who bow down" (2:43).

2. "Thee do we serve and Thee do we beseech for help. Guide us on the right path" (1:4, 5).

3. "And when thou art among them and leadest the prayer for them, let a party of them stand with thee and let them take their arms; then when they have prostrated themselves let them go to your rear and let another party who have not prayed come forward and pray with thee"(4:102).

The prayer-service of Islām is essentially a congregational service, and has, besides the development of the inner self of man, through communion with God, other ends as well in view, which show what a unique force the Islamic prayer is in the unification of the human race. In the first place, this gathering of all people living in the same vicinity five times daily in the mosque, is a great help to the establishment of healthy social relations, the circle becoming wider in the Friday service, and still more extensive in the 'Īd gatherings. But the jamā'ah not only promotes social relations: what is far more important it levels down social differences. In the congregational prayer all Muslims stand shoulder to shoulder before their Maker, the king along with his poorest subject, the rich arrayed in costly robes with the beggar clad in rags, the white man along with his black brother. Nay, the king or the rich man standing in a back row is required to lay his head, when prostrating himself before God, at the feet of a slave or a beggar standing in the front row There could be no greater levelling influence in the world. In fact, congregational prayers are meant, among other things, to carry into practice the theoretical lessons of equality and fraternity for which Islām stands, and however forcibly Islām may have preached in words the equality of man and the fraternity of the community of Islām, all this would have ended in mere talk, had it not been translated into everyday life through the institution of five daily congregational prayers.

The stress laid by the Holy Qur'ān on jamā'ah is evident not only from the express command contained in v. 1; the very word used in it for the observance of prayers is evidence that congregation is of the essence of prayer. Wherever the institution of prayer is spoken of, one of the derivatives of the word iqāmah which signifies the putting (of an affair) into a right state or the keeping up or establishing of it, is used to indicate its proper observance. This very word iqāmah technically signifies the pronouncement of certain sentences before the congregational service is held, for which see the preceding chapter. The word iqāmah being thus associated with congregational service by the Holy Prophet himself is a clear indication that by the iqāmah of prayer in the Holy Qur'ān is meant the establishment of the congregational service. In fact, the stress laid on jamā'ah by the Holy Qur'ān is evident from its prayers, which all aim at the development of the community as a whole--v. 2 which contains the most frequently repeated prayer of Islām affords an example of this. V. 3 shows that the importance attached to congregational prayer is so great that even when facing the enemy in the battle-field, Muslims are required to say their prayers in congregation.

Of the hadīth related in this chapter, the first three lay stress on the importance of the congregational prayer; h. 4 shows that when the congregational prayer it being said, no prayer shall be said singly, H. 5 speaks of the excellence of congregational prayer, while h. 6 shows that when it would be hard on people to gather together in the mosque they should be allowed to say their prayers in their abodes. Hh. 7, 8 show that even women were required to join the congregation, while h. 14 requires that women should form a separate row by themselves. Hh. 9,-12 relate to the arrangement of ranks, while h. 13 shows that a single man shall not form a row by himself.

1. Abū Hurairah reported that The Messenger of Allāh, peace and blessings of Allāh be on him, said:

"I swear by Him in Whose hand is my soul, I had almost determined that I should order that wood should be collected, then I should order that a call should be sounded for prayer, then I should order a man that he should lead the prayer, then I should go to the people who have absented themselves and burn their houses on them."[121]

(B. 10:29.)

2. Abu-1-Dardā' said, The Messenger of Allāh, peace and blessings of Allāh be on him, said:

"There are not three people, either in the town or in the desert, among whom prayer is not said in congregation but the devil will surely overcome them; so stick to the congregation for the wolf eats the one that has strayed away from the flock."

(AD.-Msh. 4:21)

3. Mālik said, Two men who intended going out on a journey came to the Prophet, peace and blessings of Allāh be on him, and the Prophet, peace and blessings of Allāh be on him, said:

"When you go out, give out a call for prayer, then recite the iqāmah, then let the senior of you lead the prayer."

(R 10:18.)

4. Abū Hurairah said, The Messenger of Allāh, peace and blessings of Allāh be on him, said:

When the iqāmah for prayer has been called, no prayer but the one that is obligatory shall be said."

(M-Msh 4:21)

5. Ibn 'Umar reported that The Messenger of Allāh, peace and blessings of Allāh be on him, said.

"Prayer said in congregation excels the prayer said alone by twenty-seven degrees."

(B. 10:30.)

6. Nāfi' said,

Ibn 'Umar gave a call for prayer in Dzajnān on a cold night, then said, Say prayers in your abodes; and he informed us that the Messenger of Allāh, peace and blessings of Allāh be on him, used to order a mu'adhdhin, on a cold or rainy night and during journey, to give a call for prayer, then say, on finishing it, Beware! Say prayers in (your) abodes.[122]

(B. 10:18.)

7. Ibn 'Umar reported on the authority of the Prophet, peace and blessings of Allāh be on him, (who) said

"When your women ask your permission to go to the mosque at night, give them permission."[123]

(B. 10:162.)

8. 'Ā'ishah reported that The Messenger of Allāh, peace and blessings of Allāh be on him, used to say the morning prayer when it was yet dark; so the women of the believers returned while they could not be recognised on account of darkness, or they did not recognise one another.

(B. 10:164.)

9. Anas reported on the authority of the Prophet, peace and blessings of Allāh be on him, (who) said:

"Arrange your ranks properly, for the proper arrangement of ranks is part of the keeping up of prayer." (B. 10:74.)

10. Abū Hurairah reported that The Messenger of Allāh, peace and blessings of Allāh be on him, said:

"Did people know the importance of the adhān and of being in the first row, and they had no choice but to draw lots for it, they would draw lots for it."

(B. 10:9.)

11. Abn Mas'ūd said,

The Messenger of Allāh, peace and blessings of Allāh be on him, used to touch our shoulders at the time of prayer, and used to say:

"Keep straight and do not be uneven, for in that case your hearts would disagree. Let those from among you, who are possessed of understanding and wisdom, stand nearest to me, then those who are next to them, then those who are next to them."

(M-Msh. 4:24.)

12. Anas said,

The Messenger of Allah, peace and blessings of Allāh be on him, said:

"Complete the first row, then the one that is next to it, and whatever deficiency there is, let it be in the last row."

(AD-Msh. 4:24.)

13. Wābisah said,

The Messenger of Allāh, peace and blessings of Allāh be on him, saw a man praying alone behind the row; so he commanded him to say the prayer over again.[124]

(Ah.-Msh. 4:24.)

14. Anas said,

I and an orphan in our house prayed behind the Prophet, peace and blessings of Allāh be on him, (in one row), and my mother Umm Sulaim was behind us.[125]

(B. 10:78).

THE IMĀM

1. And when his Lord tried Abraham with certain words, he fulfilled them. He said, Surely I will make thee a leader (imām) of men. Abraham, said, And of my offspring? My covenant does not include the unjust, said He." (2: 124.)

Imām is literally one who is imitated or whose example is followed from i'tamma bi-hī, he followed or imitated him. It generally means a head or a chief or a leader whether he follows the right way or not. In relation to congregational prayers, the imām is the person who leads the prayer. Abraham is spoken of as having been made an imām because he fulfilled the Divine commandments--and every imām should try to follow his example; and an unjust person did not deserve to be made a leader--even though he may be of high parentage (v. 1).

That the man who leads the prayers is called an imām shows that he should be one occupying the highest place of honour in his community on account of his righteousness. While alive, the Holy Prophet himself acted as imām; and when he was unable during his last illness to perform that function, he ordered that Abū Bakr should act as imām (h. 1).

The honour of acting as an imām should be conferred upon the man who occupies the highest place of honour in a community (h. 1): it is further laid down that the man having the greatest knowledge of the Qur'ān should be chosen as imām (hh. 2, 3), even though he be a slave (h. 4). He should not be paid any remuneration for leading prayers (H. vi:12), It is not, however, prohibited to say prayers behind an imām who is either a usurper (h. 5) or an unrighteous person (b. 6). A blind man is not unfit to lead the prayers (h. 7), nor is a woman (h. 8). The imām should have regard for the weak and the sick among those who follow him (h. 9). Those who follow the imām shall not anticipate him in any movement (h. 10). When a person joins the congregational service, he should start his prayer where he finds the imām (h. 11). The position which the imām occupies in relation to the congregation is explained in hh. 12-14. There is no harm if a wall intervenes between the imām and the congregation (b. 15).

1. Abū Mūsā said, The Prophet, peace and blessings of Allāh be on him, fell ill and his illness became severe; so he said:

"Tell Abū Bakr that he should lead the prayer for the people."[126] ... So the messenger came to him, and he (Abū Bakr) led the prayer for the people in the lifetime of the Prophet, peace and blessings of Allāh be on him.

(B. 10:46.)

2. Abū Mas'ūd said, The Messenger of Allāh, peace and blessings of Allāh be on him, said

"The man who knows most the Book of Allāh shall act as imām of a people;[127] and if there are persons equal in their knowledge of the Qur'ān, then he who has greater knowledge of the Sunnah; and if they are equal in their knowledge of the Sunnah, then he who is first in hijrah; [128] and if they are equal in hijrah, then he who is older in years; and a man shall not lead another in prayer in the place where he (the latter) is in authority,[129] and no one shall occupy the place of honour in another man's house except with his permission.

(M-Msh. 4:26.)

3. Ibn 'Abbās said, The Messenger of Allāh, peace and blessings of Allāh be on him, said:

"The most virtuous among you shall deliver the adhān, and those having most knowledge of the Qur'ān shall act as imams."[130]

(AD-Msh 4:26.)

4. Ibn 'Umar said, When the first emigrants came to 'Usbah, a place in Qubā', before the coming of the Messenger of Allāh, peace and blessings of Allāh be on him, the slave of Abu Hudhaifah, used to act as their imām, and he had the greatest knowledge of the Qur'ān.[131]

(B. 10: 54)

5. 'Ubaid Allāh reported that He entered upon 'Uthmān ibn 'Affān and he was then besieged (by the rebels). He said, Thou art the imām of the people and to thee has happened what thou seest, and the rebel imām leads our prayers and we consider this to be a sin. He said, Prayer is the best of things which people do; so when people do a good work, do thou also do the good with them, and when they do evil, do thou shun their evil.

(B. 10:56.)

6. Abū Hurairah said, The Messenger of Allāh, peace and blessings of Allāh be on him, said:

"Jihād is incumbent on you under every commander whether he is virtuous or wicked, even though he be guilty of heinous sins and prayer is incumbent on you behind every Muslim whether he is virtuous or wicked, even though he be guilty of heinous sins;[132] and the holding of a (funeral) service on every Muslim is incumbent whether he is virtuous or wicked, even though he be guilty of heinous sins."

(AD-Msh. 4:26)

7. Anas reported that The Prophet, peace and blessings of Allāh be on him, left Ibn Umm Maktūm after him to act as imām of the people, and he was a blind man.

(AD. 2:64.)

8. It is reported about Umm Waraqah who had learned the Qur'ān by heart that The Prophet, peace and blessings of Allāh be on him, commanded her that she should act as imām of the people of her house, and she had a mu'adhdhin and she used to act as imām of the people of her house.[133]

(Ah. VI, 405)

9. Abū Hurairah reported that The Messenger of Allāh, peace and blessings of Allāh be on him, said:

"When one of you leads the prayer for the people, he should lighten it, for among them is the weak one and the sick one and the old one; and when one of you prays alone, he may lengthen (it) as he likes."

(B. 10:62.)

10. Barā' said,

It was the practice that when the Messenger of Allāh, peace and blessings of Allāh be on him, said samiʿ Allāhu li-man hamidahū, none of us bent down his back (for falling down in prostration) until the Prophet, peace and blessings of Allāh be on him, fell down in prostration, and then we fell down in prostration after him."

(B. 10:52.)

11. Abū Hurairah said,

The Messenger of Allāh, peace and blessings of Allāh be on him, said:

"When you come to prayer, and we have fallen down in prostration, fall down in prostration and do not count it as anything, and whoever joins in one rak'ah joins the prayers."[134]

(AD-Msh. 4:28.)

12. Samurah said,

The Messenger of Allāh, peace and blessings of Allāh be on him, commanded us that when we were three, one of us should stand in the front.

(Tr-Msh. 4:25.)

13. Abū Hurairah said,

The Messenger of Allāh, peace and blessings of Allāh be on him, said:

"Keep the imām in the middle and close the openings."[135]

(AD-Msh. 4:24.)

14. Ibn 'Abbās said,

I said my prayers with the Prophet, peace and blessings of Allāh be on him, on a certain night and I stood on his left, and the Messenger of Allāh, peace and blessings of Allāh be on him, took hold of my head from, behind me and placed me on his right hand, then he said prayers.[136]

(B. 10:77.)

15. 'Ā'ishah said,

The Messenger of Allāh, peace and blessings of Allāh be on him, used to say his prayers at night in his enclosure, and the wall of the enclosure was low, so the people saw the person of the Prophet, peace and blessings of Allāh be on him, (standing in prayers), and some people got up and followed him in his prayers.[137]

(B. 10:80)

INSTITUTION OF PRAYER

1. "Recite that which has been revealed to thee of the Book, and establish prayer: surely prayer keeps one away from indecency and evil" (29:45).

2. "And establish prayer in the two parts of the day and in the first hours of the night; surely good deeds take away evil deeds this is a reminder to the mindful" (11:114).

3. "Establish prayer, from the declining of the sun till the darkness of the night, and the morning recitation; surely the morning recitation is witnessed" (17:78).

4. "Surely prayer is a timed ordinance for the believers" (4:103).

5. "Guard (your) prayers and the most excellent prayer, and stand up truly obedient to Allāh" (2:238).

6. "Woe to the praying ones, who are unmindful of their prayers, who pray to be seen, and withhold alms" (107:4-7).

In this chapter I have collected the hadīth relating to the times of prayer and other external circumstances relating to it, while the prayer-service itself is dealt with in the next chapter.

Prayer was made an institution by Islām. It was not left to individual choice to resort to prayer when and how one liked. The order to establish prayer as an institution is very frequent in the Holy Qur'ān, the first three verses quoted above being given as an example. The purification of the mind is the great aim (vv. 1, 2: hh. 1, 2). which is attained by resorting to the remembrance of Allāh time after time in the midst of one's worldly pursuits. The spirit to serve humanity is also imbibed through prayer; and unless that spirit is imbibed, prayer is simply a show (v. 6). The times of prayer were fixed by Divine ordinance (v. 4). There is a continuity in prayer from the declining of the sun till the darkness of the night (v. 3)--early afternoon late afternoon, after sunset and early hours of the night (h. 3)-- and then there is a break till dawn (v. 3), which is the time of the fifth prayer (h. 3). p. 120 To say prayer purposely when the sun is rising, or when it is setting, is prohibited (h. 5). The two afternoon prayers and the two early night prayers may be combined (h. 6). The morning and the late afternoon prayer must not be missed on any account (h. 7). When a prayer has been unavoidably missed (h. 8), or when one forgets the saying of a prayer (h. 9), the prayer must be said at the first opportunity. It is undesirable to sleep before the 'Ishā' prayer or engage in unnecessary talk after it (h. 10). Everything must be avoided which may distract one's attention from prayer (hh. 11-13). One must not hurry for prayer, for it would destroy the calm of mind which is so essential for prayer (h. 14): nor should one when taking food make haste and leave his food for the sake of prayer (h. 15). Prayer may be said even when riding (h. 16), in a boat or a railway carriage. As regards dress, a man may wear any dress that he can afford or that is convenient for him, and prayer may be said even in knickers and shirt (h. 17) It is not proper for any one to pass in front of the man who is praying (h. 18) and a sutra may be set up when prayer is said in an open place.

1. Abū Hurairah reported that He heard the Messenger, peace and blessings of Allāh be on him, say:

"Tell me if there is a stream at the door of one of you, in which he bathes five times every day, what dost thou say, will it leave anything of his dirt? "

They said, It would not leave anything of his dirt. He said:

"This is the likeness of the five prayers, with which

Allāh blots out (all) faults."

(B. 9:6.)

2. Anas reported

The Prophet, peace and blessings of Allāh be on him, said:

"When one of you says prayers, he holds confidential intercourse with his Lord."

(B. 9:8.)

3. Ibn 'Abbās said, The Messenger of Allāh, peace and blessings of Allāh be on him, said:

"Gabriel acted as imām for me twice in the (Sacred) House; so he said the Zuhr Prayer with me when the sun had declined from the meridian and (the shadow) was the measure of a thong, and he said the 'Asr prayer with me when the shadow of everything was the like of it, and he said the Maghrib prayer with me when one who fasts breaks the fast, and he said the 'Ishā' prayer with me when redness in the horizon had disappeared, and he said the Fajr prayer with me when food and drink are prohibited to one who fasts. When it was the next day, he said with me the Zuhr prayer when the shadow (of a thing) was the like of it, and he said with me the 'Asr prayer when the shadow (of a thing) was its double, and he said with me the Maghrib prayer when one who fasts breaks the fast, and he said with me the 'Ishā' prayer when one-third of the night had passed, and he said with me the Fajr prayer when the dawn was bright. Then he turned to me and said, O Muhammad! This is the time of the prophets before thee, and the time is between these two times."[138]

1. This hadīth should be interpreted in the light of the Qur'ān which says, as quoted in the heading "Prayer keeps one away from indecency and evil" (v. 1). By the blotting out of faults is therefore meant curbing the tendency to go against Divine injunctions. The man who feels himself in the Divine presence five times a day, has his mind purified of all dross, just as the bather is purified of physical dirt.

2. That is the essence of prayer; a man should feel when praying that he is alone before his Maker. and he should open his mind to Him in its fulness.

(AD., Tr-Msh. 4:1.)

4. Ibn Abbās reported that The Prophet, peace and blessings of Allāh be on him, forbade prayer after the morning prayer till the sun brightens, and after 'Asr till it sets.'

(B. 9:30.)

5. Ibn 'Umar said,

The Messenger of Allāh, peace and blessings of Allāh be on him, said:

"Do not purposely seek in your prayer the rising of the sun or the setting of it."[139]

4. The Fajr prayer is the last prayer of the night, and the 'Asr the last prayer of the day. As h. 7 shows, these two prayers are given a special importance.

(B. 9:30)

6. Ibn 'Abbās reported that

The Prophet, peace and blessings of Allāh be on him, said prayers in Madīnah seven (rak'ahs) and eight (rak'ahs) Zuhr and 'Asr and Maghrib and 'Ishā'.[140]

(B. 9:12.)

7. Fadzālah said, The Messenger of Allāh, peace and blessings of Allāh be on him, taught me, and there was in what he taught me (the command). "And be mindful of the five prayers." He said, I said, These hours are such that I have (other) business to attend to therein, so command me something comprehensive so that when I have done it, it should suffice me. He said: "Be mindful of the two 'Asr prayers." This was not known in our idiom. So I said, what are the two 'Asr prayers? He said: "A prayer before the rising of the sun and a prayer before the setting of it."[141]

(AD. 2:2.)

8. Jābir reported that

'Umar ibn al-Khattāb came on the day of the Ditch[142] after the sun had set, and he began to abuse the disbelieving Quraish. He said, O Messenger of Allāh! I could not manage to say the 'Asr prayer until the sun was about to set. The Prophet, peace and blessings of Allāh be on him, said. "I call Allāh to witness that I (too) have not said it." Then we got up towards Buthān, and he performed ablutions for prayer, and we too performed ablutions for it, and he said the 'Asr (prayer) after the sun had set, and after that he said the Maghrib (prayer).[143]

(B. 9:36.)

9. Anas reported on the authority of the Prophet, peace and blessings of Allāh be on him, (who) said

"Whoever forgets (the saying of) a prayer, let him say the prayer when he remembers it; there is no atonement for it but this, 'Establish the prayer for My remembrance'."[144]

(B. 9:37.)

10. Abū Barzah reported that The Messenger of Allāh, peace and blessings of Allāh be on him, disliked sleeping before the 'Ishā' (prayer) and conversation after it.[145]

(B. 9:21)

11. Anas said,

'Ā'ishah had a figured curtain of red wool, with which she had covered a side of her apartment. The Prophet, peace and blessings of Allāh be on him, said:

"Remove from us thy curtain, for its figures come before me in my prayers."[146]

(B. 8:15.)

12. 'Ā'ishah said,

I asked the Messenger of Allāh, peace and blessings of Allāh be on him, about casting side glances in prayer. He said:

"That is a snatching from the prayer of the servant, which the devil snatches away by deceit."[147]

(B. 10:91)

13. Zainab, wife of Abd Allāh ibn Mas'ūd, said,

The Messenger of Allāh, peace and blessings of Allāh be on him, said to us: "When one of you goes to the mosque, let her not use scent."[148]

(M-Msh. 4:23)

14. Abū Qatādah said,

While we were saying our prayers with the Prophet, peace and blessings of Allāh be on him, he suddenly heard noise of (running) people. When he finished the prayer, he said, "What was the matter with you?"

They said, We were hastening for the prayer. He said:

"Do not do so; when you come to prayer, you should be perfectly calm; then whatever part of it you overtake, say (it with the imām), and complete the part that has escaped you."[149]

(B. 10:20.)

15. Ibn 'Umar said,

The Prophet, peace and blessings of Allāh be on him, said ."When one of you is taking food, let him not hasten until he satisfies his need, even though the iqāma for prayer has been recited."

(B. 10:42.)

16. Jābir said,

The Prophet, peace and blessings of Allāh be on him, used to say his prayers on his riding camel in whichever direction it turned with him; but when he intended to say the obligatory prayer, he got down and faced towards the Qiblah.[150]

(B. 8:31.)

17. Abū Hurairah said,

A man got up before the Prophet, peace and blessings of Allāh be on him, and asked him about praying in one garment. He said: "Can every one of you get two garments?" Then a man asked 'Umar, and he said, When Allāh gives ample, then you should use amply; a man wore his garments, a man prayed in a waist-wrapper and an outer garment, in a waist-wrapper and a shirt, in a waist-wrapper and a cloak, in trousers and outer garment, in trousers and a shirt, in trousers and a cloak, in knickers and a cloak, in knickers and a shirt, and I think he said, in knickers and an outer garment.[151]

(B. 8:9.)

18. Abū Juhaim said,

The Messenger of Allāh, peace and blessings of Allāh be on him, said:

"Did the passer in front of one who is praying know what burden is on him, it would be better for him to wait for forty (days) than that he should pass in front of him."[152]

(B. 8:101)

PRAYER-SERVICE

1. "O you who believe! Go not near prayer when you are intoxicated until you know what you say" (4:43).

2. "And when you journey in the earth, there is no blame on you if you shorten the prayer" (4:10).

3. "And when thou art amongst them and leadest them in prayer, let a party of them stand up with thee .... then when they have prostrated themselves, let them go to your rear, and let another party who have not prayed come forward and pray with thee" (4:102).

4. "And they who pass the night prostrating themselves before their Lord and standing" (25:64).

5. "Thou wilt see them bowing down, prostrating themselves, seeking grace from Allāh and pleasure" (48:29).

6. "O you who believe! Bow down and prostrate yourselves and serve your Lord" (22:77).

7. "Those who remember Allāh, standing and sitting." (3:190).

Every prayer-service consists of two, three or four units (h. 1), the unit being called a rak'ah (lit., an act of bowing) which consists of qiyām (standing) rukū' (bowing of the head and body). sajdah (prostration) and jalsah or qa'dah (sitting), in the order in which they are mentioned. These are all the worshipful positions which a man can adopt, and they are mentioned in the Holy Qur'ān in different places, not of course in this order (vv. 3-7.) It will be noted that after giving the number of rak'ahs in a particular prayer it is added. "and after it two rak'ahs" (h. 1). This latter is the supererogatory part (nafl), which is said singly and is commonly known as sunnah (the Prophet's practice), as distinguished from the congregational prayer which is called maktūbah (obligatory) (H. vii:4), and is commonly known as fardz. There is perfect agreement in the whole Muslim world as to the number of rak'ahs in the congregational service. In the case of prayers consisting of four fardz rak'ahs, the number of rak'ahs is halved when journeying, while the sunnah may be dropped altogether (v. 2; h. 32). A full description of the different postures of the rak'ahs--a practical revelation to the Holy Prophet (H. ix:3)--and the arrangement in which they follow each other are given in h. 3. Further details relating to these postures are contained in hh. 4-7.

Every posture or change from one posture to another is connected with some kind of dhikr,[153] and the man who prays should know its significance (v. 1; h. 8). The most frequently occurring dhikir in prayer is the takbīr (magnifying). i.e., the utterance of Allāhu Akbar (Allāh is the Greatest). These words are uttered first when a man begins the prayer-service and then on every change from one position to another, except when he rises from rukū' (h. 9). An additional dhikr after rising from rukū' is mentioned in h. 19. After the first utterance of Allāhu Akbar, one or other of the dhikrs mentioned in hh. 10, 11 is uttered in a voice audible to oneself only. The latitude given in this matter shows that any other prayer may be added. It is, however, with the Fātihah that the service really opens (h. 12). It is so essential to prayer, that without it no prayer is acceptable (h. 13). The recital of the Fātihah is followed by Āmīn, which should be uttered in a loud voice when the Fātihah is recited in a loud voice (h. 14). In the first two rak'ahs the Fātihah is followed by the recital of any portion of the Holy Qur'ān (hh. 15, 16). There are many forms of dhikr for rukū' and sajdah (hh. 17, 18). to which any prayer in any language may be added, especially in sajdah in which state a person is enjoined to make most petitions, as he is nearest to God when he humbles himself most (h. 21). in fact, the whole of the prayer-service is a petition to the Divine Being, and any prayer may he addressed in any position, so much so that the Holy Prophet used to address prayers even when reciting the Holy Qur'ān (b.18). Special intercessory prayers were offered on rising from rukū (h. 20). A prayer is also addressed in the respite between the two sajdahs (h. 22). Prayers are also offered in the sitting position (hh. 23-26). But like a petitioner who takes advantage of an opportunity for being heard, some sort of dhikr is resorted to even after the prayer is finished (hh 28, 29). The service ends with taslīm (h. 27).

Some points of minor importance are added at the end. The first relates to the procedure to be adopted when a mistake is made through forgetfulness (hh. 30, 31); the second to prayer when journeying and to the duration of the journey (hh. 32, 33).

1. Ibn 'Umar said,

I prayed with the Messenger of Allāh, peace and blessings of Allāh be on him, when staying at home and when journeying; so he said the Zuhr prayer, when staying at home, four rak'ahs and after it two rak'ahs and he said the 'Asr prayer four rak'ahs and there was nothing after it, and he said the Maghrib prayer three rak'ahs and after it two rak'ahs and he said the 'Ishā' prayer four rak'ahs; and he said the Zuhr prayer, when journeying, two rak'ahs and after it two rak'ahs, and the 'Asr two rak'ahs and there was nothing after it, and the Maghrib three rak'ahs and after it two rak'ahs, and the 'Ishā' two rak'ahs and after it two rak'ahs.[154]

(Ah. 11, 90.)

2. 'Ā'ishah reported that

The Prophet, peace and blessings of Allāh be on him, never omitted saying four rak'ahs before Zuhr and two rak'ahs before Fajr.[155]

(B. 19:34.)

3. Abū Hurairah reported that

A man entered the mosque, and the Messenger of Allāh, peace and blessings of Allāh be on him, sitting in a corner of the mosque; .... he said, Teach me, O Messenger of Allāh! He said:

"When thou risest for the prayer, then perform the ablution in a right manner, then turn thy face towards the Qiblah, then say Allāhu Akbar, then recite what thou canst afford of the Qur'ān, then bow down until thou art at rest in bowing down (rukū'), then raise thyself up until thou art firm in the standing posture, then fall down in prostration until thou art at rest in prostration, then raise thyself up until thou art at rest in sitting, then fall down in prostration until thou art at rest in prostration, then raise thyself up until thou art at rest in sitting[156]; and, according to one report, then raise thyself up until thou art firm in the standing posture; then do this in the whole of thy prayer."

(B. & M-Msh. 4:10.)

4. Abū Humaid al-Sā'idī said,

I best guard the prayer of the Messenger of Allāh, peace and blessings of Allāh be on him. When he said Allāhu Akbar[157] I saw him raise his hands to his shoulders; and When he performed the rukū', he firmly held his two knees with his two hands, and he bent his back (levelling it with his head); then when he raised his head, he stood erect until every bone of the spine returned to it regular place; and when he performed the sajdah, he laid his forearms (on the ground), not spreading them out as a bed, nor contracting them (to his sides), and he made the tips of the toes of his two feet face towards the Qiblah; and when he sat after (finishing) two rak'ahs, he sat on his left foot and made the right one stand erect; and when he sat after the last rak'ah, he brought forward his left foot and made the other stand erect, and sat on his sitting-place.[158]

(B. 10:145.)

5. Sahl ibn Sa'd said,

Order was given to the people that in prayer a

man should place his right hand on his left forearm.[159]

(B. 10:87.)

6. Ibn 'Abbās said,

The Prophet, peace and blessings of Allāh be on him, was commanded that he should perform sajdah on seven members of the body, the forehead[160], the two hands, the two knees and the two feet, and that. he should not arrange hair nor garments (while praying).

(B. 10:131)

7. Ibn 'Umar said,

When the Messenger of Allāh, peace and blessings of Allāh be on him, sat in tashahhud[161], he used to place his left hand on his left knee and his right hand on his right knee.[162]

(M-Msh. 4:15.)

8. Anas reported on the authority of the Prophet, peace and blessings of Allāh be on him, (who said):

"When a person is drowsy in his payers, let him go to sleep until he knows what he recites."[163]

(B. 4:51)

9. Abu Hurairah said,

When the Messenger of Allāh, peace and blessings of Allāh be on him, got up for prayer, he used to say Allāhu Akbar when he assumed qiyām then he said Allāhu Akbar when he bowed down for rukū'; then he said, "Allāh listens to him who praises Him", when he raised his back from rukū'; then he said while he was standing, "Our Lord, Thine is the praise then he said Allāhu Akbar when he fell down (In sajdah); then he said Allāhu Akbar when he raised his head; then he said Allāhu Akbar when he performed the (second) sajdah; then he said Allāhu Akbar when he raised his head; then he did this in the whole of his prayer until he finished it, and he said Allāhu Akbar when he rose from the sitting posture after two (rak'ahs[164]).

(B. 10:117.)

10. Abū Hurairah said, The Messenger of Allāh, peace and blessings of Allāh be on him, used to remain silent between the (opening) takbīr and the recital (of the Qur'ān)--I think, he said--a little. I said, May my father and my mother be thy sacrifice, O Messenger of Allāh! thy silence between the takbīr and the recital, what sayest thou (in that interval)? He said, "I say:

'O Allāh! Keep faults as distant from me as the east is distant from the west; O Allāh! cleanse me of all faults as a white cloth is cleansed of dirt; O Allāh! wash away my faults with water and snow and hail."[165]

(B. 10:89.)

11. 'Ā'ishah said,

The Messenger of Allāh, peace and blessings of Allāh be on him, used to say, when he opened the prayer:

"Glory to Thee, O Allāh! and Thine is the praise, and blessed is Thy name and exalted is Thy majesty and there is none to be served besides Thee"

(AD-Msh. 4:11.)

12. Anas reported that

The Prophet, peace and blessings of Allāh be on him, and Abu Bakr and 'Umar used to open the prayer with al-hamdu lillāhi Rabbi-l-'ālamīn.[166]

(B. 10:89.)

13. 'Ubādah reported that

'The Messenger of Allāh, peace and blessings of Allāh be on him, said:

"There is no prayer for him who does not recite the Opening (chapter) of the Book."[167]

(B. 10:95.)

14. Abu Mūsā said,

The Messenger of Allāh, peace and blessings of Allāh be on him, said:

"When you pray, set right your ranks; then one of you should act as your imām, so when he says the takbīr, say the takbīr, and when he says ghairi-l-maghdzūb-i 'alai-him wa la-dzzāllīn, say āmīna,[168] Allāh will accept your prayer.

(M-Msh. 4:12.)

15. Abū Qatādah reported that

The Prophet, peace and blessings of Allāh be on him, used to recite Umm al-Kitāb (the Fātihah) and along with it another sūrah in the first two rak'ahs of Zuhr and 'Asr prayers, and now and then he made us hear a verse, and he used to lengthen (recital) in the first rak'ah.[169]

(B. 10:109.)

16. Abū Rāfi' said,

I said with Abu Hurairah the 'Ishā' prayer, and he recited Idha-l-samā' u-nshaqqat (ch. 84), and performed sajdah[170]. I enquired from him, and he said, I performed the sajdah behind Abu-l-Qāsim, peace and blessings of Allāh be on him, and I will continue to perform the sajdah in it until I meet him.

(B. 10:100.)

17. 'Ā'ishah said,

The Prophet, peace and blessings of Allāh be on him, used to say in his rukū' and in his sajdah:

"Glory to Thee, O Allāh, our Lord! And Thine is the praise; grant me protection, O Allāh!"

(B. 10:121)

18. Hudhaifah reported that

He prayed with the Prophet, peace and blessings of Allāh be on him, and he (the Prophet) used to say in his rukū', 'Glory to my Lord, the Great', and in his sajdah, 'Glory to my Lord, the Most High', and he did not recite any verse speaking of Divine mercy but he paused and asked (for mercy), and he did not recite any verse speaking of Divine punishment but he paused and sought refuge (in Allāh).[171]

(Tr-Msh. 4:13.)

19. Rifā'ah said,

We were one day praying behind the Prophet, peace and blessings of Allāh be on him, So when he raised his head from rukū' (and) said, 'Allāh listens to him who praises Him," a man behind him said, Our Lord! And Thine is the praise, abundant praise, most excellent, blessed therein. When he finished (the prayer), he said, "Who uttered (the words)?" The man said, I. He said, I saw over thirty angels hastening who should write them first."[172]

(B. 10:126.)

20. Abū Hurairah said, O And when the Messenger of Allāh, peace and blessings of Allāh be on him, raised his head saying, "Allāh listens to him who praises Him, our Lord! and Thine is the praise" he used to pray for some people mentioning them by name and said:

"O Allāh! Deliver Walīd ibn al-Walīd and Salamah ibn Hishām, and 'Ayyāsh ibn Abī Rabī'ah and the weak from among the believers; O Allāh! make severe Thy hold on Mudzar and make these to them years (of draught) like the years of Joseph"[173]

(B. 10:128.)

21. Abū Hurairah said,

The Messenger of Allāh, peace and blessings of Allāh be on him, said, "The nearest that the servant is to his Lord is when he is in sajdah so make most petitions (in sajdah)."[174]

(M-Msh. 4:14.)

22. Ibn 'Abbās said,

The Messenger of Allāh, peace and blessings of Allāh be on him, used to say between the two sajdahs: "O Allāh! Forgive me and have mercy on me and guide me and grant me security and grant me sustenance."

(AD-Msh. 4:14.)

23. 'Abd Allāh said, 'When we said our prayers with the Prophet, peace and blessings of Allāh be on him, we said, Peace be on Allāh from His ser-

vants........; so the Prophet, peace and blessings of Allāh be on him, said to us:

"Do not say, Peace be on Allāh, for Allāh is the Author of peace; but say, 'All services rendered by words and bodily actions and sacrifice of wealth are due to Allāh. Peace be to Thee, O Prophet! and the mercy of Allāh and His blessings. Peace be to us and the righteous servants of Allāh,'--for when you say this, it reaches every servant (Of Allāh) in heaven and in earth--'I bear witness that none deserves to be worshipped but Allāh, and I bear witness that Muhammad is His servant and His Messenger.' Then one should choose any petition which he likes most and pray (to Allāh).[175]

(B. 10:150.)

24. Abd Allāh ibn Mas'ūd said,

I was saying prayers, and the Prophet, peace and blessings of Allāh be on him, was present and Abu Bakr and 'Umar were with him. When I assumed the sitting posture, I began with extolling Allāh, then I repeated salā on the Prophet, peace and blessings of Allāh be on him, then I prayed for myself." The Prophet, peace and blessings of Allāh be on him, said, "Ask (and) thou wilt be given, ask (and) thou wilt be given."[176]

23. This, of course, was as taught by the Holy Prophet himself. The extolling of Allāh is as taught in h. 23, the salā on the Holy Prophet as taught in h. 25 and the prayer for oneself as taught in h. 26 and other hadīth.

(Tr-Msh. 4:16.)

25. 'Abd al-Rahmān said,

We' said, O Messenger of Allāh! How should we offer you salā? .... He said, "Say:

'O Allāh! Exalt Muhammad and the true followers of Muhammad as Thou didst exalt Abraham and the true followers of Abraham, for Thou are Praised, Magnified. O Allāh! Bless Muhammad and the true followers of Muhammad as Thou didst bless Abraham and the true followers of Abraham, for Thou are Praised, Magnified."[177]

(B. & M.-Msh. 4:16.)

26. 'Ā'ishah reported that

The Messenger of Allāh, peace and blessings of Allāh be on him, used to say in his prayers:

"O Allāh! I seek refuge in Thee from the punishment of the grave,[178] and I seek refuge in Thee from the tribulation of al-Masīh al-Dajjāl[179] (the Anti-Christ), and I seek refuge in Thee from the trials of life and the trials of death; O Allāh! I seek refuge in Thee from sins and from being in debt."

(B. 10:149.)

27. 'Abd Allāh said,

The Messenger of Allāh, peace and blessings of Allāh be on him, used to utter taslīm on his right hand side, "Peace be on you and the mercy of Allāh", until the white of his right cheek could be seen, and on his left, "Peace be on you and the mercy of Allāh", until the white of his left cheek could be seen.[180]

(AD-Msh. 4:17.)

28. Ibn 'Abbās reported that

The raising of voices with dhikr when the people turned away from the obligatory prayer was the practice in the time of the Prophet, peace and blessings of Allāh be on him.

(B. 10:155.)

29. Thaubān said,

When the Messenger of Allāh, peace and blessings of Allāh be on him, turned back from his prayer, he used to resort to istighfār thrice, and said:

"O Allāh! Thou art the Author of peace and from Thee is peace, Blessed art Thou, O Lord of Glory and Honour."

(M-Msh. 4:18.)

30. Abd Allāh ibn Buhainah ...... said,

The Prophet, peace and blessings of Allāh be on him, led them in the Zuhr (prayer), and he stood up after the first two raka'ahs and did not sit, and the people stood up with him. When he finished the prayer and the people waited for taslīm, he uttered the takbīr while sitting and performed two sajdahs before he pronounced the taslīm, then he pronounced the taslīm.[181]

29. This hadīth and h. 29 speak of the dhikr uttered individually in a loud voice when the congregational service was over. The practice now generally in vogue--the imām and the congregation raising hands in silent prayer--cannot be traced to the Holy Prophet.

(B. 10:146)

31. Abū Sa'īd said,

The Messenger of Allāh, peace and blessings of Allāh be on him, said:

"When one of you has a doubt about his prayer and he does not know how many rak'ahs he has said, whether three or four, let him dismiss the doubt and proceed on what he is certain, then let him perform two sajdahs before he pronounces the taslīm."

(M-Msh 4:20.)

32. Hafs ibn 'Āsim said,

I asked Ibn 'Umar. He said, I have been in the company of the Prophet, peace and blessings of Allāh be on him, and I never saw him saying the sunnah while journeying.[182]

(B. 18:10)

33. Ibn 'Abbās said,

The Prophet, peace and blessings of Allāh be on him, stayed for nineteen days shortening the prayer, so when we were in journey for nineteen days we shortened, and when it was above that we completed (the prayer).[183]

(B. 18:l.)

FRIDAY SERVICE

"O you who believe! When the call is given for prayer on Friday, hasten to the remembrance of Allāh and leave off business" (62: 9).

Jumu'ah (from jama'a, he gathered together) is literally congregation; it is the name by which the sixth day of the week is known. The verse quoted above contains an express commandment to all Muslims to leave off business of every kind to join it. The prevalent idea that Friday service can be held only in big towns or under Muslim rule has no sanction in the Holy Qur'ān, which requires all Muslims wherever they may be to join it. Hadīth makes it further clear. In the Holy Prophet's time, Friday service was held at Juwāthā, a village in Bahrain (h. 1). It was held even in a place where some Muslims had settled temporarily for management of a tract of land (h. 2). Omitting the Friday service without good reason is considered as one of the gravest sins (h. 3). Even women should try to attend the Friday service (h. 4), and also those who are journeying (h. 5), But when the inconvenience is too great, attendance is not compulsory (B. 11:13). Time for the Friday service is the same as that for the Zuhr prayer (h. 6) though on account of the larger numbers attending the service an additional adhān has become the practice (h. 7), Every Muslim must try to take bath before attending the congregation and cleanse his mouth and use scent if possible (h. 8). Two sunnahs must be said before the service is held (h. 9). The service must be preceded by a sermon which constitutes an integral part of it (hh. 10-13). The service itself consists of two rak'ahs (h. 14), in which the Holy Qur'ān is recited in a loud voice (h. 15).

1. Ibn 'Abbās said,

The first Friday service, after the Friday service in the mosque of the Messenger of Allāh, peace and blessings of Allāh be on him, was that held in the mosque of 'Abd al-Qais at Juwāthā in Bahrain.[184]

(B. 11:11.)

2. Yūnus said, Ruzaiq ibn Hukaim wrote to Ibn Shihāb,

What is thy opinion--should I hold the Friday service? And Ruzaiq was manager of a certain land on which be worked and there was a party of Negroes and others besides them there, and Ruzaiq was then the governor of Ailah. So Ibn Shihāb wrote, while I heard, commanding him to hold the Friday service.[185]

(B. 11:11)

3. Abu-l-Ja'd said, The Messenger of Allāh, peace and blessings of Allāh be on him, said:

"Whoever omits three Friday services making light of it, Allāh sets a seal on his heart."

(AD-Msh. 4:41)

4. Ibn 'Umar said,

A wife of 'Umar used to attend the morning and 'Ishā' prayers in congregation in the mosque. It was said to her, Why dost thou go forth and thou knowest that 'Umar does not like this and is averse (to it). She said, What prevents him from prohibiting me? He said, What prevents him is the saying of the Messenger of Allāh:

"Do not prohibit the handmaids of Allāh from attending the mosques of Allāh."

(B. 11:12.)

3. Women were required to attend the 'Īd gatherings, and their presence at the Friday service is of the utmost importance for the welfare of the Muslim community; and, therefore, even if it may not be obligatory for them, they should generally attend the Friday service so far as is consistent with their duties. The words of the Holy Prophet quoted here include the Friday service along with other prayers.

5. It is reported on the authority of Zuhrī,

When the Mu'adhdhin gives a call for prayer on Friday, and there is one who is journeying, it is incumbent on him that he should attend.

(B. 11:17.)

6. Anas reported that

The Messenger of Allāh, peace and blessings of Allāh be on him, used to hold the Friday service when the sun declined.

(B. 11:15)

7. Sā'ib said,

The first call on Friday, in the time of the Prophet, peace and blessings of Allāh be on him, and Abu Bakr and 'Umar, was sounded when the imām ascended the pulpit; but when (the time of) 'Uthmān came and the number of people became very great, he added a third call at the Zaurā.[186]

(B. 11:21.)

8. Abū Sa'īd said,

I bear witness to the Messenger of Allāh, peace and blessings of Allāh be on him, saying,

"It is incumbent on every one who has attained to puberty that he should take a bath on Friday, and that he should use the tooth-brush, and that he should use scent if he can get it."

(B. 11:3.)

9. Jābir said, A man came while the Prophet, peace and blessings of Allāh be on him, was delivering the sermon to the people on Friday. So he said, "Hast thou said the prayer, O such a one?" He said, No. He said, "Get up and say two rak'ahs of prayer."[187]

(B. 11:32.)

10. Abū Sa'īd al-Khudrī reported that

The Prophet, peace and blessings of Allāh be on him, one day ascended the pulpit and we sat around him.[188]

(B. 11:27.)

11. Ibn 'Umar said,

The Prophet, peace and blessings of Allāh be on him, used to deliver the sermon standing, then he sat down, then he stood up again, as you do now.[189]

(B. 11:26.)

12. Salmān said on the authority of the Prophet, peace and blessings of Allāh be on him, "One should remain silent when the imām speaks."

(B. 11:35)

13. Anas said,

While the Prophet, peace and blessings of Allāh be on him, was delivering the Friday sermon, a man stood up and said, O Messenger of Allāh! Horses have perished, goats have perished; pray to Allāh that He may send us rain. So he raised his hands and prayed.

(B. 11:34.)

14. Abu Hurairah said,

The Messenger of Allāh, peace and blessings of Allāh be on him, said:

"Whoever joins in one rak'ah of the Friday service, he should add to it another, and whoever misses both rak'ahs, he should say four (rak'ahs)," or he said, "the Zuhr."

(DQ-Msh. 4:45.)

15. Ibn 'Abbās reported on the authority of the Prophet, peace and blessings of Allāh be on him,

He used to recite (on Friday) al-Sajdah (ch. 32) and Hal atā 'ala-l-insāni (ch. 76) in the morning prayer, and al-Jumu'ah (ch. 62) and al-Munāfiqūn (ch. 63) in the Friday service.[190]

(Ah. I, 340.)

8. The Friday service thus consists of two rak'ahs of prayer, and whoever misses both should say the Zuhr prayer.

'ĪD SERVICE

1. "It is not their flesh nor their blood that reaches Allāh, but to Him is acceptable righteousness on your part" (22:37).

2. "When they fall down eat of them and feed the poor man who is contented and the beggar" (22:36).

The word 'Īd (from 'āda, he or it returned) is literally "the time of return of joy and of grief" (LL), and hence it comes to indicate a festival or a periodical festival, The word 'Īd itself occurs in the Holy Qur'ān only in connection with the prayer of Jesus for bread for his disciples in the sense of an ever-recurring happiness (5:114). There are two festivals among the Muslims (h. 3), the festival of sacrifices, called 'Īd al-Adzhā, (dzuhā meaning early part of the day, and dzāhhā, he sacrificed a victim in the time of dzuhā, and the festival of breaking fasts, called 'Īd al-Fitr (fatara meaning he split a thing, and aftara, he broke the fast). In the Holy Qur'ān, a reference to 'Īd al-Adzhā is contained in the course of the mention of the sacrifice which is the chief feature of that day (v. 1-2).

The dates for the two 'Īds are determined with reference to the appearance of the new moon, and hence certain rules are laid down when there is doubt about it (hh. 1, 2) The festivals start, not with any physical enjoyment but with an act of bowing before God. so that the spiritual awakening thus brought about may serve as a restraint on physical enjoyment (h. 3). A sermon is delivered by the imām after two rak'ahs of prayer have been said. and stress is laid in it on matters relating to the welfare of the community (hh. 3, 4). No adhān is delivered, nor the iqāmah; a number of additional takbīrs is, however, pronounced during the service (hh. 5. 6). Women and children are also required to join in the service and listen to the sermon (hh. 7, 8). The 'Īd service is held wherever there is a number of Muslims, whether it is a town or a village or a solitary place (h. 8). In the 'Īd al-Fitr it is necessary to take some food before going out to pray (h. 9). The taking of a bath is also necessary (h. 10). The 'Īd prayer should be said at an early hour, say by breakfast time (h 11). The Holy Prophet generally took a different route on returning from the place of prayer (h. 12). Sacrifice should not be offered until prayer has been said (h. 13), Everyone who has the means is required to sacrifice an animal (h. 14). Some details regarding the animals to be sacrificed are given in (hh. 15, 16). One goat or one sheep is sufficient for one man or one household, but seven men may be partners in one cow or one camel (h. 17). The animals may be sacrificed either on the day of 'Īd or on the two following days (h. 18). A part of the meat of the animal sacrificed is distributed among the poor, and the price of the skin must be devoted to charitable objects (H. xviii:26). A charitable institution is also connected with the 'Īd al-Fitr in the form of Fitr charity which must be collected at a central place and then distributed (hh. 19, 20). When the 'Īd occurs on a Friday, the Friday service becomes optional (h. 21). A little music or sport is not prohibited on the 'Īd day (h. 22).

1. Ibn 'Umar reported that,

The Messenger of Allāh, peace and blessings of Allāh be on him, mentioned Ramadzān and said:

"Do not keep the fast until you see the new moon, and do not discontinue the keeping of fast until you see it (again), and if it be veiled to you (by cloud, etc.), have it measured."

(B. 30:11.)

2. Ibn 'Umar reported that,

The Messenger of Allāh, peace and blessings of Allāh be on him, said:

"The month is (sometimes) twenty-nine nights, so do not keep the fast until you see (the new moon), and if it be veiled to you (by cloud, etc.), then complete the number thirty."[191]

(B. 30:11)

3. Abū Sa'īd said,

The Prophet, peace and blessings of Allāh be on him, used to go forth on the day of the Fitr and the Adzhā to the Musallā; so the first thing that he did was the saying of prayer; then he turned and stood facing the people while the people were sitting in their rows, and he admonished them and gave them injunctions and commands; then if he intended to raise an army, he gave the orders for it, or if he intended to command any (other) thing, he commanded it; then he returned.[192]

(B. 13:6.)

4. Ibn 'Abbās reported that,

The Prophet, peace and blessings of Allāh be on him, said two rak'ahs of prayer on the day of the Fitr, and he did not say any prayer before it, nor after it; then he came to the women and with him was Bilāl, and he commanded them to give charity; so they began to throw away (their ornaments),--a woman gave away her ear-ring and her necklace.[193]

(B. 13:8)

5. Jābir ibn Samurah said,

I said both the 'Īd prayers with the Prophet, peace and blessings of Allāh be on him, not once or twice, without adhān and without iqāmah.

(M-Msh. 4:47.)

6. Kathīr reported on the authority of his grandfather that,

The Prophet, peace and blessings of Allāh be on him, uttered takbīrs in both 'Īd services seven times in the first (rak'ah) before the recitation (of the Fātihah), and five times in the second (rak'ah) before recitation.'

(Tr-Msh. 4:47.)

7. Umm 'Atiyyah said,

We (women) were commanded to go forth on the day of 'Īd, in so far as to make a virgin leave her curtain and to require (even) menstruating women to turn out; and they (the women) were behind the men, and they uttered the takbīr, along with their takbīr, and they made their supplications along with their supplications, hoping for the blessings of that day and its purification.[194]

(B. 13:12)

4. According to another hadīth, four takbīrs were uttered (AD-Msh. 4:47).

8. Anas ordered his slave

Ibn Abū 'Utbah at Zāwiya, so he gathered together the people of his household and his sons, and held prayer service just as the residents of the towns hold prayer service and utter takbīrs.

(B. 13:25)

9. Anas said,

The Messenger of Allāh, peace and blessings of Allāh be on him, did not go out on the morning of the day of the Fitr till he had eaten some dates.[195]

(B. 13:4.)

10. Ibn 'Abbās said,

The Messenger of Allāh, peace and blessings of Allāh be on him, used to take a bath on the day of the Fitr and the day of the Adzhā.

(IM. 5:166)

11. It is reported on the authority of 'Abd Allāh ibn Busr that,

He went forth with the people on the day of the Fitr or the Adzhā, and disapproved of the delay of the imām and said, We used to have finished by this time; and it was the time of the prayer after sunrise.[196]

(IM. 5:170)

12. Jābir said,

The Prophet, peace and blessings of Allāh be on him, used to change the route on the day of the 'Īd.

(B. 13:24.)

13. Barā' said,

I heard the Prophet, peace and blessings of Allāh be on him, delivering a sermon, so he said

"The first thing that we do on this day of ours is that we say prayers, then we go back and sacrifice (an animal); so whoever does (this) abides by our sunnah."[197]

8. He went to the place of prayer by one way and came back by another, so that greater numbers of the public might see with their own eyes that Muslims sought communion with the Divine Being even in their festivals.

(B. 13:3.)

14. Abū Hurairah said,

The Messenger of Allāh, peace and blessings of Allāh be on him, said:

"Whoever has the means but does not sacrifice (an animal), let him not come to our place of prayer."

(Ah. II, 321.)

15. Jābir said, The Messenger of Allāh, peace and blessings of Allāh be on him, said:

"Do not slaughter but a musinnah, unless it is difficult for you (to get it); in that case, slaughter a jadha'ah from among the sheep.[198]

(M-Msh. 4:48.)

16. Barā ibn 'Āzib reported that,

The Messenger of Allāh, peace and blessings of Allāh be on him, was asked as to what sacrifices should be avoided. He pointed out with his hand and said:

"Four: The lame one whose limping is manifest and the blind of one eye whose disfigurement is manifest, and the diseased one whose disease is manifest, and the emaciated one which has no marrow left in its bones."[199]

(AD-Msh. 4:48.)

17. Jābir reported that,

The Prophet, peace and blessings of Allāh be on him, said,

"(Sacrifice of)[200] a cow (suffices) for seven, (persons) and that of a camel for seven (persons).

(M-Msh. 4:48.)

18. Ibn 'Umar said,

Al-Adzhā 'lasts two days after the day of Adzhā.[201] (M-Msh. 4:48.)

19. Ibn 'Umar said,

The Messenger of Allāh, peace and blessings of Allāh be on him, made the charity of the Fitr-one sā' of dates or one sā' of barley -obligatory on every slave and free man, male and female, minor and major, from among Muslims, and ordered that it should be paid before people go out for ('Īd) prayer." (13. 24. 70.)

14. Charity, like prayer, constitutes a distinguishing characteristic of both 'Id festivals. In the 'Īd al-Adzhā, charity takes the form of the distribution of the meat of the sacrificed animal, and the price of its skin which must be devoted to some charitable object; and in the 'Īd al-Fitr, it is made obligatory in the form of Fitr charity. The sā' was an Arab measure for grain weighing about four seers. Under present conditions money-value of the sā' would be about four annas in Pakistan, and that may safely be taken as the standard for Fitr charity for each individual, including children.

20. Abū Hurairah said,

The Messenger of Allāh, peace and blessings of Allāh be on him, appointed me to guard the charity of Ramadzān.[202]

(B. 40:10)

21. Ibn 'Umar said,

Two 'Īds occurred together[203] in the time of the Messenger of Allāh, peace and blessings of Allāh be on him, So he performed the ('Īd) prayer with the people, then said: "Whoever desires to come to the Friday service, he may come; and whoever desires to remain absent, he may remain absent."

(I M. 5:166.)

22. 'Ā'ishah reported that,

'Abū Bakr paid her a visit in the days of Minā, and with her were two girls playing on a tambourine and beating (it), and the Prophet, peace and blessings of Allāh be on him, covered himself up with his cloth. Abu Bakr upbraided them, but the Prophet, peace and blessings of Allāh be on him, uncovered his face and said: "Leave them alone, O Abū Bakr! for these are the days of 'Īd."

(B. 13:25.)

SUPEREROGATORY PRAYERS (TAHAJJUD, WITR AND TARĀWĪH)

1. "And during part of the night forsake sleep by prayer, beyond what is incumbent on thee; maybe thy Lord will raise thee to a position of great glory" (17:79).

2. "The rising by night is the firmest way to tread and the best corrective of speech" (73:6).

3. "Surely thy Lord knows that thou passest in prayer nearly two-thirds of the night, and (sometimes) half of it, and (sometimes) one-third of it, and also a part of those who are with thee" (73: 20).

Tahajjud, from hajada meaning he remained wakeful in the night, is the prayer which is offered during the latter part of the night, before daybreak. It is a supererogatory prayer, but special stress is laid on it in the Holy Qur'ān (vv. 1, 2). Witr, (lit. an odd number), originally a part of the Tahajjud prayer. is a supererogatory prayer of three rak'ahs, generally said after the 'Ishii' prayer. Tarāwīh (pl. of tarwihah meaning rest) is a supererogatory prayer of eight or twenty rak'ahs said during the month of Ramadzān immediately after the 'Ishā' prayer.

The Tahajjud prayer is said, after one has enjoyed sleep, during the latter third of the night (h. 1), This prayer consists of eleven rak'ahs (h. 2). but may be shortened to nine or seven or even less (hh. 3. 4), there being a break after every two rak'ahs. As all people could not afford to get up in the latter part of the night, three rak'ahs of witr were added to the 'Ishā' prayer, being the final act of devotion before going to sleep (hh. 5, 6). The last rak'ah of witr war, characterized by a special prayer offered before or after rukū' and called the qunūt (h. 7).

The Tarāwīh prayer really takes the place of Tahajjud, in the case of those who cannot get up for Tahajjud, in the month of Ramadzān. In its present form, it was introduced in the time of 'Umar (h. 8).

1. Abn Hurairah reported,

The Messenger of Allāh, peace and blessings of Allāh be on him, said,

"Our Lord, blessed and exalted is He, descends every night to the nearest heaven when the latter one-third of the night remains, (and) says, Is there any one who calls upon Me so that I may accept of him, who asks of Me so that I may grant him, who seeks forgiveness of Me so that I may forgive him?[204]

(B. 19:14.)

2. 'Ā'ishah reported,

The Messenger of Allāh, peace and blessings of Allāh be on him, used to say eleven rak'ahs of prayer-- this was his prayer, see meant, at night; and he used to remain in sajdah so long, before he raised his head, that one of you could recite fifty verses; and he said two rak'ahs before the morning prayer, then he lay down on his right side until the mu'adhdhin came to him for the (congregational) prayer.[205]

(B. 14:1.)

3. Masrūq said,

I asked 'Ā'ishah about the prayer of the Prophet, peace and blessings of Allāh be on him, at night. She said, (Sometimes) seven (rak'ahs), (sometimes) nine and (sometimes) eleven,

besides the two (sunnah) rak'ahs of the Fajr.

(B. 19:10.)

4. Ibn 'Umar said,

A man asked the Prophet, peace and blessings of Allāh be on him, while he was on the pulpit, What dost thou say about the night prayer? He said:

"Two (rak'ahs) at a time; and when one of you knows (that) the dawn (is near), he should add one (rak'ah)-this will make his prayer witr."

(B. 8:84.)

5. Ibn 'Umar reported,

The Prophet, peace and blessings of Allāh be on him, said:

"Let the witr be your last prayer at night."

(B. 14:4.)

6. Abn Hurairah said,

The Messenger of Allāh, peace and blessings of Allāh be on him, commanded me to say the witr before going to sleep.[206]

(B. 14:2.)

7. Al-Hasan ibn 'Alī said,

The Messenger of Allāh, peace and blessings of Allāh be on him, taught me sentences to be repeated in the qunūt[207] in witr:

"O Allāh! Guide me among those whom Thou hast guided, and preserve me among those whom Thou hast preserved, and befriend me among those whom Thou hast befriended, and bless me in whom Thou hast granted, and save me from the evil of what Thou hast ordered, for Thou dost order, and no order overrides Thy order; surely he is not disgraced whom Thou befriendest; blessed art Thou, our Lord! and highly exalted."

(AD-Msh. 4:35.)

8. 'Abd al-Rahmān said,

I went out with 'Umar ibn al-Khattāb to the mosque on a certain night in Ramadzān, and the people had formed themselves into different groups-- one man saying prayer alone and another saying prayers with a number of people following his prayer. So 'Umar said, I think if I gather them together behind one reciter, it would be much better. Then he made his decision and gathered them together behind Ubayy ibn Ka'b. Then I went out with him on another night and the people were following the prayer of their reciter.

'Umar said, This innovation is very good; and the part (of the night) in which they sleep is better than that in which they stand saying prayers--he meant the latter part of the night; and the people stood praying in the first part.[208]

(B. 31:1.)

MISCELLANEOUS PRAYERS (ISTIKHĀRAH. SALĀT AL-KUSŪF, ISTISQĀ')

ISTIKHĀRAH (lit. the asking of khair, i.e., good or blessing) means the asking of Divine blessing in the doing of a thing which a man intends to do. Kusūf means the eclipse of the sun or the moon. Istisqā' (from saqy, giving to drink) is a prayer for rain.

1. Jābir said,

The Messenger of Allāh, peace and blessings of Allāh be on him, used to teach us istikhārah in all matters, as he used to teach us a chapter of the Qur'ān. He said:

"When one of you intends the doing of a thing, he should say two rak'ahs[209] besides the obligatory prayers, then he should pray--'O Allāh! I desire Thy blessing by Thy knowledge, and I beg of Thee to give me power (to do it) by Thy power, and I ask of Thee Thy great grace, for Thou hast the power while I have not the power, and Thou knowest while I do not know, and Thou art the Great Knower of the unseen things. O Allāh! If Thou knowest that this affair is good for me in the matter of my religion and my living and the result of my affair--or he said, in the present state of my affair and in its future--then ordain it for me and make it easy for me and bless (me) therein; and if Thou knowest that this affair is evil for me in the matter of my religion and my living and the result of my affair--or he said, in the present state of my affair and in its future--then turn it away from me and turn me away from it and ordain what is good for me wheresoever it is, and make me contented with it.'

He (the Prophet) said,

"And he should say what he wants."[210]

(B. 19:25.)

2. Abd Allāh ibn 'Amr said 'When the sun was eclipsed in the time of the Messenger of Allāh, peace and blessings of Allāh be on him, a call was given that prayer-service gathering together (people) was going to be held.

(B. 16:3.)

3. 'Ā'ishah said,

'The Prophet, peace and blessings of Allāh be on him, recited aloud his qirā'at in the eclipse prayer and when he finished his recital he pronounced the takbīr and performed the rukū'; and when he raised (his head) from the rukū', he said, "Allāh listens to him who praises Him. Our Lord! And Thine is the praise." Then he returned to the recital (of the Qur'ān). In the eclipse prayer there are four rukū's and four sajdahs in two rak'ahs.[211]

(B. 16:19.)

4. Abd Allāh reported,

I saw the Prophet, peace and blessings of Allāh be on him, on the day he went out to pray for rain. He said, He (the Prophet) turned his back to the people and faced the Qiblah praying, then he turned over his outer wrapping garment, then he said with us two rak'ahs of prayer reciting therein the qirā'at aloud.[212]

(B. 15:17.)

BURIAL SERVICE

1. "And give good news to the patient ones who, when a misfortune befalls them. say: We are Allāh's and to Him shall we return. These are they on whom are blessings and mercy from their Lord. and these are the followers of the right course" (2:155-157).

2. "Our Lord! Forgive us and those of our brethren who had precedence of us in faith" (59:10).

3. "And never hold a burial service for any one of them who dies and do not stand (to pray) on his grave: surely they disbelieve in Allāh and his Messenger" (9:84).

When news of death is received, one should repeat the words innā li-llāh-i wa innā ilai-hi rāji'ūn (v. 1). The asking of forgiveness for the departed ones is a Muslim's duty towards a Muslim (v. 2), and this is done by the holding of a burial service at death. Burial service is prohibited in the case of those who disbelieve in Allāh and His Messenger (v. 3), the particular people referred to in the verse being hypocrites whose disbelief had become manifest.

Details as to the duties of the living towards the dying and the dead are given in Hadīth. Visiting the sick is a duty laid upon every Muslim (h. 11). When signs of the approach of death are witnessed in a person, the Holy' Qur'ān may be recited by his bedside (h. 1). Speaking well of the dead or a sick person when a visit is paid to him is recommended (h. 2). Grief for the dying or the dead is but natural. and one may weep when overcome (hh. 3. 4). but wailing, slapping the cheeks, tearing garments, etc., are forbidden (hh. 5, 6). Death of children is spoken of as a blessing in disguise (h. 7). The dead body must be washed and cleaned of all impurities and then wrapped up in clean cloth (hh. 8, 9). Following the bier is an act of great merit (h. 10), and a duty which a Muslim owes to his dead brother (h. 11). Respect must be shown to the bier, whether it be of a Muslim or of a non-Muslim (hh. 12, 13). A burial service may be held even in the absence of the dead body (h. 14). Women were advised not to follow a bier but there is no prohibition against it (h. 15). The bier may be followed on foot or riding (h. 16). Those who follow the bier arrange themselves into ranks behind the imām at the burial service (h. 17).

The service consists of four takbīrs and taslīm while standing, there being no rukū' or sajdah but wudzū' must be performed before joining it (bb. 17, 18). The bier is placed before the imām who stands opposite the middle. or the breast, of the dead body (b. 19). The first takbīr is followed by the recital of the Fātihah in a soft voice audible to oneself (preceded by the istiftāh, as in prayer); the second by the recital of al salāt 'ala-l-Nabī; the third by an intercessory prayer for the dead one in particular, but it includes the living as well; and the fourth by taslīm (hh. 20-23). Burial service must be held even on a Muslim who is guilty of heinous sins (H. viii:6). The committing of suicide is, according to Islām. a criminal act. but even such a person may not be deprived of the burial service (h. 24). In the battle-field the washing, the shrouding and the burial service were dispensed with, and two men were buried in one grave (h. 25). What should be said and done at the burial is related in (hh. 26, 27). The tomb should be raised a little above the ground and should be gibbous in shape (h. 28). The plastering of tombs or construction of buildings on them is discouraged (h. 29). The gathering of friends and relatives to console the bereaved family is allowed. and so also is the preparation for them of food, at which only those very nearly related should be present (hh. 30, 31). Abusing the dead is forbidden (h. 32). Charity on behalf of the dead is allowed (hh. 33, 34). When visiting graves, one must pray for the dead (h. 35).

1. Ma'qil said, of

The Messenger Allāh, peace and blessings of Allāh be on him, said:

Recite the Sūrah Yāsīn before the dying among you."[213]

(Ah-Msh. 5:3.)

2. Umm Salamah said,

The Messenger of Allāh, peace and blessings of Allāh be on him, said:

"When you visit a sick person or a dead one, speak well (of him), for the angels say āmīna to what you say."

(M-Msh. 5:3.)

3. 'Ā'ishah said,

'The Messenger of Allāh, peace and blessings of Allāh be on him, kissed 'Uthmān ibn Maz'ūn while he was dead, and he wept, so that the tears of the Prophet, peace and blessings of Allāh be on him, flowed over the face of 'Uthmān.[214]

(M-Msh. 5:3.)

4. Anas said,

Along with the Messenger of Allāh, peace and blessings of Allāh be on him, we visited Abū Saif, the blacksmith, and he was Ibrāhīm's foster-father.

The Messenger of Allāh, peace and blessings of Allāh be on him, took Ibrāhīm (in his arms) and kissed him and smelt him. Then we visited him after this while Ibrāhīm was yielding up his spirit; so tears began to flow from the eyes of the Messenger of Allāh, peace and blessings of Allāh be on him, 'Abd al-Rahmān ibn 'Auf said to him, And thou too, O Messenger of Allāh? He said, "O Ibn 'Auf! That is compassion." Then he wept again and said:

"Surely the eye sheds tears and the heart grieves and we do not say but what the Lord is pleased with; and we, O Ibrāhīm! are full of grief on account of thy separation."[215]

(B. 23:41)

5. 'Abd Allāh said,

'The Prophet, peace and blessings of Allāh be on him, said:

"He is not of us who slaps the cheeks and tears the garments and mourns like the mourning of the (days of) Ignorance."

(B. 23:35.)

6. 'Umar said,

'Leave them (the women) alone, weeping over Abu Sulaimān, so long as there is not throwing of dust on heads or wailing.[216]

(B. 23:33.)

7. Anas said, The Messenger of Allāh, peace and blessings of Allāh be on him, said:

"There is, from among the people, no Muslim who has three of his (children) dead before they have reached majority but Allāh will make him enter paradise by His gracious mercy on their account."

(B. 23:6.)

8. Umm 'Atiyyah said,

The Messenger of Allāh, peace and blessings of Allāh be on him, came to us while we were washing (the body of) his daughter; so he said:

"Wash her thrice or five times or more than that with water having (leaves of) the lote tree (boiled in it), and the last time put in camphor; and when you have finished, inform me."

So when we had finished we informed him, and he threw towards us his waist-wrapper and said "Put it next to her body."

(B. 23:9.)

9. 'Ā'ishah reported,

The Messenger of Allāh, peace and blessings of Allāh be on him, was shrouded

in three pieces of white washed cotton cloth,[217] made in Yaman; there was neither shirt in them nor turban.

(B. 23:18.)

10. Abū Hurairah said,

The Messenger of Allāh, peace and blessings of Allāh be on him, said:

"Whoever stays with a bier until he joins the burial service over it, he has one portion; and whoever remains present till the body is buried, he has two portions."

(B. 23:58.)

11. Barā ibn 'Āzib said,

The Prophet, peace and blessings of Allāh be on him, commanded us....to follow biers (to their last resting-place), to visit the sick person, to accept (the invitation of) one who invites (to a dinner), to help the oppressed one, to execute the oath, to return the salutation, and to utter a prayer for the sneezer.[218]

(B. 23:2.)

12. 'Āmir reported,

The Prophet, peace and blessings of Allāh be on him, said:

"When one of you sees a bier then, if he does not accompany it, he should stand until he leaves the bier behind or the bier leaves him behind, or it is put down before it leaves him behind."

(B. 23:47.)

13. Jābir said,

A bier passed by us and the Prophet, peace and blessings of Allāh be on him, stood up for it, and we (also) stood up. Then we said, O Messenger of Allāh! it is the bier of a Jew. He said:

"When you see a bier, stand up."[219]

(B. 23:49.)

14. Abū Hurairah reported, The Messenger of Allāh, peace and blessings of Allāh be on him, gave the news of the death of the Negus on the day on which he died. He went forth to the place of prayer and made the people stand in ranks and uttered four takbīrs.[220]

(B. 23:4)

15. Umm 'Atiyyah said,

We were forbidden to follow biers, and it was not a decisive prohibition.[221]

(B. 23:29)

16. Al-Mughīrah reported,

The Prophet, peace and blessings of Allāh be on him, said:

"The rider shall go behind the bier; and he who walks on foot may go behind it and before it and on its right and on its left, remaining near to it."

(AD-Msh. 5:5.)

17. Ibn 'Abbās reported,

The Prophet, peace and blessings of Allāh be on him, came to a grave apart from other graves, so he arranged the people into ranks and pronounced four takbīrs.[222]

(B. 23:54.)

18. The Prophet, peace and blessings of Allāh be on him, said:

"Whoever prays on the bier"............He called it salāt (prayer), and there is no rukū' in it, nor sajdah; and no one should talk during the service; and there is in it takbīr and taslīm; and Ibn 'Umar would not pray (on the bier) unless he had performed the wudzū'.

(B. 23:56.)

19. Samurah reported,

A woman died in childbirth, and the Prophet, peace and blessings of Allāh be on him, held a burial service over her, and stood opposite the middle (of the bier)."

(B. 6:29.)

20. Talhah said,

I prayed on a bier behind Ibn 'Abbās, and he recited the Fātihah and said, (I have done this) so that you may know that it is the Sunnah.[223]

11. This hadīth is again related by Bukhārī in 23:64 under the heading "Where to stand in the case of the woman and the man." This shows that the same position should be adopted by the imām, whether the bier is that of a mate or a female. Imām Abū Hanīfa interpreted the middle as meaning the breast, and that is the right position of the imām according to him, both in the case of the female and the male.

(B. 23:65.)

21. Abu Hurairah said.

The Messenger of Allāh, peace and blessings of Allāh be on him, said:

"When you pray over the dead one, be sincere in your prayer for him."[224]

(AD-Msh. 5:5.)

22. Abel Hurairah said,

The Messenger of Allāh, peace and blessings of Allāh be on him, used to say when he held a burial service over a bier:

"O Allāh! Forgive our living ones and our dead ones, and those of us who are present and those who are absent, and our young ones and our old ones, and our males and our females. O Allāh! Whom Thou keepest living among us cause him to live in submission to Thee, and whom Thou causest to die from among us make him die in faith. O Allāh! Do not deprive us of his reward, and do not make us fall into a trial after him."

(AD-Msh. 5:5.)

23. Hasan said,

The Fātihah should be recited over the child and then one should say, O Allāh! Make him for us a cause of recompense in the world to come and as one going before and a reward.[225]

(B. 23:65.)

24. Abū Hurairah said,

The Prophet, peace and blessings of Allāh be on him, said:

"Whoever strangles himself strangles himself into fire, and whoever stabs himself with a spear stabs himself into fire."[226]

(B. 23:81)

25. Jābir said,

The Prophet, peace and blessings of Allāh be on him, gathered together in one cloth two men out of those who were killed in (the battle of) Uhud. Then he asked, "Which of them knew more of the Qur'ān"? When one of them was pointed out to him, he gave him precedence in the lahd, and said, "I shall be a witness of these on the Day of Resurrection". And he commanded that they should be buried with their blood (on them) and they were not washed, nor was a burial service held over them."

(B. 23:72.)

26. Ibn 'Umar reported,

When the dead body was placed in the grave, the Prophet, peace and blessings of Allāh be on him, used to say:

"In the name of Allāh and with Allāh and according to the religion of the Messenger of Allāh."

(Ah-Msh, 5:6.)

27. Muhammad reported without tracing it up to the Holy Prophet,

The Prophet, peace and blessings of Allāh be on him, threw on the dead body (at its burial) three handfuls of dust with both his hands, and he caused water to be sprinkled on the grave of his son Ibrāhīm, and placed pebbles on it.

16. Lahd (from lahada, he inclined to a thing) is an oblong excavation in the side of the grave, a lateral hollow, in which the dead body is placed, the opening into the grave being then closed with bricks, so that when the grave is filled with earth the body remains intact. As this hadīth shows, preference was given to the lahd, the other body being placed in the shaqq, the pit itself, and therefore burial in the shaqq is not disallowed. In the case of a coffin, the shaqq alone would serve the Purpose.

The martyrs of Uhud were neither washed nor was a burial service held over them, and the same rule may be followed in the exigency of war or other exigencies. Towards the end of his life, however, the Holy Prophet held a burial service on the grave of the martyrs of Uhud.

(Msh. 5:6.)

28. Sufyān, the date-seller, reported:

He saw the grave of the Prophet, peace and blessings of Allāh be on him, gibbous-shaped.[227]

(B. 23: 96.)

29. Jābir said,

The Messenger of Allāh, peace and blessings of Allāh be on him, forbade the plastering of the grave, and the construction of a building on it, and sitting on it.[228]

(M-Msh. 5:6.)

30. 'Ā'ishah, wife of the Prophet, peace and blessings of Allāh be on him, reported:

When a person of her family died and the women gathered together over it, then they dispersed, except the family of the dead and those closely related to him, she used to order a cooking-pot of talbīnah which was cooked, then tharīd was made and the talbīnah was cast over it then she would say, Eat of it, for I heard the Messenger of Allāh, peace and blessings of Allāh be on him, say "The talbīnah gives rest to the heart of the sick one and takes away some of the grief."'[229]

(B. 70:24.)

31. 'Ā'ishah said,

'When the news came to the Prophet, of Allāh, peace and blessings of Allāh be on him, that Ibn Hārithah and Ja'far and Ibn Rawāhah were killed, he sat (in the mosque), and grief could be seen in his face, and I saw (him) through the opening at the pivot of the door.[230]

(B. 23:40.)

32. 'Ā'ishah said,

The Prophet, peace and blessings of Allāh be on him, said:

"Do not abuse the dead, for they have gone on to what they sent before."[231]

(B. 23:97.)

33. 'Ā'ishah reported,

A man said to the Prophet, peace and blessings of Allāh be on him, My mother died a sudden death, and I am sure that if she had been able to speak she would have given in charity; will she have a reward if I give in charity on her behalf? He said "Yes".[232]

(B. 23:94.)

34. It is reported on the authority of Sa'd ibn 'Ubādah that

His mother died while he was absent. So he said, O Messenger of Allāh! My mother died while I was absent; will it benefit her if I give in charity on her behalf? He said, "Yes". He said, Then I make thee a witness that my orchard Mikhrāf is a charity on her behalf.

(B. 55:15.)

35. Buraidah said,

The Messenger of Allāh, peace and blessings of Allāh be on him, used to teach them (to say), when they went forth to the graves:

"Peace be with you, Dwellers of this abode! from among the faithful and the Muslims; and we, if it please Allāh, will join you; we ask of Allāh security for ourselves and for you."

(M-Msh. 5:8.)

CHARITY AND ZAKĀT

1. "The parable of those who spend their property in the way of Allāh is as the parable of a grain growing seven ears with a hundred grains in every ear, and Allāh multiplies for whom He pleases, and Allāh is Ample-giving, Knowing" (2:261).

2. "O you who believe! Give in charity of the good things you earn and of what We have brought forth for you out of the earth, and do not aim at giving in charity what is bad" (2:267).

3. "If you give in charity openly it is well, and if you hide it and give it to the poor it is better for you. (2:271).

4. "Righteousness is this that one believes in Allāh and the last day and the angels and the Book and the prophets, and gives away wealth out of love for Him to the near of kin and the orphans and the needy and the wayfarer and the beggars and for the emancipation of the captives, and keeps up prayer and pays the zakāt" (2:177).

5. "(Zakāt) charity is only for the poor and the needy, and the collectors appointed for its collection, and those whose hearts are made to incline to truth, and the ransoming of captives, and those in debt. and for the way of Allāh, and (for) the wayfarer" (9:60).

The Arabic word for charity is sadaqah (from sidq, meaning truth). Zakāt, is originally zakawah, of the same measure as sadaqah, and its primary significance is increase or purification. Technically zakāt is a fixed portion of one's wealth which it is obligatory to give away annually for the benefit of the poor; the giving away of wealth to the needy is thus regarded as bringing about its purification and increase. Charity is likened to the sowing of seed which brings immense reward (v. 1). Only that charity is acceptable to God which is given out of one's lawful earnings (v. 2). It may be given either openly or in secret (v. 3). Zakāt is obligatory charity in addition to voluntary charity, and it forms with the keeping up of prayer the basis of Islām (v. 4; h. 10). Those appointed to collect the zakāt are included among the persons who are entitled to receive the zakāt (v. 5); and thus it is definitely laid down that the zakāt must be collected as public money. and distributed as such, under the directions of the head of the state or the head of a community.

Hadīth gives equal conspicuousness to this subject. Charity is here given the broadest possible significance, including the doing of any good to a fellowman or to an animal, refraining from doing evil, meeting one's brother with a cheerful countenance and so on (hh. 1-6). The giving of charity in secret is praised (h. 7). Asking for other people's charity is disapproved, earning one's livelihood by hard labour being far more preferable (h. 8).

Zakāt is a tax distinct from voluntary charity and the most important obligation next to prayer (H. ii:5, 6; hh. 9, 10). The minimum limit on which zakāt is payable is in silver about Rs. 50 (h. 11). Zakāt is payable at the rate of 2½ p.c. on all savings (h. 12) over which a year has passed (h. 13). A woman must pay zakāt out of her ornaments (h. 14). A trader is also liable to pay zakāt on his goods (h. 15), and being a tax on property it is payable out of the property of an orphan (h. 16). The zakāt is payable to the Muslim state or some other authority; it must be collected at some central place and then distributed (hh. 17, 18). One-third or one-fourth of zakāt may be left in the hands of the person who pays the zakāt, for distribution according to his choice (h. 19). The tax on land-produce is one-tenth or one-twentieth (h. 20), while in the case of treasure-trove or minerals it is one-fifth (hh. 21, 22).

1. Abū Mūsā reported,

The Prophet, peace and blessings of Allāh be on him, said:

"Sadaqah is incumbent on every Muslim."

They (his companions) said, O Prophet of Allāh! And (what about him) who has not got (anything to give)? He said:

"He should work with his hand and profit himself and give in charity."

They said, If he has nothing (in spite of this). He said:

"He should help the distressed one who is in need."

They said, If he is unable to do this. He said:

"He should do good deeds and refrain from doing evil--this is charity on his part."

(B. 24:31.)

2. Abū Hurairah reported,

The Prophet, peace and blessings of Allāh be on him, said:

"On every bone of the fingers charity is incumbent every day: One assists a man in riding his beast or in lifting his provisions to the back of the animal, this is charity; and a good word and every step which one takes in walking over to prayer is charity; and showing the way (to another) is charity.

(B. 56:72.)

3. Abū Hurairah reported,

The Prophet, peace and blessings of Allāh be on him, said:

"Removal from the way of that which is harmful is charity."

(B. 46:24.)

4. Jābir said,

The Messenger of Allāh, peace and blessings of Allāh be on him, said:

"Every good deed is charity, and it is a good deed that thou meet thy brother with a cheerful countenance and that thou pour water from thy bucket into the vessel of thy brother."

(Ah-Msh. 6:6.)

5. Abū Hurairah said,

The Prophet, peace and blessings of Allāh be on him, said:

"The man who exerts himself on behalf of the widow and the poor one is like the one who struggles in the way of Allāh, or the one who keeps awake in the night (for prayers) and fasts during the day."

(B. 69:1.)

6. Abū Hurairah said,

The Messenger of Allāh, peace and blessings of Allāh be on him,

"A prostitute was forgiven--she passed by a dog, panting with its tongue out, on the top of a well containing water, almost dying with thirst; so she took off her boot and tied it to her head-covering and drew forth water for it; she was forgiven on account of this."

It was said: Is there a reward for us in (doing good to) the beasts? He said:

"In every animal having a liver fresh with life there is a reward."[233]

(B. & M-Msh. 6:6.)

7. Abū Hurairah said on the authority of the Prophet, peace and blessings of Allāh be on him, (who said):

"There is a man who gives a charity and he conceals it so much so that his left hand does not know what his right hand spends."

(B. 24:11)

8. Zubair reported,

The Prophet, peace and blessings of Allāh be on him, said:

"If one of you should take his rope and bring a bundle of fire-wood on his back and then sell it, with which Allāh should save his honour, it is better for him than that he should beg of people whether give him or do not give him." (B. 24:50.)

9. Fātimah bint Qais said,

The Messenger of Allāh, peace and blessings of Allāh be on him, said:

"In (one's) wealth there is a due besides the zakāt;" then he recited:

"It is not righteousness that you turn your faces towards the East and the West (2: 177.)"[234]

(Tr-Msh. 6:6.)

10. Ibn 'Abbās reported,

The Prophet, peace and blessings of Allāh be on him, sent Mu'ādh to Yaman and said:

"Invite them to bear witness that there is no god but Allāh and that I am the Messenger of Allāh; if they accept this, tell them that Allāh has made obligatory on them five prayers in every day and night; if they accept this, tell them that Allāh has made obligatory in their wealth a charity which is taken from the wealthy among them and given to the poor among them."

(B. 24:1)

11. Abū Sa'īd said,

The Prophet, peace and blessings of Allāh be on him, said:

"There is no zakāt in what is less than five auqiyah (of silver), nor is there any zakāt in the case of less than five camels, nor is there any zakāt in what is less than five wasaq."[235]

(B. 24:4.)

12. 'Ali said,

'The Messenger of Allāh, peace and blessings of Allāh be on him, said:

"I remit (zakāt on) horses for riding and slaves for service; but pay the zakāt on silver, one dirham out of every forty dirhams; and there is no zakāt if there are 190 dirhams, but when it reaches two hundred, there are (to be paid) out of it five dirhams (of zakāt).

(Tr-Msh. 6:I.)

13. Ibn 'Umar said:

The Messenger of Allāh peace and blessings of Allāh be on him, said:

"Whoever acquires wealth, there is no zakāt on it until a year has passed over it."[236]

(Tr-Msh. 6.)

14. Umm Salamah said,

I used to wear ornaments of gold. So I said, O Messenger of Allāh! Is this hoard? He said:

"Whatever reaches the limit that thou shouldst pay zakāt out of it, and the zakāt is paid thereon it is not hoarding."[237]

(AD-Msh. 6:1.)

15. Samurah reported,

The Messenger of Allāh, peace and blessings of Allāh be on him, commanded us that we should pay zakāt out of that which we provided for trade.[238]

(AD-Msh 6:1.)

16. 'Amr ibn Shu'aib reported on the authority of his grandfather,

The Prophet, peace and blessings of Allāh be on him, addressed the people and said:

"Beware! Whoever is the guardian of an orphan who has property, should trade with it, and should not leave it (undeveloped), so that the zakāt should consume it."[239]

(Tr-Msh. 6)

17. Abū Hurairah said

When the Messenger of Allāh, peace and blessings of Allāh be on him, died and Abū Bakr became (his successor), and those of the Arabs who would disbelieve disbelieved, 'Umar said, How dost thou fight people (who profess Islām), and the Messenger of Allāh, peace and blessings of Allāh be on him, said "I have been commanded to continue fighting against people until they say, There is no god but Allāh8; whoever says this will have his property and his life safe unless there is a due against him and his reckoning is with Allāh." (Abū Bakr) said, By Allāh! I shall fight those who make a difference between prayer and zakāt, for zakāt is a tax on property; By Allāh! if they withhold from me even a she-kid which they used to make over to the Messenger of Allāh, peace and blessings of Allāh be on him, shall fight against them for their withholding it. 'Umar said, By Allāh! Allāh opened the heart of Abū Bakr (to receive the truth), so I knew that it was true.[240]

(B. 24:1.)

8. For what this means, see H. xix:17.

18. Abn Humaid said,

The Messenger of Allāh, peace and blessings of Allāh be on him, pointed a man from among the Asad to collect the zakāt of Banū Sulaim--he was called Ibn al-Lutbiyyah--so when he came to him, he called him to account for it.[241]

(B. 24:67.)

19. Sahl reported,

The Messenger of Allāh, peace and blessings of Allāh be on him, said "When you have formed an opinion, then take (the zakāt) and leave one-third; if you do not leave one-third, leave one fourth."[242]

(Tr-Msh. 6:l.)

20. 'Abd Allāh reported,

The Prophet, peace and blessings of Allāh be on him, said:

"In (the produce of) lands watered by rain and springs or in what is watered by water running on the surface of the ground is one-tenth, and (in) what is watered by wells one-twentieth."[243]

(B. 24:55.)

21. Abū Hurairah reported,

The Prophet, peace and blessings of Allāh be on him, said:

"............In treasure-trove (or minerals) one-fifth (shall be taken by the state)."[244]

(B. 24:66.)

22. Ibn 'Abbās said

Amber is not treasure-trove; it is a thing which the sea casts forth.

And Hasan said, In amber and pearls one-fifth (shall be taken by the state).[245]

(B. 24:65)

FASTING

1. "O you who believe! Fasting is prescribed for you as it was prescribed for those before You, so that you may guard (against evil); ...... and those who find it hard to do so may effect a redemption by feeding a poor man" (2:183, 184).

2. "The month of Ramadzān is that in which the Qur'ān was revealed; ...... Therefore, whoever of you witnesses the month, he shall fast during it, and whoever is sick or on a journey (he shall fast) a (like) number of other days" (2:185).

3. "It is made lawful to you to approach your wives on the night of the fast: they are an apparel for you and you are an apparel for them ...... and eat and drink until the whiteness of the day becomes distinct to you from the blackness of the night at dawn, then complete the fast till night" (2:187).

The directions relating to fasts are all contained in vv. 2:183-187. Fasts are to be kept during the 29 or 30 days of Ramadzān (v. 2). The Fast consists in abstaining daily, from dawn till sunset, from food and drink and sexual intercourse (v. 3). Fasting is recognised in hadīth as one of the pillars of Islām (H. ii:5, 6), but too much voluntary fasting is prohibited (H. ii:3.). While tasting, one must cultivate the habit of abstaining from evil, from foul talk and falsehood (hh. 1. 2), and of charity to fellow-men (h. 3). Fasting starts with the first day of Ramadzān and ends with the last day of it. Ramadzān being a lunar month, its beginning and end depend on the appearance of the new moon (H. xii. 1, 2). Fast must not be kept on a doubtful day (h. 4). The fast begins when dawn appears (h. 5), and ends when the sun sets (h. 6). When fasting, it is recommended that one should have a meal in the morning (h. 7). a little before dawn (h. 8).

Breaking the fast when one is journeying is permitted. but fasting is allowed in such a case unless it entails hardship (hh. 9. 10). One who is ill, the pregnant woman, the woman who gives suck, and a very old person may feed a needy person instead of fasting (h. 11). A woman should not fast when she is menstruating, but she should fast for the same number of days afterwards (h. 12).

When for some reason. the number of fasts is to be completed after Ramadzān, it may be done at any time before the next Ramadzān (h. 13). Fasting on 'Īd days is strictly prohibited (h. 14). When a person eats or drinks forgetting that he is fasting, the fast is not broken (h. 15). Cooling oneself, taking a bath, gargling or rinsing the mouth, and tasting of the food in the cooking-pot do not break the fast (h. 16), nor does vomiting (h. 17). I'tikāf or keeping to the mosque during the last ten days of Ramadzān, and not going out of it except for a need, may be resorted to by those who fast, and it is in these nights that the Laila al-Qadr must be sought (hh. 18,19).

1. Abū Hurairah reported,

The Messenger of Allāh, peace and blessings of Allāh be on him, said:

"Fasting is an armour with which one protects oneself; so let not him (who fasts) utter immodest (or foul) speech, nor let him act in an ignorant manner; and if a man quarrels with him or abuses him, he should say twice, I am fasting. And by Him in Whose hand is my soul, the odour of the mouth of one fasting is sweeter in the estimation of Allāh than the odour of muskh--gives up his food and his drink and his (sexual) desire for MY sake; fasting is for Me and I will grant its reward; and a virtue brings reward ten times like it."

(B. 30:2.)

2. Abū Hurairah said,

The Messenger of Allāh, peace and blessings of Allāh be on him, said:

"He who does not give up uttering falsehood and acting according to it, Allāh has no need of his giving up his food and his drink."

(B. 30:8.)

3. Ibn 'Abbās said,

The Messenger of Allāh, peace and blessings of Allāh be on him, was the most generous of all people, and he was most generous in Ramadzān, when Gabriel met him, and he met him in every night of Ramadzān and read with him the Qur'ān; so the Messenger of Allāh, peace and blessings was of Allāh be on him, more generous in the doing of good than the wind which is sent forth (on every body).

(B. 1:1.)

4. Silah said, reporting on the authority of 'Ammār,

Whoever keeps fast on a doubtful day, disobeys

Abu-l-Qāsim[246], peace and blessings of Allāh be on him.

(B. 30:11.)

5. 'Adiyy ibn Hātim said,

'When it was revealed, "Until the khait al-abyadz becomes distinct to you from the khait al-aswad", I betook myself to a black cord and a white cord[247] and put them under my pillow, and I looked at them (now and then) during the night but I could not distinguish between them; then I came to the Messenger of Allāh, peace and blessings of Allāh be on him, in the morning and I mentioned this to him. He said," By this is meant only the blackness of the night and the whiteness of the day."

(B. 30:16)

6. Umar said, 'The Messenger of Allāh, peace and blessings of Allāh be on him, said:

"When the night comes on from there and the day departs on this side and the sun goes down, the one who is fasting should break the fast."

(B. 30:43.)

7. Anas said,

The Prophet, peace and blessings of Allāh be on him, said:

"Have the meal before dawn, for there is blessing in the meal before dawn."

(B. 30:20.)

8. Abū Hāzim said that he heard Sahl ibn Sa'd saying, I used to have my meal before dawn in my family, then I used to hasten to overtake the morning prayer with the Messenger of Allāh, peace and blessings of Allāh be on him.

(B. 9:27)

9. Anas said,

We used to be on journey with the Prophet, peace and blessings of Allāh be on him, and he who kept the fast did not find fault with him who broke it, nor did he who broke the fast find fault with him who kept it.

(B. 30:37.)

10. Jābir said,

The Messenger of Allāh. peace and blessings of Allāh be on him, was on a journey, and he saw a crowd and a man who was placed under a shade. He said, "What is this?" They said, He is one fasting. He said

"There is no great virtue. in fasting when on journey."

(B. 30:36.)

11. 'Atā' said,

One should break the fast on account of illness, whatever it may be, as Allāh has said. And Hasan and Ibrāhīm said, concerning the woman who gives suck and the one with child, when they fear about themselves or their child, they should break the fast, then fast on other days. And as to the very old man when he cannot bear fasting--Anas, after he became old, fed one who was needy, for a year or two daily with bread and meat, and broke the fast.

(B. 65:ii, 25.)

12. Abu-l-Zinād said,

The menstruating woman has to fast afterwards, and she has not to perform any prayer (for the prayers omitted).

(B. 30:41.)

13. Abū Salamah said,

I heard 'Ā'ishah say, I used to be under obligation to fast on account of (the fasts omitted in) Ramadzān, and I was not able to perform this obligation except in Sha'bān."

(B. 30:40)

14. Abū 'Ubaid said,

I was present at 'Īd with Umar and he said, The Messenger of Allāh, peace and blessings of Allāh be on him, forbade fasting on these two days, the ('Īd) day of your breaking the fast and the other ('Īd) day on which you eat of your sacrifices.

(B. 30:66.)

3. Sha'bān is the month preceding Ramadzān.

15. Abū Hurairah reported,

The Prophet, peace and blessings of Allāh be on him, said:

"When one forgets and eats and drinks, he should complete his fast, for Allāh made him eat and drink."

(B. 30:26.)

16. Ibn 'Umar moistened a cloth and cast it over him while he was fasting; and Sha'bī entered a bath while he was fasting. Ibn 'Abbās said, There is no harm that one should taste of the food in the cooking-pot and anything else. And Hasan said, There is no harm in rinsing the mouth with water, and getting cooled, by one who fasts.

(B. 30:25.)

17. Abū Hurairah said,

When a person vomits, he should not break the fast.

(B. 30:32.)

18. 'Ā'ishah said,

The Messenger of Allāh, peace and blessings of Allāh be on him, used to confine himself (to the mosque) in the last ten days of Ramadzān, and he would say: "Seek the Lailat al-Qadr in the last ten days of Ramadzān."[248]

(B. 32:1)

19. 'Ā'ishah said,

The Messenger of Allāh, peace and blessings of Allāh be on him, would cause his head to get to me while he was in the mosque, and I would comb his hair; and he did not enter the house when performing i'tikāf except for a need.

(B. 33:1)

PILGRIMAGE (HAJJ AND 'UMRAH)

1. "Surely the first House appointed for men is the one at Makkah, blessed and a guidance for the nations.....And pilgrimage to the House is incumbent upon men for the sake of Allāh, upon every one who is able to undertake the journey to it" (3:95, 96).

2. "The pilgrimage is performed in the well-known months; so whoever determines the performance of the pilgrimage therein. there shall be no amorous speech, nor abusing, nor disputing in the pilgrimage and make provision" (2:197).

The word hajj means literally qasd (betaking oneself to a person or a place), and technically it means betaking oneself at a particular time to Makkah to perform certain devotional acts required by Islām. 'Umrah, from 'amara meaning he paid a visit to a place, means a visit to Makkah at any time of the year, and consists of some of the devotional acts of hajj. The Sacred House, called the Ka'bah a rectangular building 40 ft. by 35 ft., and the Haram, including Makkah and some adjacent territory, form the centre of the devotional acts of hajj and 'umrah.

The Ka'bah is called the first House of Divine worship on earth, and a pilgrimage to it is made incumbent upon every Muslim who has the means to undertake the journey to it (v. 1). Pilgrimage is spoken of as one of the basic institutions of Islām (H. ii:6), and its performance once in a lifetime is obligatory (h. 1). If a person is unable to perform it personally, he can do it through a substitute (h. 2). One must provide oneself beforehand with what is required for the journey (h. 3). Hajj can be performed only at a fixed time (h. 4) 'umrah may be performed at any time. Ihrām is the condition in which the pilgrim puts himself; what is to be done or not done in this state is described in hh. 5-8. There are particular places on the different routes to Makkah, where the pilgrim must enter into the state of ihrām (h. 9). The particular dhikr of hajj is the utterance of labbaika in a loud voice (h. 10). Making circumambulations of the Ka'bah, or tawāf, is the first devotional act of hajj or 'umrah (h. 11); it is performed by men and women together (h. 12). and may be made while riding (h. 13). The tawāf is commenced at the corner where the

Black Stone is fixed, which is kissed at the start by making a sign with something (h 13). In kissing it there is no idea of paying Divine honour to it; the other corners were also kissed (bb. 14, 15). The tawāf, as a devotional act, is likened to prayer, and therefore a menstruating woman should postpone it (hh. 16-17). In the tawāf the first three circuits are made running and the last four walking (h. 18). Running between the Safā and the Marwah, known as sa'y, is the next devotional act of hajj and 'umrah, and with this the 'umrah ends (h. 18) The hajj proper begins on the 8th Dhu-l-Hijjah, which is called the yaum al-tarwiyah when the pilgrims proceed to Minā, and here they say their Zuhr and 'Asr prayers (hh. 19, 20), On the 9th Dhu-l-Hijjah, called yaum al-'arafah, the pilgrims proceed from Minā to 'Arafāt where they say the Zuhr and 'Asr prayers, and the imām delivers the Khutbah (h. 21.) 'Arafāt is left after sunset, and the Maghrib and 'Ishā' prayers on that day and the Fajr prayer on the following day, are said at Muzdalifah (hh. 22, 23), which is left before sunrise for Minā where the animals are sacrificed at about breakfast time. Then the tawāf al-ifādzah is performed and after this the pilgrim gets out of the state of ihrām (h. 24). The flesh of the animals sacrificed may be eaten, stored or distributed. and their skins must be given in charity (h. 25, 26). The head is shaven or the hair is clipped as a sign of getting out of the state of ihrām (h. 27). The 10th Dhu-l-Hijjah and the following two or three days, called the ayyām al-tashrīq, are spent in Minā. During these days the pilgrims may occasionally visit the Ka'bah (h. 28). Stones are thrown at three places known as the Jamrah and the pilgrim prays to God to keep the Evil one away from him (h. 29). The final act of hajj is the tawāf al-wadā', the circumambulation of the Ka'bah when leaving Makkah (h. 30). The pilgrim is allowed to do any business before or after the hajj (h. 31).

1. Ibn 'Abbās reported,

Al-Aqra' asked the Prophet, peace and blessings of Allāh be on him, O Messenger of Allāh! Is the pilgrimage to be performed every year or only once? He. said: "Only once; and whoever does it more than once, it is supererogatory."

(AD. 11:I.)

2. Ibn 'Abbās said,

Fadzl was riding behind the Messenger of Allāh, peace and blessings of Allāh be on him, when a woman of (the tribe of) Khath'am came.........and she said, O Messenger of Allāh! The ordinance regarding pilgrimage made obligatory by Allāh for His servants found my father a very old man unable to sit firmly on a riding camel, shall I perform a pilgrimage on his behalf? He said, "Yes". And this happened in the Farewell Pilgrimage.

(B. 25:l.)

3. Ibn 'Abbās said,

The people of Yaman used to go to pilgrimage while they had no provisions with them and they said, We are those who trust (in Allāh). But when they came to Makkah they begged of people, so Allāh revealed: "And make provision, for the benefit of provision is the guarding oneself."

(B. 25:6.)

4. Ibn 'Umar said,

The months of hajj are Shawwāl and Dhul-l-Qa'dah and (the first) ten days of Dhu-l-Hijjah. And Ibn 'Abbās said, It is the Sunnah that a man shall not enter the state of ihrām[249] except in the months of pilgrimage.

(B. 25:34.)

5. Ibn 'Umar reported about the Prophet, peace and blessings of Allāh be on him,

A man asked him, What should a man wear in the state of ihrām? He said:

"He shall not wear shirt, nor turban, nor trousers, nor head-gear, nor any cloth dyed with wars or saffron; and if he does not find shoes, let him wear leather stockings, and he should cut them off so that they may be lower than the ankles."[250]

(B. 3:51)

6. Ibn 'Abbās said,

One in a state of ihrām may smell sweet-smelling plants, and look in the looking-glass, and use medicines out of what he eats, (such as) olive oil and butter; and 'Atā' said, He can wear a ring and carry a purse; and Ibn 'Umar made circuits, while he was in a state of ihrām, and he had girdled his belly with a cloth; and 'Ā'ishah's opinion was that there was no harm in wearing knickerbockers.[251]

(B. 25:18.)

7. Ibn 'Umar reported,

He heard the Messenger of Allāh, peace and blessings of Allāh be on him, forbidding women in a state of ihrām wearing gloves, and veil, and garments dyed with wars and saffron, and (saying) that they might wear besides this what they liked of garments coloured with safflower, or made of silk (or silk and wool), or ornaments, or trousers, or shirt.[252]

(AD. 11:29.)

8. Abū Allāh said,

'I heard the Messenger of Allāh, peace and blessings of Allāh be on him, uttering labbaika with glued hair.[253]

(B. 25:19.)

9. Ibn 'Abbās said, The Prophet, peace and blessings of Allāh be on him, appointed for the people of Madīnah Dhu-l-Hulaifah as the place where they should enter into the state of ihrām; for the people of Syria, Juhfah; for the people of Najd, Qarn al-Manāzil, and for the people of Yaman, Yalamlam. These are for them and for those who come upon them from other places, of those who have determined the performance of the hajj and 'umrah; and for him who is on the nearer side (of Makkah), the appointed place is from where he starts, so that for the people of Makkah it is Makkah.[254]

(B. 25:7.)

10. Ibn 'Umar reported,

The uttering of labbaika[255] by the Messenger of Allāh, peace and blessings of Allāh be on him, was thus:

"I am at Thy service, O Allāh! I am at Thy service.

"I am at Thy service; Thou hast no associate, I am at Thy service.

"Thine is the praise and Thine the favour and Thine the kingdom, Thou hast no associate."

(B. 25:26.)

11. Urwah said,

'Ā'ishah informed me that when the Prophet, peace and blessings of Allāh be on him, entered (Makkah on pilgrimage), the first thing that he did was that he performed ablutions, then he made circuits (round the Ka'bah),[256] and there was no 'umrah.

(B. 25:62.)

12. Ibn Juraij reported,

When Ibn Hishām forbade women making circuits along with men, 'Atā' said, How dost thou forbid them while the wives of the Prophet, peace and blessings of Allāh be on him, made circuits along with men? I said, Was it after the (verses relating to) curtain (were revealed) or before (it)? He said, By my life! I found this after the curtain (orders). I said, How did men mix with them? He said, They did not mix with them; 'Ā'ishah used to make circuits remaining aside from the men, not mixing with them; ... but when they intended to go into the (Sacred) House, they stopped before entering (it) till the men were turned out.[257]

(B. 25: 61)

13. Ibn 'Abbās said,

The Prophet, peace and blessings of Allāh be on him, made circuits of the House riding on a camel, and every time that he came to the Corner, he made a sign with something which he had with him and said, Allāhu Akbar.[258]

(B. 25:61.)

14. Ibn 'Umar reported,

'Umar said, speaking of the Corner (the Black Stone), I call Allāh to witness that I know that thou art a stone-thou canst not harm or profit; and if I had not seen the Messenger of Allāh, peace and blessings of Allāh be on him, kissing thee, I would not have kissed thee, then he kissed it.

(B. 25:56)

15. Ibn 'Umar said,

I have not given up the kissing of these two corners[259], in difficulty and in ease, since I saw the Messenger of Allāh, peace and blessings of Allāh be on him, kissing them both.

(B. 25:56.)

16. Ibn 'Abbās reported,

The Prophet, peace and blessings of Allāh be on him, said: "The making of circumambulations round the House is like prayer except that you talk in it; and whoever talks in it, let him not talk anything but good,"[260]

(Tr.-Msh. 11:3.)

17. 'Ā'ishah said,

'We went out with nothing in view but hajj, and when we reached Sarif, I menstruated. The Messenger of Allāh, peace and blessings of Allāh be on him, entered upon me and I was weeping. He said, "What is the matter with thee? Hast thou menstruated?" I said, Yes. He said:

"This is a matter that Allāh has ordained for the daughters of Adam, so do what the pilgrims do, except that thou shalt not make circuits round the House."

(B. 6:l.)

18. Ibn 'Umar reported,

When the Messenger of Allāh, peace and blessings of Allāh be on him, made circuits in the hajj and the 'umrah, on first coming (to Makkah), he started with three circuits at a fast pace, and made four circuits walking; then he said two rak'as of prayer; then he ran between the Safā and the Marwah.[261]

(B. 25:62)

19. Jābir said,

We came with the Prophet, peace and blessings of Allāh be on him, we were not in a state of ihrām till the day of tarwiyah, and with Makkah to our back we uttered labbaika for the hajj.[262]

(B. 25:81.)

20. Abd al-'Azīz said,

I asked Anas, Inform me about something which thou hast known about the Prophet, peace and blessings of Allāh be on him, where did he say the Zuhr and the 'Asr prayers on the day of tarwiyah? He said, At Minā.

(B. 25:82.)

21. Sālim reported,

Hajjāj ibn Yūsuf, in the year in which he attacked Ibn al-Zubair, asked 'Abd Allāh, How dost thou do in the halting-place on the day of 'Arafah?[263] Sālim said, If thou wilt follow the Sunnah, say the prayer at an early hour on the day of 'Arafah. Then 'Abd Allāh ibn 'Umar said, He is right; they used to combine the Zuhr and 'Asr prayers according to Sunnah.[264] (B. 25:88.)

22. Ibn 'Umar said,

The Prophet, peace and blessings of Allāh be on him, combined the Maghrib and 'Ishā' prayers at Muzdalifah-the iqāma was called out for each one of them; and he did not say any supererogatory prayer between them, nor after any one of them.²⁶⁵

(B. 25:96.)

23. 'Amr ibn Maimūn said,

I was present with 'Umar; he said the morning prayer at Muzdalifah.

(B. 25:100.)

24. Ibn 'Umar said,

In the Farewell pilgrimage the Messenger of Allāh, peace and blessings of Allāh be on him, profited by combining the 'umrah with the hajj .... So he performed the tawāf when he came to Makkah; and the first thing that he did was that he kissed the Corner, then he ran in the first three circumambulations and walked in four; then when he had finished the tawāf of the House, he said two rak'ahs of prayer near the Standing-place (of Abraham), then he uttered taslīm; and when he had done this, he came to the Safā, and made tawāf of the Safā and the Marwah seven times; then nothing that was forbidden to him (in ihrām) became lawful to him until he completed his hajj, and sacrificed the animal on the day of Sacrifice,²⁶⁶ and he returned and performed the tawāf of the House;²⁶⁷ then everything that was forbidden to him (in ihrām) became lawful for him.

(B. 25:104.)

25. 'Alī said.

The Prophet, peace and blessings of Allāh be on him, appointed me, so I superintended the sacrifice of camels; and he ordered me so I distributed their flesh; then he ordered me and i distributed their coverings and their skins.²⁶⁸

(B. 25:120.)

26. Jābir said,

We used not to eat of the flesh of our sacrifices beyond the three days of Minā; then the Prophet, peace and blessings of Allāh be on him, gave us permission and said: "Eat and take it as a provision (for the journey)." So we ate and took it as a provision.[269]

(B. 25:124.)

27. 'Abd Allāh said,

The Prophet, peace and blessings of Allāh be on him, and a party of his companions, had their heads shaven, and some of them had their hair clipped.[270]

(B. 25:127.)

28. Ibn 'Abbās reported,

The Prophet, peace and blessings of Allāh be on him, used to visit the House in the days of Minā.[271]

(B. 25:129.)

29. Jābir reported,

The Prophet, peace and blessings of Allāh be on him, threw stones in the forenoon on the day of Sacrifice, and after this he threw stones in the afternoon.[272]

(B. 25:134.)

30. Anas reported,

The Prophet, peace and blessings of Allāh be on him, said the Zuhr and the 'Asr and the Maghrib and the 'Ishā' prayers, then slept a little at Muhassab; then he rode to the House and performed tawāf.[273]

(B. 25:144.)

31. Ibn 'Abbās reported,

Dhu-l-Majāz and 'Ukāz were markets for trade (during the pilgrimage) in the days of Ignorance. When Islām came, they (the Muslims) disliked this until it was revealed: "There is no blame on you if you seek bounty from your Lord", (that is to Say), at the time of pilgrimage.[274]

(B. 25:150.)

JIHĀD

1. "And those who strive hard for Us, We will certainly guide them in Our ways" (29:69).

2. "Strive hard against them a mighty striving with it (the Qur'ān)" (25:52).

3. "And from among you there should be a party who invite to good and enjoin what is right and forbid the wrong. and these it is that shall be successful" (3:103).

4. "There is no compulsion in religion" (2:256).

5. "And fight in the way of Allāh with those who fight with you and do not exceed this limit" (2:190).

6. "And they will not cease fighting with you until they turn you back from your religion if they can" (2:217).

7. "And fight with them until there is no persecution and all religions are only for Allāh" (8:39).

8. "And if they incline to peace, do thou incline to it and trust in Allāh And if they intend to deceive thee, then surely Allāh is sufficient for thee" (8:61, 62).

9. "He it is who has sent His Messenger with the guidance and the true religion that He may make it overcome all (other) religions." (61:9).

Jihād means the exerting of one's power in repelling the enemy or in contending with an object of disapprobation. It carries a twofold significance in Islām, being applied to both. the purely missionary activities of a Muslim and his defence of the Faith. when necessary, in a physical sense. The first duty--the duty to invite people to Islām--is a permanent duty laid upon all Muslims of all ages; while the second is a duty which arises upon certain contingencies. The Holy Qur'ān calls attention to both these duties in the clearest and most forceful words. In the first place, it speaks of a jihād to attain to Allāh (v. 1). Then it speaks of carrying on a jihād against unbelievers by means of the Holy Qur'ān, and this it calls jihād-an kabīr-an, a very great jihād (v. 2). Islām's greatest jihād is, therefore, not by means of the sword, but by means of the Holy

Qur'ān, i.e., a missionary effort to establish Islām. We are further told that there should always be among Muslims a party who invite people to Islām (v. 3). Thus the missionary jihād of Islām is to be carried on in all circumstances.

The sword could never be used to force Islām on others. compulsion in religion being forbidden in clear words (v. 4). Fighting was undoubtedly allowed but it was expressly allowed only as a defensive measure against those who were bent upon annihilating Islām by the sword, not to compel people to accept Islām (vv. 5, 6). When persecution ceased and everyone was at liberty to profess whatever religion he liked, the sword had to be sheathed (v. 7). Even in the midst of the war, if the enemy wanted peace, war was to be discontinued (v. 8). The good news is finally given that not only will Islām not be annihilated but it would ultimately be ascendant over all other religions (v. 9).

Hadīth also speaks of both kinds of jihād. It is a Muslim's foremost duty, and the most excellent deed a Muslim can do (hh. 1, 2). A promise is given that if Muslims exerted themselves to their utmost to uphold the cause of Islām, they would be in the ascendant (hh. 3, 4). There is a further promise that divinely inspired persons, called rnujaddids, shall appear among Muslims to revive the faith (h. 5), and that a Messiah shall appear among them to carry the message of Islām to the Christian nations of the world in particular (h. 6).

Guiding a man to truth is spoken of as a Muslim's greatest treasure (h. 7), and the Holy Prophet himself wrote letters to kings in the 6th year of Hijrah, inviting them to accept Islām (h. 8). He never threatened any of them with invasion if his message was not accepted (h. 9). Muslims had to fight their battles, but this they had to do simply to defend Islām which unbelievers wanted to annihilate (vv. 5. 6) The cause of Truth was, however, to be defended unto death (h. 10), and Muslims were told to be always ready, if the need arose, to defend the Faith with the sword, that being the way to Paradise (h. 11). The Holy Prophet's own soul yearned after martyrdom in defence of the Truth and if possible. to come back to life and die again defending the Truth (h. 12), and such should, therefore, be the desire of every Muslim. Martyrdom could, however, be attained in other ways too (h. 13). Even women took part in the battles which were being fought in defence of Islām (hh. 14, 15), Non-combatants were not to be killed in battle, there being a prohibition against the killing of women and children (h. 16). Fighting was to cease if the enemy offered peace, even though his intention might be to deceive (v. 8), or if the enemy entered the brotherhood of Islām (h. 17).

1. Abu Hurairah said,

A man came to the Messenger of Allāh, peace and blessings of Allāh be on him, and said,

Guide me to a deed which is equal to jihād. He said, "I do not find it." (Then) he said: "Is it in thy power that when the one engaged in jihād goes forth, thou shouldst enter thy mosque and stand in prayer and have no rest, and that thou shouldst fast and break it not?" He said, Who can do it?

(B. 56:l.)

2. Abū Sa'īd al-Khudrī said,

It was said, O Messenger of Allāh! Who is the most excellent of men? The Messenger of Allāh, peace and blessings of Allāh be on him, said, "The believer who strives hard in the way of Allāh with his person and his property."

(B. 56:2)

3. Mughīrah reported,

The Prophet, peace and blessings of Allāh be on him, said,

"Some people from among my community shall remain in the ascendant, until the command of Allāh comes to them and they shall be triumphant."[275] (B. 61:28.)

4. 'Imrān ibn Husain said,

'The Messenger of Allāh, peace and blessings of Allāh be on him, said

"A party of my community shall not cease fighting for the Truth--they shall be triumphant over their opponents."²⁷⁶

(AD-Msh. 18.)

5. Abū Hurairah reported,

The Messenger of Allāh, peace and blessings of Allāh be on him, said:

"Surely Allāh will raise for this community at the beginning of every century one who shall revive for it its faith."²⁷⁷

(AD. 36:1.)

6. Abū Hurairah said,

The Messenger of Allāh, peace and blessings of Allāh be on him, said

"How would you feel when the son of Mary makes his appearance among you, and he is your imām from among yourselves."⁴ (B. 60:49.)

7. Sahl reported,

He heard the Messenger of Allāh, peace and blessings of Allāh be on him, say:

4. This is a further prophecy relating to the ascendancy of Islām. The son Of Mary is the Messiah, and Muslims are told that a Messiah would appear among them. This Messiah is called imāmu-kum min-kum i.e., your imām from among yourselves. In a hadīth of the Sahih Muslim on the same subject, the words are wa amma-kum min-kum, i.e., he (the Messiah) shall be your imām from among yourselves, leaving no doubt that a member of the Muslim community would be raised to the dignity of the Messiah. These words were no doubt added by the Holy Prophet to remove the possible misconception that the Israelite Messiah would appear among Muslims.

The prophecy relating to the advent of a Messiah among Muslims, generally known as the second advent of the Messiah, is on all fours with the prophecy relating to the second advent of Elias among the Israelites: "Elijah went up by a whirlwind into heaven" (II Kings 2:11); "I will send you Elijah the prophet before the coming of the great and dreadful day of the Lord" (Mal. 4:5). When Jesus Christ was confronted with this difficulty-- "Why then say the Scribes that Elias must first come?" (Mt. 17: 10),--he simply replied: "Elias is come already but they knew him not"......"Then the disciples understood that he spake unto them of John the Baptist" (Mt. 17:11-13); because, as further explained, John the Baptist came "in the spirit and power of Elias" (LK. 1:17). The appearance of the Messiah among Muslims thus meant only the appearance of a mujaddid "in the spirit and power" of the Messiah.

The Messiah's work is thus described in the Bukhārī "The son of Mary will appear among you as a judge, doing justice (between people), and he will break the Cross and kill the swine" (B. 60:49). This clearly shows that the Messiah would come when the religion of the Cross will be in the ascendant, and that his work will be to spread Islām among the Christian nations of the world in particular. which in other Hadīth is described as the rising of the sun in the West, the sun standing for the Sun of Islām and the West for the Western nations. Thus this prophecy speaks in fact of the final ascendancy of Islām in the world. ". . . Then invite them to Islām, and inform them of what is incumbent on them; for, by Allāh, if a single man is guided aright through thee, it is better for thee than red camels."[278]

(B. 56:102.)

8. Ibn 'Abbās reported,

The Messenger of Allāh, peace and blessings of Allāh be on him, wrote to the Cæsar inviting him to Islām, and sent his letter to him with Dihyah al-Kalbī, and the Messenger of Allāh, peace and blessings of Allāh be on him, ordered him to make it over to the Chief of Busrā that he might send it to the Caesar.[279]

(B. 56:102.)

9. Ibn 'Abbās reported,

... And this (letter) ran as follows:

"In the name of Allāh, the Beneficent, the Merciful. From Muhammad, the servant of Allāh and His Messenger, to Heraclius, the Chief of the Roman Empire. Peace be with him who follows the guidance. After this, I invite thee with invitation to Islām. Become a Muslim and thou wilt be in peace-- Allāh will give thee a double reward; but if thou turnest away, on thee will be the sin of thy subjects. And, O followers of the Book! Come to an equitable proposition between us and you that we shall not serve any but Allāh, and that we shall not associate aught with Him, and that some of us shall not take others for lords besides Allāh; but if they turn back, then say: Bear witness that we are Muslims."

(B. 1:1.)

10. Salamah said,

I swore allegiance to the Prophet, peace and blessings of Allāh be on him, then I turned to the shade of a tree. When the crowd diminished, he (the Prophet) said, "O Ibn al-Akwa'! Will thou not swear allegiance?" He said, I said, I have already sworn allegiance, O Messenger of Allāh! He said, "And do it again." So I swore allegiance to him a second time. I (the reporter) said to him, O Abu Muslim! For what did you swear allegiance (to him) then? He said, For death.[280]

(B. 56:110.)

7. B. 1:1 is a very long hadīth, only the part relating to the letter spoken of in the last hadīth is produced here. The subject-matter of the letter is a clear proof that invitation to Islām was not accompanied by any threat of hostilities. Similar letters were written to other rulers.

11. Abd Allāh ibn Abū Aufā reported,

The Messenger of Allāh, peace and blessings of Allāh be on him, said:

And know that paradise is beneath the protection of the swords."[281]

(B. 56:22.)

12. Abū Hurairah said,

I heard the Prophet, peace and blessings of Allāh be on him, say

"By Him in Whose hand is my soul, were it not that there are men among the believers who cannot bear to remain behind me--and I do not find that on which to carry them--I would not remain behind an army that fights in the way of Allāh; and by Him in Whose hand is my soul, I love that I should be killed in the way of Allāh then brought to life, then killed again then brought to life, then killed again then brought to life, then killed again."

(B. 56:7.)

13. Abū Hurairah said,

The Messenger of Allāh, peace and blessings of Allāh be on him, said:

Whom do you count to be a martyr among you?" They said, O Messenger of Allāh! Whoever is killed in the way of Allāh is a martyr. He said:

"In that case the martyrs of my community shall be very few--he who is killed in the way of Allāh is a martyr; he who dies a natural death in the way of Allāh is a martyr; he who dies of the plague (in the way of Allāh) is a martyr; he who dies of cholera (in the way of Allāh) is a martyr."[282]

(M-Msh. 18.)

14. Anas said,

On the day that battle was fought at Uhud, (some) people fled away from the Prophet, peace and blessings of Allāh be on him. He said, And I saw 'Ā'ishah, daughter of Abu Bakr and Umm Sulaim, and they had both tucked up their garments, so that I could see the anklets on their shanks, and they were carrying skins (full of water) on their backs, and they poured water into the mouths of the people then they went back and filled them again, then came and poured them into the mouths of the people.[283]

(B. 56:65.)

15. Rubayyi' daughter of Mu'awwidh said,

We used to be with the Prophet, peace and blessings of Allāh be on him, (in his battles), giving drink to and tending the wounded, and removing the slain to Madīnah.

(B. 56:67)

16. 'Abd Allāh reported,

A woman was found among the killed in one of the battles of the Prophet, peace and blessings of Allāh be on him, so the Messenger of Allāh, peace and blessings of Allāh be on him, forbade the killing of women and children.[284]

(B. 56:147.)

17. Ibn 'Umar reported, The Messenger of Allāh, peace and blessings of Allāh be on him, said:

'I have been commanded that I should fight these people till they bear witness that there is no god but Allāh and keep up prayer and pay zakāt. When they do this, their blood and their property shall be safe with me except as Islām requires, and their reckoning is with Allāh."[285]

(B. 2:16.)

MARRIAGE

1. "And He it is Who has created man from the water, and He has made for him blood-relationship and marriage-relationship" (25:54).

2. "And marry those among you who are single" (24:32)

3. "Do not prevent them (the divorced women) from marrying their husbands when they agree among themselves in a lawful manner" (2:232).

4. "And they (your wives) have made with you a firm covenant" (4:21).

5. "He it is Who created you from a single being, and of the same kind did He make his mate that he might incline to her" (7:189).

6. "And one of His signs is that He created mates for you from yourselves that you may find quiet of mind in them and He put between you love and compassion" (30:21).

7. "He made mates for you from among yourselves .... multiplying you thereby" (42:11).

8. "And the chaste from among the believing women and the chaste from among those who have been given the Book before you are lawful for you when you have given them their dowries, taking them in marriage, not fornicating, nor taking them for paramours in secret" (5:5).

9. "Forbidden to you are your mothers, and your daughters, and your sisters, and your paternal aunts, and your maternal aunts, and brothers' daughters, and sisters' daughters, and your mothers that have suckled you, and your foster-sisters, and mothers of your wives, and your step-daughters who are in your guardianship born of your wives to whom you have gone in--but if you have not gone in to them, there is no blame on you--and the wives of your sons who are of your own loins, and that you should have two sisters together except what has already passed...........and all married women except those whom your right hands possess" (4:23, 24). p. 267

10. "And give women their dowries as a free gift but if they of themselves be pleased to give you a portion of them, then eat it with enjoyment and with wholesome result" (4:4).

11. "And you have given one of them a heap of gold, take not from it anything" (4:20).

12. "There is no blame on you about what you mutually agree after what is appointed of dowry. (4:24).

13. "And if you fear that you cannot act equitably towards orphans, marry such women as seem good to you, two and three and four; but if you fear that you will not do justice between them, then (marry) only one or what your right hands possess. (4:3).

14. "And whoever among you has not within his power ampleness of means to marry free believing women, (he may marry) of those whom your right hands possess from among your believing maidens............So marry them with the permission of their masters and give them their dowries justly" (4:25).

The Arabic word for marriage is nikāh which means, originally 'aqd or uniting. It is recognised in Islām as the basis of human society, and marriage-relationship is given the same importance as blood-relationship (v. 1). Celibate life its against the teachings of the Holy Qurān which requires every Muslim to live in a married state (v. 2: h. 1), Castration is forbidden (hh. 2, 3), Marriage is a sacred contract (v. 4), which a man and a woman enter into by mutual agreement (v. 3). It is a contract entered into for life, temporary marriage being forbidden (h. 4). It serves a double purpose, being the means of the moral uplift of man and the means of the multiplication. of the human race (vv. 5-7). Marriage may be contracted with a non-Muslim woman (v. 8). It is prohibited within certain degrees of relationship (v. 9). The rule is the marriage of one man with one woman, but in exceptional cases a man may marry up to four women (v. 13). Marriage with slave-girls was allowed in case a man had not the means to marry a free woman (v. 14).

Marriage should be preceded by a proposal (h. 5). It is recommended that before making a proposal, a man should satisfy himself as to the desirability of the match (hh. 6, 7). The guardian must obtain the woman's consent (h. 8); where a woman was given in marriage by tier father and she disliked the match, the marriage was annulled (b. g). Marriage among equals is recommended, but all Muslims being equal there is no limitation as to the choice of the mate (b. 10). Nobility of character is the most valuable gift of a woman which should be taken into consideration in marrying her (b. 11). A dowry must be settled upon the woman, there being no limitation as to the amount (vv. 10, 11; h. 5): it may be increased or decreased by mutual consent after marriage (v. 12). Any conditions may be laid down at the time of marriage. so long as they are not against the law of Islām (h. 12). Shighār is prohibited (h. 13). The marriage must be publicly proclaimed, and it is recommended that it should be held in a public place and announced with the beat of duff, a musical instrument (h. 14). The contract is sanctified by a sermon before the parties announce their acceptance (h. 15). Gatherings on the occasion of marriage are also a means of making it publicly known (h. 16). Music is allowed at the marriage ceremony (h. 17). Gifts may also be given on this occasion (h. 18). A feast is recommended when the bride comes to the husband's house (hh. 19, 20), Prayer to God for Divine blessings is recommended at the first meeting of the husband and the wife (h. 21). Birth-control is allowed when it becomes a necessity (hh. 22, 23). When a baby is born, adhān must be called out into its ears (h. 24), and the naming and the tahnīk follow (h. 25). 'Aqīqah must also be performed if one can afford (hh. 26-28).

1. 'Alqamah said,

While I was going along with 'Abd Allāh, he said, We were with the Prophet, peace and blessings of Allāh be on him, and he said:

"He who is able to marry should marry, for it keeps the eye cast down and keeps a man chaste; and he who cannot, should take to fasting, for it will have a castrating effect upon him.[286]

(B. 30:10.)

2. Ibn Mas'ūd said,

We used to fight along with the Prophet, peace and blessings of Allāh be on him, and we had not (our) wives (with us); so we said, May we not castrate, O Messenger of Allāh? And he forbade us doing so.[287]

(B. 67:64)

3. Sa'd said, The Messenger of Allāh, peace and blessings of Allāh be on him, repudiated Uthmān ibn Maz'ūn's remaining celibate, and if he had permitted him, we would have been emasculated.

(B. 67:8.)

4. 'Alī reported,

The Messenger of Allāh, peace and blessings of Allāh be on him, forbade temporary marriage with women, and the eating of domestic asses. on the day of Khaibar.[288]

(B. 64:40.)

5. 'Ā'ishah reported,

In the pre-Islamic times marriage was in four ways; one of these being as the people's marriage to-day, a man asking another man for marriage with his ward or his daughter, then he settles on her a dowry, then marries her.[289]

(B 67:37.)

6. Jābir said,

The Messenger of Allāh, peace and blessings of Allāh be on him, said When one of you asks a woman in marriage, then if he is able that he should look into what invites him to have her in marriage, he should do it."

(AD. 12:17.)

7. Mughīrah reported,

He made a proposal of marriage to a woman, and the Prophet, peace and blessings of Allāh be on him, said:

"See her, for this is more likely to bring about agreement between you."

(Tr. 9:5.)

8. Abū Hurairah reported,

The Prophet, peace and blessings of Allāh be on him, said

"The widow shall not be married until she is consulted, and the virgin shall not be married until her consent is obtained."

They said, O Messenger of Allāh! How shall her consent be obtained? He said. "(It is sufficient) that she remains silent."[290]

(B. 67:42.)

9. Khansā' reported,

Her father gave her away in marriage, and she was a thayyib, and she did not like it. So she came to the Messenger of Allāh, peace and blessings of Allāh be on him, and he annulled her marriage.[291]

(B. 67:43.)

10. 'Ā'ishah said,

The Messenger of Allāh, peace and blessings of Allāh be on him, said:

"Select (fit) women (in respect of character) for your seed, and marry (your) equals and give (your daughters) in marriage to them."[292]

(IM. 9:46.)

11. Abū Hurairah reported,

The Prophet, peace and blessings of Allāh be on him, said:

"A woman is married on account of four things; on account of her wealth, and on account of (the nobility of) her family, and her beauty, and on account of her character,[293] so attain success with the one possessing nobility of character." (B. 67: 16.)

12. 'Uqbah said,

The Messenger of Allāh, peace and blessings of Allāh be on him, said:

"The conditions which are most worthy that you should fulfil are those with which you legalize sexual relations."[294]

(B. 54:6.)

13. Ibn 'Umar reported,

The Messenger of Allāh, peace and blessings of Allāh be on him, forbade, shighār; and shighār is this that a man gives his daughter in marriage to another man on condition that the latter shall give his daughter in marriage to him, neither of them paying dowry.[295]

(B. 67:29.)

14. 'Ā'ishah said,

The Messenger of Allāh, peace and blessings of Allāh be on him, said:

Make the marriage publicly known, and perform it in mosques, and beat at it with duff."[296]

(Tr-Msh. 13:3.)

15. Abd Allāh said:

'The Messenger of Allāh, peace and blessings of Allāh be on him, taught us the marriage sermon (which is thus):[297]

"All praise is due to Allāh; we beseech Him for help, and we ask for His protection, and we seek refuge in Him from the mischiefs of our souls; whomsoever Allāh guides, there is none who can lead him astray and whomsoever Allāh finds in error, there is none to guide him; and I bear witness that there is no god but Allāh and that Muhammad is His servant and His Messenger. 'O you who believe! Be careful of your duty to Allāh, by Whom you demand one of another your rights, and to the ties of relationship; surely Allāh watches over you. 'O you who believe! Be careful of your duty to Allāh with the care which is due to him, and do not die unless you are Muslims.' 'O you who believe! Be careful of your duty to Allāh and speak the right word; He would put for you your deeds into a right state and forgive you your faults; and whoever obeys Allāh and His Messenger, he indeed achieves a mighty success."

(AD. 12:31.)

16. Anas said,

The Prophet, peace and blessings of Allāh be on him, saw women and children coming from a wedding, so the Prophet, peace and blessings of Allāh be on him, stood up erect and said: "O Allāh! You are the most loved of all people to me." He said this three times.[298]

(B. 63:5.)

17. 'Ā'ishah said,

She conducted the bride to a man from among the Ansār. And the Prophet of Allāh, peace and blessings of Allāh be on him, said, "O 'Ā'ishah! Why had you no music with you, for the Ansār love music?[299]

(B. 67:64.)

18. Anas said,

The Messenger of Allāh, peace and blessings of Allāh be on him, had Zainab conducted to him on the occasion of his marriage with her; so Umm Sulaim said to me, What i if we send a present to the Messenger of Allāh? peace and blessings of Allāh be on him, I said to her, Do it. So she took dates and butter and cheese, and made a preparation mingling them in a cooking-pot, and sent me with it to him. And I went with it to him, and he said, Place it (here[300])."

(B. 67:65.)

19. Anas said,

Zainab bint Jahsh was conducted as a bride to the Prophet, peace and blessings of Allāh be on him, and bread and meat were served, and I was sent to invite people to the feast. A party came and had the meal, then went out; then another party came and had the meal and went out; I went on thus inviting until I could not find any one whom I should invite.[301]

(B. 65-33:8.)

20. Ibn 'Umar reported,

The Messenger of Allāh, peace and blessings of Allāh be on him, said:

"When one of you is invited to a marriage feast, he should go to it."

(B. 67:72.)

21. Ion 'Abbās said, carrying it back to the Prophet, peace and blessings of Allāh be on him, (who) said:

"If one of you, when he goes in to his wife, should say, 'In the name of Allāh; O Allāh! Ward off from us the Devil and ward off the Devil from that which Thou grantest us, then offspring is decreed for them, it (the Devil) will not harm it."

(B. 4:8.)

22. Jābir said,

We used to resort to 'azl[302] in the time of the Prophet, peace and blessings of Allāh be on him, and the Qur'ān was then being revealed.

(B. 67:97.)

23. Abū Sa'īd said,

.... We resorted to 'azl, then we asked the Messenger of Allāh, peace and blessings of Allāh be on him, and he said:

"What! Do you do it?" He said this thrice.

"There is no soul that is to be till the day of Resurrection but it will come into life."

(B. 67:97)

24. Abū Rāfi' said,

I saw the Messenger of Allāh, peace and blessings of Allāh be on him, calling out adhān for prayer in the ear of Hasan ibn 'Alī, when Fātimah gave birth to him.[303]

(Tr-Msh. 19:1)

25. Abū Mūsā said,

A son was born to me and I brought him to the Prophet, peace and blessings of Allāh be on him, He named him Ibrāhīm, and he chewed a date and rubbed thereby his palate, and prayed for blessings for him and gave him back to me.[304]

(B. 71:I.)

26. Salmān ibn 'Āmir said,

I heard the Messenger of Allāh, peace and blessings of Allāh be on him, say:

"In the case of the boy is 'aqīqah, so pour blood for him and remove from him the uncleanness."[305]

(B. 71:2.)

27. Umm Kurz said,

I heard the Messenger of Allāh, peace and blessings of Allāh be on him, say:

"In the case of a boy, two goats, and in the case of a girl, one goat (should be sacrificed.)"[306]

(Tr-Msh. 19:3.)

28. Ibn 'Abbās said,

The Messenger of Allāh, peace and blessings of Allāh be on him, sacrificed a ram each in the case of Hasan and Husain.

(AD-Msh. 19:3.)

DIVORCE

1. "And if you fear a breach between the two, then appoint a judge from his people and a judge from her people; if they both desire agreement, Allāh will effect harmony between them" (4:35).

2. "And if a woman fears ill usage or desertion on the part of her husband, there is no blame on them if they effect a reconciliation between themselves, and reconciliation is better. And if they separate, Allāh will render them both free from want out of His ampleness" (4:125-130).

3. "When you divorce women, divorce them for their prescribed time. Do not drive them out of their houses, nor should they themselves go forth, unless they commit an open indecency" (65:1).

4. "And the divorced women shall keep themselves in waiting for three qurū......and their husbands have a better right to take them back in the meanwhile if they wish for reconciliation" (2:228).

5. "And when you have divorced women and they have ended their term of waiting, do not prevent them from marrying their husbands when they agree among themselves in a lawful manner" (2:232).

6. "Divorce may be pronounced twice; then keep them in good fellowship or let them go with kindness: and it is not lawful for you to take any part of what you have given them, unless both fear that they cannot keep within the limits of Allāh; then if you fear that they cannot keep within the limits of Allāh, there is no blame on them for what she gives up to become free thereby ...... Then if he divorces her, she shall not be lawful to him afterwards until she marries another husband; if he (too) divorces her, there is no blame on them if they return to each other if they think that they can keep within the limits of Allāh" (2:229, 230).

7. "And if you wish to have one wife in the place of another and you have given one of them a heap of gold, take not from it anything would you take it by slandering her and doing her manifest wrong? (4:20).

8. "O you who believe! When you marry the believing women, then divorce them before you touch them, you have in their case no term which you should reckon" (33:49.)

9. "So when they have reached their prescribed time retain them with kindness or separate them with kindness, and call to witness two just ones from among you" (65:2).

10. "And for those of your women who have despaired of menstruation, if you have doubt, the prescribed time shall he three months, and of those too who have not had their courses; and as for the pregnant women, their prescribed time is that they lay, down their burden" (65:4).

Talāq (lit., undoing of a knot), or dissolution of marriage, is permitted by Islām, bur the right should be exercised under exceptional circumstances (hh. 1. 2). When differences arise between husband and wife, every effort should first be made for reconciliation, and private judges should be appointed for the purpose (v. 1). Divorce may be resorted to only if reconciliation cannot be effected (v. 2) The wife can claim a divorce for any good reason (vv. 2, 6; h. 2), even though there is no ill-treatment on the part of the husband. (h. 3). The procedure laid down requires that divorce should be pronounced, during the period of cleanness (h. 4), and must be followed by 'iddah, a waiting period of three qurū', about three months; and during this period the woman should remain in the house of her husband, and the parties may re-establish marital relations (vv. 3, 4). In the case of women who do not menstruate, the 'iddah is three months, and in the case of pregnant women it lasts till delivery (v. 10). There is no 'iddah when the divorce takes place before the parties have come together (v.8). After the 'iddah has passed away, the parties may remarry (v. 5). But the option for re-establishment of marital relations and remarriage is limited to two occasions, if the husband after benefiting of the permission on two occasions resorts to divorce a third time the divorce becomes irrevocable and reconciliation cannot be effected, nor can the parties remarry. An exception in this case is, however, made when the wife has married another husband and becomes eligible again for marriage through a divorce (v. 6), or any other reason. Halālah is an un-Islamic practice, and it was denounced by the Holy Prophet (h. 8). The dowry settled on the wife at the time of marriage cannot be taken back by the husband on divorce. unless the wife is guilty of adultery (v. 7), or she wants a divorce without any fault on the part of her husband (b. 3). The divorce must be pronounced in the presence of witnesses (v. 8; h. 9). Divorce should be pronounced only once; its utterance thrice on one occasion is un-Islamic (hh. 5, 6). The three divorces allowed are separate acts between which there must be an interval (h. 7). To give the wife option of freeing herself from the marital tie is not a divorce, unless the wife exercises the right (h. 10). The wife is considered to be divorced if the husband is mafqūd (h. 11). Divorce also takes place when li'ān is resorted to. but in this case the husband cannot claim the return of dowry (h. 12). If a man resorts to ilā' (temporary cessation of marital relations), without naming a period, he is bound either to reestablish the normal relations after four months or to divorce the wife after the lapse of this period (h. 13).

1. Ibn 'Umar reported,

The Prophet, peace and blessings of Allāh be on him, said

"With Allāh, the most detestable of all things permitted is divorce."[307]

(AD. 13:1)

2. Thaubān said,

The Messenger of Allāh, peace and blessings of Allāh be on him, said:

"Whatever woman asks for divorce from her husband without any harm, the sweet odour of paradise shall be forbidden to her."[308]

(Ah. 5, 277.)

3. Ibn 'Abbās reported,

The wife of Thābit Ibn Qais came to the Prophet, peace and blessings of Allāh be on him, and said, O Messenger of Allāh! I do not find fault in Thābit ibn Qais regarding his morals or faith, but I hate disbelief in Islām. The Messenger of Allāh, peace and blessings of Allāh be on him, said: "Wilt thou return to him his orchard?" She said, Yes. So the Messenger of Allāh, peace and blessings of Allāh be on him, said (to Thābit): "Accept the orchard and divorce her."[309]

(B. 68:12.)

4. Ibn 'Umar reported,

He divorced his wife while she was menstruating. 'Umar mentioned this to the Messenger of Allāh, peace and blessings of Allāh be on him, so the Messenger of Allāh, peace and blessings of Allāh be on him, became displeased on account of this and said:

"He should take her back, then keep her until she is clean, then menstruates and (again) becomes clean, if it then appears to him that he should divorce her, he should divorce her while she is in a clean condition before he approaches her. This is the 'iddah as Allāh has commanded it."[310]

(B. 65:65.)

5. Ibn 'Abbās said,

The (procedure of) divorce in the time of the Messenger of Allāh, peace and blessings of Allāh be on him, in that of Abū Bakr and for two years in the caliphate of 'Umar ibn al-Khattāb, was that divorce uttered thrice (on one occasion) was considered as one divorce. Then 'Umar said, People have made haste in a matter in which there was moderation for them; so we may make it take effect with regard to them. So he made it take effect with regard to them.[311]

(Ah. I, 314.)

6. Mahmūd ibn Labīd said,

The Messenger of Allāh, peace and blessings of Allāh be on him, was informed about a man who divorced his wife, divorcing (her) three times together, so he stood up in displeasure and said:

"Is the Book of Allāh being sported with while I am in your midst?"

(Ns. 27:6.)

7. Rukānah ibn 'Abd Yazīd reported,

He divorced his wife Suhaimah thrice and informed the Prophet, peace and blessings of Allāh be on him, about it and said, I call Allāh to witness that I intended only a single (divorce). The Messenger of Allāh, peace and blessings of Allāh be on him, said

"Dost thou call Allāh to witness that thou didst not intend but a single (divorce)?" He said, Yes, I call Allāh to witness that I did not intend but a single (divorce). So the Messenger of Allāh, peace and blessings of Allāh be on him, returned her back to him, and he divorced her a second time in the time of 'Umar, and a third time in the time of 'Uthmān.[312]

(AD. 13: 13.)

8. 'Ali said,

The 'Messenger of Allāh, peace and blessings of Allāh be on him, cursed the man who committed halālah and the one for whom halālah was committed.'

(Tr. 9:25)

9. Mutarrif reported,

'Imrān was asked about a man who divorced his wife, then he had intercourse with her, and he did not call in witnesses on the occasion of the divorce, nor on taking her back. 'Imrān said, Thou divorcest against the Sunnah and takest back against the Sunnah; have witnesses on the occasion of her divorce and on taking her back.[313]

(IM. 10:5.)

7. In pre-Islamic Arabia the divorce was pronounced thrice and was irrevocable, and remarriage between the parties required the wife to go through a temporary marriage with another husband who divorced her after having sexual connection with her. This practice was called halālah (lit., making a thing lawful). Without going through it, it was not lawful for the divorced pair to return to marital relationship. Islām did not recognise temporary marriage (H. xx:4), and therefore halālah was denounced. The marriage after an irrevocable divorce spoken of in 2:230 is quite different, being a perpetual marital tie.

10. 'Ā'ishah said,

The Messenger of Allāh, peace and blessings of Allāh be on him, gave us option; so we chose Allāh and His Messenger; this was not reckoned for us as anything.[314]

(B. 68:5.)

11. Ibn al-Musayyab said.

When a person is found missing while fighting, his wife shall wait for one year.[315]

(B. 68:22.)

12. 'Abd Allāh reported,

A man from among the Ansār accused his wife of adultery; so the Prophet, peace and blessings of Allāh be on him, asked them both to take an oath, then he ordered them to be separated from each other.[316]

(B. 68:27.)

13. Ibn 'Umar used to say, with respect to ilā' about which Allāh has spoken,

It is not lawful for any one after the prescribed time (of four months) has passed away, except that he should either keep (the wife) in good fellowship or resolve upon divorce.[317]

(B. 68:21.)

BUYING AND SELLING (BUYŪ')

1. "Men shall have the benefit of what they earn, and women shall have the benefit of what they earn" (4:32).

2. "Do not devour your property among yourselves falsely except that it be trading by your mutual consent" (4:29).

3. "Men whom neither merchandise nor selling diverts from the remembrance of Allāh" (24:37).

4. "And when the prayer has been ended, disperse abroad in the land and seek of Allāh's bounty" (62:10).

5. "Give a full measure when you measure out and weigh with a fair balance" (17:35).

The Arabic word for trading is bai' which means both buying and selling. Every man must earn his own living (v. 1, h. 1) and every profession is, therefore, honourable, even that of the hewer of wood (H. xvi:8). A man may follow any worldly pursuit that he likes but duty to Allāh shall take precedence of all other duties (v. 3; h. 2). Among means of livelihood, trade occupies the most prominent place, the honest merchant being one of the righteous servants of Allāh (v. 2, h. 3). The seller is required to be just in weighing (v. 5), generous in dealing (h. 4), giving respite even to those in easy circumstances and forgiving those in straitened circumstances (h. 5). If there is a defect in the thing sold, it must be made manifest to the purchaser (h. 6). Two kinds of sale prevalent before Islām, munābadhah and mulāmasah, in which the purchaser was deprived of the occasion to examine the thing purchased. were made unlawful (h. 7). The taking of oaths in selling things is forbidden (h. 8). Special directions are given as to the sale of cereals, because they are the prime need of every man, rich or poor. They should be sold in the market so that they may be had at the price which the producer obtained (h. 9). Speculation in this prime need of humanity is disallowed, it being necessary that cereals shall be sold only after their possession has been obtained (h. 10). The withholding of cereals to raise their price artificially is prohibited (h. 11). Najsh or deceiving a purchaser through a third party offering a higher price is forbidden (h. 12), but auction or open sale to the highest bidder is allowed (h. 13). Similarly enhancing the price of milch animals by leaving them unmilked before their sale is forbidden (h. 14). Advance prices or earnest money could be paid only when the measure or weight and time of delivery were definitely settled (h. 15). Immovable property, it is recommended, should only be sold if the seller intends investing money in other immovable property (h. 16). Trade in idols and in things which are forbidden as food, such as wine, swine and that which dies of itself, is disallowed (h. 17), but as there is an express direction that the skin of a dead animal should nor be thrown away and advantage should be derived therefrom (h. 18), trade in it is evidently not prohibited, and the same rule may be followed in other things prohibited as food, such as the bones and fat of a dead animal, etc.

1. Miqdām reported,

The Messenger of Allāh, peace and blessings of Allāh be on him, said:

"No one eats better food than that which he eats out of the work of his hand."[318]

(B. 34:15.)

2. Qatādah said, People used to buy and sell and carry on trade (in goods), but when it was the turn of a duty out of the duties imposed by Allāh, neither merchandise nor selling diverted them from the remembrance of Allāh, so that they performed their duty to Allāh (first).[319]

(B. 34:8.)

3. Abū Sa'īd reported,

The Prophet, peace and blessings of Allāh be on him, said:

"The truthful, honest merchant is with the prophets and the truthful ones and the martyrs."[320]

(Tr. 12:4.)

4. Jābir reported,

The Messenger of Allāh, peace and blessings of Allāh be on him, said:

"May Allāh have mercy on the man who is generous when he buys and when he sells and when he demands (his due)."

(B. 34:16.)

5. Hudhaifah said,

The Prophet, peace and blessings of Allāh be on him, said:

"The angels met the soul of a man from among those who were before you, (and) they said, Hast thou done any good? He said, I used to give respite to the one in easy circumstances and forgive one who was in straitened circumstances. So they forgave him."

(B. 34:17.)

6. Hakīm ibn Hizām said,

The Messenger of Allāh, peace and blessings of Allāh be on him, said:

"The buyer and the seller have the option (of cancelling the contract) as long as they have not separated, then if they both speak the truth and make manifest,[321] their transaction shall be blessed, and if they conceal and tell lies, the blessing of their transaction shall be obliterated."

(B. 34:19.)

7. Abū Sa'īd reported, The Messenger of Allāh, peace and blessings of Allāh be on him, forbade munābadhah, and this was the throwing of a person his cloth in sale to another before he examined it or looked at it; and he forbade mulāmasah, and mulāmasah was the touching of a cloth without looking at it.[322]

(B. 34:62.)

8. Abū Hurairah said,

I heard the Messenger of Allāh, peace and blessings of Allāh be on him, say

"The taking of oaths makes the commodities sell, but it obliterates the blessing (therein)."

(B. 34:26.)

9. Ibn 'Umar reported,

They used to buy cereals from the camel-owners in the time of the Prophet, peace and blessings of Allāh be on him, and he used to send to them a person who forbade them selling it where they purchased it, until it was brought to the place where cereals were sold.

(B. 34:49.)

10. Ibn 'Umar said,

The Prophet, peace and blessings of Allāh be on him, said:

"Whoever buys cereals, he shall not sell them until he obtains their possession."

(B. 34:54.)

11. Ma'mar said,

The Messenger of Allāh, peace and blessings of Allāh be on him, said,

"Whoever withholds cereals that they may become scarce and dear, is a sinner."[323]

(M-Msh. 12:8.)

12. Abū Hurairah said,

The Messenger of Allāh, peace and blessings of Allāh be on him, forbade the dweller of the town selling for one coming from the desert, and (he said):

"Do not resort to najsh; and let not a man carry on a transaction against his brother's transaction."[324]

(B. 34:58.)

13. Anas reported,

The Messenger of Allāh, peace and blessings of Allāh be on him, purchased a piece of hair-cloth and a bowl, and he said:

'Who will buy this piece of hair-cloth and bowl?"

A man said, I take them for one dirham.

The Prophet, peace and blessings of Allāh be on him, said: "Who will give more than one dirham? Who will give more than one dirham?"

A man gave him two dirhams and bought them from him.[325]

(Tr. 12:10.)

14. Abū Hurairah reported on the authority of the Prophet, peace and blessings of Allāh be on him:

"Do not leave the camels and the goats unmilked,[326] and whoever buys them after (they have been so left), he has the option of doing one of the two things when he milks them; if he pleases he may keep them and if he pleases he may give them back (to the owner) with sā' of dates.

(B. 34:64.)

15. Ibn 'Abbās said,

The Prophet, peace and blessings of Allāh be on him, came to Madīnah, and they used to pay two and three years in advance for dates.[327] So he said:

"He who pays in advance for a commodity, (he should do it) for a specified measure and a definite weight to be delivered at a fixed time."

(13. 35:2.)

16. Sa'īd ibn Huraith said,

The Messenger of Allāh, peace and blessings of Allāh be on him, said:

"Whoever sells a house or a land yielding revenue, then he does not invest the price on a thing akin to it, he is not likely to be blessed therein."[328]

(Ah. IV. 307.)

17. Jābir reported,

He heard the Messenger of Allāh, peace and blessings of Allāh be on him, say, while he was at Makkah in the year of the conquest (of Makkah):

Allāh and His Messenger have forbidden trade in wine and the dead (animals) and swine and Idols."[329]

(B. 34:112.)

18. Ibn 'Abbās said, The Prophet, peace and blessings of Allāh be on him, saw a dead goat which had been given to a maid of Maimūnah out of zakāt. The Prophet, peace and blessings of Allāh be on him, said: "Why did you not benefit by its skin?" They said, It was dead. He said: "Only the eating thereof is forbidden."[330]

(B. 24:61)

CULTIVATION OF LAND (AL-HARTH WA-L-MUZĀRA'AH)

1. "Do they not consider that We drive the water to a land having no herbage, then We bring forth thereby seed produce of which their cattle and they themselves eat" (32:27).

2. "And He it is Who produces gardens (of vine), trellised and untrellised, and palms and seed-produce, of which the fruits are of various sorts, and olives and pomegranates, like and unlike" (6:142).

3. "Like seed produce that puts forth its sprout then strengthens it, so it becomes stout and stands firmly on its stem, delighting the sowers" (48:29).

Harth is the tilling of land, and muzāra'ah (from zara'a, he sowed the seed) is the making of a contract with another for labour on land to sow and till it for a share of its produce. The Holy Qur'ān draws attention to the necessity of turning waste-land into gardens by making arrangements for watering it, and growing good crops (vv. 1-3). Hadīth speaks of it as an act of great merit (h. 1), but it gives a warning at the same time that a people who give themselves up entirely to agriculture neglecting other lines of their development. are not capable of great and glorious deeds (h. 2). Impetus is given to the cultivation of wasteland (h. 3). It is allowed to let to another person land for cultivation for a part of the produce (hh. 4, 5), or for money (h. 6). but it is at the same time recommended that a person who can afford it should give land rent-free to his poor brother (h. 7). A person having his land on a water channel is entitled to water his fields. but he must allow the water to pass on to others when his need is satisfied (h. 8). The digging of a well is an act of great merit (h. 9). A neighbour's right to land must be respected very scrupulously (h. 10).

1. Anas said,

The Messenger of Allāh, peace and blessings of Allāh be on him, said

"There is no Muslim who plants a tree or cultivates land, then there eat of it birds or a man or an animal but it is a charity for him."

(B. 41:1.)

2. It is reported about Abū Umāmah that he said, when he saw a plough and some other agricultural implements, I heard the Prophet, peace and blessings of Allāh be on him, say:

"This does not enter the house of a people but it brings ingloriousness with it."[331]

(B. 41:2.)

3. 'Ā'ishah reported,

The Prophet, peace and blessings of Allāh be on him, said:

"Whoever cultivates land which is not the property of any one has a better title to it."

(B. 41:15.)

4. Abū Ja'far said,

There was not in Madīnah any house of the emigrants but they cultivated (land) on one-third and one-fourth (of the produce) .... And 'Umar employed people (for cultivation) on condition that if 'Umar supplied the seed from his pocket, he should have one-half (of the produce), and if they supplied the seed, they should have such and such a portion.[332]

(B. 41:8.)

5. Ibn 'Umar reported,

The Messenger of Allāh, peace and blessings of Allāh be on him, granted (the lands of) Khaibar to the Jews on condition that they worked thereon and cultivated them and they should have half of the produce.

(B. 41:11)

6. Rāfi' reported,

They used to have land cultivated in the time of the Prophet, peace and blessings of Allāh be on him, taking what grew on the water-courses or anything which the owner of the land reserved for himself. So the Prophet, peace and blessings of Allāh be on him, forbade this. I (the reporter) said to Rāfi', How is it if it is done on payment of dinārs and dirhams? Rāfi' said, There is no harm in taking dinārs and dirhams.

(B. 41:19.)

7. 'Amr said,

I said to Tā'ūs, Thou shouldst give up Mukhābrah, for they say that the Prophet, peace and blessings of Allāh be on him. forbade it. He said ......, Ibn 'Abbās informed me that the Prophet, peace and blessings of Allāh be on him, did not forbid this but he only said:

"If one of you gives it as a gift to his brother, it is better for him than that he takes for it a fixed payment."[333]

(B. & M-Msh. 12:13)

8. Abū Hurairah reported,

The Messenger of Allāh, peace and blessings of Allāh be on him, said:

"Excess of water should not be withheld, arresting thereby the growth of herbage."[334]

(B. 42:2.)

9. The Prophet, peace and blessings of Allāh be on him, said

"Whoever digs the well of Rūma, for him is paradise." So 'Uthmān had it dug.[335]

(B. 62:7.)

10. Ibn 'Umar said,

The Prophet, peace and blessings of Allāh be on him, said:

Whoever takes any part of land without having a right to it, he shall be, as a punishment for it, sunk down into earth on the day of resurrection to the depth of seven earths."[336]

(B. 46:13.)

MATTERS RELATING TO SERVICE (IJĀRĀT)

1. "My father invites thee that he may give thee remuneration for thy having watered for us" (28:25).

2. "The best of those that thou canst take into service is the strong one, the faithful one" (28:26).

3. "Allāh commands you to make over trusts to those worthy of them" (4:58).

4. "Place me in authority over the treasures of the land, for I am a good keeper. knowing well" (12:55).

5. "He who acts unfaithfully shall bring that in respect of which he has acted unfaithfully on the day of resurrection" (3:160).

The word ijārah (from air meaning reward) signifies compensation for work done, or wages paid by one man to another for service rendered. The two basic rules laid down in this connection, both in the Holy Qur'ān and the Hadīth, are that the servant shall do his work faithfully and to the best of his ability, and that the master shall pay him fully for the service rendered (vv. 1, 2). The officials of the government are placed in the category of servants, however high their position may be. The trust spoken of in v. 3 relates to the authority placed in the hands of such servants as explained by the Holy Prophet (B. 3:2). Authority to rule must be placed in the hands of those who are fit to rule (v. 4). Unfaithfulness is severely condemned (v. 5).

Even such a service as the tending of goats is considered honourable, the Holy Prophet himself doing this work in his earlier days (h. 1), and his companions did not disdain the work of a porter (h. 2). The faithful servant carrying out the orders of his master is ranked with those who give charity (h. 3). As conditions of different kinds of service must necessarily be different, the broad rule is laid down that the master and the servant, as well as all those who make a contract, are bound by the conditions of the contract of service (h. 4). A Muslim can take a non-Muslim into his service (h. 5), and he can also enter into the service of a non-Muslim (h. 6). A man who renders a service in connection with the teaching of the Holy Qur'ān is entitled to remuneration, as is any other person engaged for any kind of service (h. 7), even a commission agent (h. 8). The withholding of remuneration for service rendered is the gravest of sins (h. 9). Unpaid remuneration may be invested in some profitable business, and the servant is entitled to all profits accruing thus (h. 10). The greatest caution must be exercised in the choice of public servants (h. 11). Such servants are only entitled to the remuneration paid by the state and they cannot accent gifts from the public (h. 12). Misappropriation or dishonestly taking any part of the master's property is condemned in very strong terms (h. 13).

1. Abū Hurairah reported, The Prophet, peace and blessings of Allāh be on him, said:

"Allāh did not raise a prophet but he pastured goats."

His companions said, And thou?

He said:

"Yes! I used to pasture them for the people of Makkah for some carats."[337]

(B. 37:2.)

2. Abū Mas'ūd said, When the Messenger of Allāh, peace and blessings of Allāh be on him, commanded us to give in charity, one of us went to the market and carried a load for which he got a mudd, and some of them are millionaires to-day.

(B. 24:10.)

3. Abū Mūsā reported that the Prophet, peace and blessings of Allāh be on him, said:

"The faithful treasurer who pays what he is ordered with a willing heart is one of those who give charity."

(B. 37:1.)

4. The Prophet, peace and blessings of Allāh be on him, said:

"Muslims shall be bound by the conditions which they make."³³⁸

(B. 37:14.)

5. 'Ā'ishah said,

The Messenger of Allāh, peace and blessings of Allāh be on him, and Abū Bakr employed a man of the Banī Dīl as a guide, a clever man, and he followed the religion of the disbelieving Quraish, so they made over to him their riding camels and told him to come to them with their riding camels at the cave of Thaur after three nights on the morning following the third night.³³⁹

(B. 37:4.)

6. Khabbāb said,

I was a blacksmith in the days of ignorance, and I had a debt due from 'Āṣ ibn Wā'il. So I came to him demanding it. He said, I will not give it to thee until thou deniest Muhammad. I said, I will not deny even if Allāh cause thee to die and thou art then raised to life

(B. 34:29.)

7. Ibn 'Abbās said, reporting on the authority of the Prophet, peace and blessings of Allāh be on him:

"The most worthy of things for which you take a remuneration is the Book of Allāh."³⁴⁰

And Ibn Sīrīn said ...:

People paid remuneration for computing by conjecture the quantity of fruit.

(B. 37:16.)

8. Ibn Sīrīn saw no harm in the remuneration of the commission agent.

And Ibn 'Abbās said, There is no harm that one should say,

Sell this cloth for me and what thou obtainest over such and such an amount, it shall be for thee.

(B. 37:14.)

9. Abū Hurairah reported, The Prophet, peace and blessings of Allāh be on him, said

"Allāh says, There are three persons whose adversary in dispute I shall be on the day of resurrection: a person who makes a promise in My name then acts unfaithfully, and a person who sells a free person then devours his price, and a person who employs a servant and receives fully the labour due from him then he does not pay his remuneration.

(B. 34:106)

10. Ibn 'Umar said,

I heard the Messenger of Allāh, peace and blessings of Allāh be on him, say

"................ And the third man said, I employed labourers and I paid them their remuneration with the exception of one man--he left his due and went away. So I invested his remuneration in a profitable business until it became abundant wealth."[341]

(B. 37:12.)

Abū Mūsā said,

11. I went to the Prophet, peace and blessings of Allāh be on him, and with me were two men from among the Ash'arīs. I said, I did not know that they wanted to be taken into service. He said: "We do not or shall not appoint a man who desires to be so appointed."[342]

(B. 37:I.)

12. Abū Humaid said,

The Prophet, peace and blessings of Allāh be on him, appointed from among the Azd, a man, called Ibn al-Utbiyyah, for the collection of zakāt. When he came, he said, This is for you and this was given to me as a gift. He (the Prophet) said:

"He should have sat down in the house of his father or the house of his mother, then he should see whether a gift is given to him or not."[343]

(B. 51:17.)

13. Abū Hurairah said,

The Prophet, peace and blessings of Allāh be on him, stood up among us, and he spoke about dishonesty and he spoke of its enormity and spoke of the enormity of its commitment.

He said:

"I should not see any one of you on the day of resurrection, there being on his neck a goat bleating, there being on his neck a horse neighing, so he should cry out, O Messenger of Allāh! come to my succour; and I would say, I do not control aught for thee, I delivered the message to thee."[344]

(B. 56:189.)

DEBTS AND MORTGAGE

1. "When you deal with each other in contracting a debt for a fixed time, write it down and let him who owes the debt dictate" (2:282).

2. "And if you are upon a journey and you do not find a scribe, then a security may be taken into possession" (2:283).

3. "Allāh has allowed trading and forbidden usury" (2:275).

4. "And if the debtor is in straitness, then let there be postponement until he is in ease; and if you remit it as alms it is better for you, if you knew" (2:280).

Lending and borrowing are a necessary condition in human transactions, and the rules relating to them are laid down in the Holy Qur'ān. Every such transaction should be written down, and the writing should be dictated by the person who owes the debt (v. 1). This latter direction guards against injustice being done to the debtor. Mortgaging of property is also allowed (v. 2). but the apparent condition of being on a journey or there being no scribe is simply a statement of the difficulties under which it becomes a necessity. The carrying on of a trade and drawing profit therefrom is placed on a different footing from lending money on interest, the first being the fruit of labour while the latter leads to ease and inordinate love of wealth (v. 3). A debtor in straitened circumstances must be dealt with leniently, and if he is unable to pay, the debt should be remitted (v. 4).

Contracting debts was discouraged. and in his prayers the Holy Prophet sought refuge from being in debt as well as sin (h. 1). When a bier was brought to him and he was told that the dead one had died in debt and had left nothing for payment thereof. he refused to conduct the service personally until someone undertook the payment of his debt (h. 2). Contracting a debt when a man did not intend to pay it is denounced (h. 3). and the Holy Prophet's anxiety to pay his debts is shown in h. 4. Granting respite to a debtor and the remission of debt when the debtor is in straitened circumstances is recommended (H. xxii:5). Payment in excess of the actual sum which a person owes is not interest; on the other hand, it is considered goodness (h. 5). Deferring payment by one who has the means is condemned as unjust (h. 6). and may even be punished (h. 7). The Muslim state is required to pay the debts of those who contract debts due to need; it must even maintain uncared-for families (h. 8). Mortgaging of property as security for payment of debt is allowed. and the mortgagee is allowed to derive benefit from it (h. 9, 10). The case of insolvency is dealt with in hh. 11, 12. Usury, even interest, is forbidden, but it is prophesied that a time would come when people generally would be involved in it (hh. 13-15).

1. 'Ā'ishah said,

The Messenger of Allāh, peace and blessings of Allāh be on him, used to pray, while saying prayers, and to say:

"O Allāh! I seek refuge in Thee from sin and from being in debt."

Someone asked him, How often dost thou, O Messenger of Allāh! seek refuge from being in debt. He said:

"When a man is in debt he speaks and tells lies, and he promises and breaks the promise."

(B. 43:10.)

2. Salamah reported:

A bier was brought to the Prophet, peace and blessings of Allāh be on him, that he may say funeral prayers over it. He said "Was he in debt?" They said, No. So he said prayers over it. Another bier was brought to him and he said: "Was he in debt?" They said, Yes. He said "Say prayers over your companion." Abu Qatādah said, I will pay his debt, O Messenger of Allāh! So he said funeral prayers over it.[345]

(B. 39:3.)

3. Abū Hurairah reported,

The Prophet, peace and blessings of Allāh be on him, said:

"Whoever contracts a debt intending to repay it, Allāh will pay it on his behalf,[346] and whoever contracts a debt intending to waste it, Allāh will bring him to ruin."

(B. 43:2.)

4. Abū Dharr said, I was with the Prophet, peace and blessings of Allāh be on him. When he saw (the mount) Uhud, he said:

'I do not like that this (mountain) should be turned into gold for me, then there should remain with me one dīnār out of it beyond three days, except a dīnār which I should keep for payment of a debt."

Then he said:

"The wealthier are the poorer except he who gives away wealth thus and thus, and they are very few."[347]

(B. 43:3.)

5. Jābir said,

I came to the Prophet, peace and blessings of Allāh be on him, while he was in the mosque; so he said:

"Say two rak'ahs of prayer." And he owed me a debt; so he paid it to me and gave me more (than was due).[348]

(B. 43:7.)

6. Abū Hurairah said,

The Messenger of Allāh, peace and blessings of Allāh be on him, said:

"Delaying the payment of debt by a well-to-do person is injustice."

(B. 43:12.)

7. The Prophet, peace and blessings of Allāh be on him, is reported to have said:

"Deferring payment by one who has the means to pay legalizes his punishment and his honour."³⁴⁹

(B. 43:11)

8. Abū Hurairah reported,

The Prophet, peace and blessings of Allāh be on him, said:

"Whoever leaves property, it is for his heirs and whoever leaves a burden, it shall be our charge."³⁵⁰

(B. 43:11.)

9. 'Ā'ishah said, The Prophet, peace and blessings of Allāh be on him, bough food from a Jew for payment to be made at an appointed time, and he mortgaged for it a coat-of-mail made of iron.

(B. 43:l.)

10. Abū Hurairah said:

The Messenger' of Allāh, peace and blessings of Allāh be on him, said:

"The mortgaged animal may be used for riding, when it is mortgaged, on account of what is spent on it, and the milk of a milch animal may be drunk when it is mortgaged, and the expenditure shall be borne by him who rides (the animal) and drinks (the milk)."³⁵¹

(B. 48:4.)

11. Abū Hurairah-said, The Messenger of Allāh, peace and blessings of Allāh be on him, said:

"Whoever finds his property itself with a man who has become insolvent, he has a greater right to it than others."

12. Sa'īd ibn al-Musayyib said,

'Uthmān decided that whoever takes his due before a man becomes insolvent, it is his, and whoever recognises his property itself with an insolvent has a greater right to it.[352]

(B. 43:14.)

13. 'Ā'ishah said.

When the verses of the chapter al-Baqarah, relating to usury, were revealed, the Prophet, peace and blessings of Allāh be on him, went forth to

the mosque and recited them to the people, then he forbade trading in intoxicating liquors.[353]

(B. 8:73.)

14. Jābir reported,

The Messenger of Allāh, peace and blessings of Allāh be on him, cursed the usurer and the man who pays usury and the writer of the transaction and the two witnesses thereof and he said:

"They are alike."[354]

(M-Msh. 12:4.)

15. Abū Hurairah reported,

The Messenger of Allāh, peace and blessings of Allāh be on him, said:

"A time will come over people when not a single person will remain who does not swallow down usury, and if one does not swallow it, its vapour will overtake him."[355]

(AD-Msh. 12:4.)

GIFTS (HIBAH AND WAQF)

1. "As for him who gives (gifts) and guards against evil and accepts the best, We will facilitate for him the easy end" (92:5).

2. "Woe to the praying ones, who are unmindful of their prayers, who do good to be seen, and withhold small gifts" (107:4-7).

Hibah is the giving of a gift whether it is given to one who is in need or to a well-to-do person. and thus it differs from sadaqah which is meant only for the needy though they may be one's relatives. The giving of gifts (including charity) is praised (v. 1). while the withholding of small gifts is denounced as against the spirit of Islām (v. 2). Stress is laid on developing the spirit of brotherhood by the giving of gifts, great or small as one can find (hh. 1, 2). Even a poor man may give a gift out of the charity he has received (h. 3). Compensation for a gift received is recommended (h. 4). The giving of a gift to one child would be an injustice to other children, and it is therefore not allowed (h. 5). A husband can give a gift to his wife and vice-versa (h. 6). A wife may give gifts out of the property she has received from her husband (h. 7). A joint gift may be given to more persons than one (h. 8), and a gift may be given out of joint property (h. 9). A gift may be given to, and received from. a non-Muslim (hh. 10. 11). It is forbidden to take back what has once been given as a gift (h. 12). A gift for life is recognised subject to certain conditions (h. 13). Property may be dedicated as waqf, becoming thus inalienable, or as waqf'ala-l-aulād (h. 14). One who receives a gift or any other good from another must give expression to thanks (h. 15).

1. Abn Hurairah reported '

The Prophet, peace and blessings of Allāh be on him, said

"O Muslim women! Let not a neighbour despise

for her neighbour (a gift), even though it be the trotters of a goat."

(B. 51:l.)

2. 'Ā'ishah reported,

The Prophet, peace and blessings of Allāh be on him, said:

"Give gifts to one another, for gifts take away rancour."

(Tr-Msh. 12:17.)

3. Anas said,

Meat was brought to the Messenger of Allāh, peace and blessings of Allāh be on him, and it was said that it was given to Barīrah as a charity. He said:

"For her it is a charity, and for us it is a gift."[356]

(B. 51:7.)

4. 'Ā'ishah said,

The Messenger of Allāh, peace and blessings of Allāh be on him, used to accept a gift and to give a compensation for it.[357]

(B. 51:11.)

5. Nu'mān said,

My father gave me a gift. 'Amrah bint Rawāhah said, I do not agree until thou make the Messenger of Allāh, peace and blessings of Allāh be on him, witness. So he came to the Messenger of Allāh, peace and blessings of Allāh be on him, and said: I gave a gift to my son from 'Amrah bint Rawāhah, and she has bidden me to make thee a witness, O Messenger of Allāh!

He said, "Hast thou given all thy sons the like of it"? He said, No. He said: "Be careful of your duty to Allāh and keep justice between your children." So he returned and took back his gift.[358]

(B. 51:13.)

6. Ibrāhīm said,

The giving of a gift by a man to his wife and by the wife to her husband is lawful.

And 'Umar ibn 'Abd al 'Azīz said, They cannot take back (the gifts).

(B. 51:14.)

7. Asmā' said,

I said, O Messenger of Allāh I have no property except what Zubair[359] gave to me; can I give (it) as charity?

He said:

"Do thou give charity (out of it) and do not withhold it, lest it be withheld from thee."

(B. 51:15.)

8. Asmā' said to Qāsim ibn Muhammad and Ibn Abi 'Atīq,

I inherited (some property) in Ghābah from

my sister 'Ā'ishah, and Mu'āwiyah offered me a hundred thousand for it this is now for you both.[360]

(B. 51:22.)

9. The Prophet, peace and blessings of Allāh be on him, and his companions gave as a gift to Hawāzin what they had gained from them in war and it was undivided.[361]

(B. 51:23.)

10. Abū Humaid said,

...... The king of Aila sent a gift to the Prophet, peace and blessings of Allāh be on him, white mare, and he gave him to wear an over-garment.[362]

(B. 24:54.)

11. Asmā' said,

My mother came to me in the time of the Messenger of Allāh, peace and blessings of Allāh be on him, and she was an idolatress. So I asked the Messenger of

Allāh, peace and blessings of Allāh be on him, I said, She is not inclined (to Islām), may I do good to her? He said, "Yes do good to thy mother."[363]

(B. 51:29.)

12. Ibn 'Abbās said,

The Prophet, peace and blessings of Allāh be on him, said:

"The man who takes back what he has gifted is like one who returns to his vomit."

(B. 51:30.)

13. Jābir said,

The Prophet, peace and blessings of Allāh be on him, decided in the matter of 'umrā that it is for him to whom it has been gifted.[364]

(B. 51:32)

14. Ibn 'Umar reported,

'Umar ibn al-Khattāb got land in Khaibar; so he came to the Prophet, peace and blessings of Allāh be on him, to consult him about it. He said, O Messenger of Allāh! I have got land in Khaibar than which I have never obtained more valuable property; what dost thou advise about it? He said: "If thou likest, make the property itself to remain inalienable, and give (the profit from) it in charity."

So 'Umar made it a charity on the condition that it shall not be sold, nor given away as a gift, nor inherited, and made it a charity among the needy and the relatives and to set free slaves and in the way of Allāh and for the travellers and to entertain guests, there being no blame on him who managed it if he ate out of it and made (others) eat, not accumulating wealth thereby.³⁶⁵

(B. 54:19.)

15. Usāmah said,

The Messenger of Allāh, peace and blessings of Allāh be on him, said:

"To whomsoever good is done and he says to the doer of it, May Allāh reward thee, he has done his utmost in praising."³⁶⁶

(Tr-Msh. 12:17.)

WILLS AND INHERITANCE

1. "Bequest is prescribed for you when death approaches one of you, if he leaves behind wealth for parents and near relatives, according to usage, a duty incumbent noon the righteous" (2:180).

2. "O you who believe! Call to witness between you, when death draws nigh to one of you, at the time of making the will two just persons from among you, or two others from among others than you" (5:106)

3. "Allāh enjoins you concerning your children: the male shall have the equal of the portion of two females; if there are more than two females, they shall have two-thirds of what he has left, and if there is one, she shall have the half: and as for his parents, each of them shall have the sixth of what he has left if he has a child; but if he has no child and only his two parents inherit from him, then his mother shall have the third; but if he has brothers, his mother shall have the sixth after the payment of any bequest he may have bequeathed or a debt............And you shall have half of what your wives leave if they have no child: but if they have a child, you shall have the fourth of what they leave after payment of any bequest they may have bequeathed or a debt: and they shall have the fourth of what you leave if you have no child, but if you nave a child, they shall have the eighth of what you leave after payment of any bequest you may have bequeathed or a debt; and if a man or a woman having no children leaves inheritance, and he (or she) has a brother or a sister, each of them two shall have the sixth; but if they are more than that, they shall be sharers in the third. after payment of any bequest that may have been bequeathed or a debt that does not harm others" (4:11, 12).

Every man who owns property is required to make a will (wasiyyah) (v. 1, h. 1) which should be properly witnessed (v. 2). The will was ordained especially for charitable purposes and limited to one-third of the property (h. 2), the heirs receiving specified portions (v. 3: h. 9), no will being allowed in their favour (h. 3). Giving away property to needy relatives is a charitable object (h. 4).

If there is a debt due from the testator for which his property is responsible, the debt shall be paid before the execution of the will (h. 5). Muslims were not allowed to inherit from non-Muslims and vice-versa, the two being then at war with each other (h. 6). Prophets leave no inheritance, (h. 7).

If anything remains after giving away the appointed portions, it goes to the nearest male relative (h. 8). Hh. 9-11 cite certain cases of inheritance as decided by the companions of the Holy Prophet. When there are no near relatives, inheritance goes to the nearest great grand ancestor's descendants, even to a freed slave: in the last resort, when no claimant is found, it goes to the Muslim state or the Muslim community (hh. 12-14). A child born crying is considered a person who can inherit or be inherited though he may die immediately afterwards (h. 15). A man who murders another cannot inherit from him (h. 16). An illegitimate child cannot inherit or be inherited (h. 17).

1. Ibn 'Umar reported,

The Messenger of Allāh, peace and blessings of Allāh be on him, said:

"It is not right for a Muslim who has property regarding which he must make a will that he should sleep for two nights (consecutively) but that his will should be written down with him.

(B. 55:1.)

2. Sa'd ibn Abī Waqqās said,

The Messenger of Allāh, peace and blessings of Allāh be on him, used to visit me at Makkah, in the year of the Farewell pilgrimage, on account of (my) illness which had become very severe. So I said, My illness has become very severe and I have much property and there is none to inherit from me but a daughter, shall I then bequeath two-thirds of my property as a charity? He said, "No". I said, Half? He said, "No". Then he said:

"Bequeath one-third and one-third is much, for if thou leavest thy heirs free from want, it is better than that thou leavest them in want, begging of (other) people; and thou dost not spend anything seeking thereby the pleasure of Allāh but thou art rewarded for it, even for that which thou puttest into the mouth of thy wife."³⁶⁷

(B. 23:36.)

3. Abū Umāmah said,

I heard the Messenger of Allāh, peace and blessings of Allāh be on him, say in his sermon in the Farewell pilgrimage: "Surely Allāh has given to every one entitled to anything his due, therefor, there shall be no bequest for one who inherits."³⁶⁸

(AD-Msh. 12:20.)

4. Anas reported, The Messenger of Allāh, peace and blessings of Allāh be on him, said to Abū Talhah:

"Give it to the needy from among thy near relatives." So he gave it to Hassān and Ubaiyy ibn Ka'b, ... and they were nearer to him than my self.³⁶⁹

(B. 55:10.)

5. It is mentioned that

the Prophet, peace and blessings of Allāh be on him, ordered the debt to be paid before the execution of the will.³⁷⁰

(B. 55:9.)

6. Usāmah reported,

The Prophet, peace and blessings of Allāh be on him, said:

"The Muslim does not inherit from the unbeliever, nor does the unbeliever inherit from the Muslim."³⁷¹

(B. 85:25.)

7. 'Ā'ishah reported,

'When the Messenger of Allāh, peace and blessings of Allāh be on him, died, the wives of the Prophet, peace and blessings of Allāh be on him, intended sending 'Uthmān to Abu Bakr, demanding their share of inheritance. 'Ā'ishah said, Did not the Messenger of Allāh, peace and blessings of Allāh be on him, say "We are not inherited whatever we leave is a charity."

(B. 85:2.)

8. Ibn 'Abbās reported,

The Prophet, peace and blessings of Allāh be on him, said:

"Give the appointed portions to those entitled to them. Then whatever remains is for the nearest male."[372]

(B. 85:4.)

9. Zaid said,

When a man or a woman leaves behind a daughter, she gets one-half; and if there are two (daughters) or more, they get two-thirds; and if there is a male with them, beginning is made with him who inherits with them and he is given his appointed portion. and what remains (is divided among the children), the male having the portion of two females.[373]

(B. 85:4.)

10. Zaid said,

The children of a son take the place of a son, when there is no son besides them; their males are like their males and their females like their females; they inherit as they inherit and they preclude (other relatives) as they preclude; and the son of a son does not inherit with the son.[374]

(B. 85:6.)

11. Ibn 'Abbās said,

My son's son inherits from me precluding my brothers, why should I not inherit from my son's son? And different opinions are related from 'Umar and 'Alī and Ibn Mas'ūd and Zaid.

(B. 85:8.)

12. Buraidah said,

A man from. among the Khuzā'ah died, and his inheritance was brought to the Prophet, peace and blessings of Allāh be on him. He said, "Search for his heir or one related to him on the female side." But they could not find a heir for him, nor one related on the female side. So the Messenger of Allāh, peace and blessings of Allāh be on him, said Give it to the nearest connected with him through a great-grand-ancestor from among the Khuzā'ah"[375]

(AD-Msh. 12:19.)

13. Ibn Abbās reported,

A man died, and he did not leave any heir except a slave whom he had set free. The Prophet, peace and blessings of Allāh be on him, said, "Has he any one (to inherit)?" They said, None, except a slave whom he had set free. So the Prophet, peace and blessings of Allāh be on him, gave his inheritance to him.

(AD-Msh. 12:19.)

14. Miqdām said,

The Messenger of Allāh, peace and blessings of Allāh be on him, said:

"I am nearer to every believer than his own self; so whoever leaves behind a debt or children to support, it shall be our charge; and whoever leaves property, it is for his heirs; and I am the heir of the person who has no heir--p. 342 I inherit his property and liberate his captivity.[376]

(AD-Msh 12:19.)

15. Jābir said,

The Messenger of Allāh, peace and blessings of Allāh be on him, said:

"When a child is born crying, funeral service is held over him and he is inherited."

(IM-Msh. 12:19.)

16. Abū Hurairah said,

The Messenger of Allāh, peace and blessings of Allāh be on him, said

"The murderer does not inherit."

(Tr.-Msh. 12:19.)

17. 'Amr ibn Shu'aib .reported,

The Prophet, peace and blessings of Allāh be on him, said:

Whoever holds illicit intercourse with a free woman or a slave-girl, the child (thus born) is illegitimate, and be does not inherit, nor is he inherited." (Tr-Msh. 12: 19.)

FOODS AND DRINKS

1. "O men! Eat the lawful and good things out of what is in the earth" (2:168).

2. "And eat and drink and be not immoderate, for He does not love the immoderate" (7:31).

3. "O you who believe! Do not forbid yourselves the good things which Allāh has made lawful for you, and do not exceed the limits" (5:87).

4. "And do not eat of that on which Allāh's name has not been mentioned." (6: 122).

5. "Forbidden to you is that which dies of itself, and blood, and flesh of swine, and that on which any other name than that of Allāh has been invoked, and the strangled animal, and that beaten to death, and that killed by a fall, and that killed by being smitten with the horn, and that which wild beasts have eaten--except what you slaughter--and what is sacrificed on stones set up for idols" (5:3).

6. "Lawful to you is the game of the sea and its food ... and the game of the land is forbidden to you so long as you are on pilgrimage" (5:96).

7. "And the food of those who have been given the Book is lawful for you and your food is lawful for them" (5:5).

8. "It is no sin in you that you eat together or separately (24:61).

9. "O you who believe! Intoxicants and games of chance are only an uncleanness, the devil's work; shun them, therefore, that you may be successful" (5:90).

There are some general principles laid down by the Holy Qur'ān regarding food. The first condition is that it should be lawful (halāl) (v. 1), which carries the double significance of being earned lawfully and not being prohibited by Law. The second is that it should be good (tayyih) (v. 1) or fit for eating, not unclean or such as offends the taste. It is further stated that the golden rule regarding what one eats and drinks is moderation (v. 2). As underfeeding affects the build-up of man, so does also the overloading of the stomach. Moderation also requires that no food should be used to excess. Self-denying practices by which a man deprives himself of certain kinds of food are expressly denounced (v. 3). Flesh is allowed if the animal is slaughtered in the name of Allāh (v. 4). Prohibited foods are detailed in v. 5. Game of land and sea is allowed with one exception (v. 6), Inter-dining with non-Muslims is allowed (v. 7). One may eat in the company of others or separately (v. 8), Intoxicants are prohibited (v. 9).

Further details are laid down in Hadīth. The name of Allāh must be mentioned when an animal is slaughtered (h. 1). It may be slaughtered with any sharp instrument which makes the blood flow (h. 2), Slaughtering consists in cutting the jugular vein of the throat, but the spinal cord must not be cut (hh. 3, 4). An afflicted animal may be slaughtered (h. 5). An animal properly slaughtered by a non-Muslim is allowed (h. 6). In a doubtful case the utterance of Allāh's name is sufficient (h. 7). Game is allowed subject to certain conditions (hh. 8, 9). Beasts of prey with teeth are prohibited (h. 10). Intoxicants are prohibited (hh. 11, 12), and they cannot be taken even in small quantities which may not intoxicate (h. 13). The hands must be washed before taking meals and again after it, when the mouth must also be rinsed (h. 14, 15). The utterance of Bismillāh when taking food and a short prayer after it was the Holy Prophet's practice (hh. 16, 17). Drink and food must not be blown into and must be kept covered (hh. 18-20). In eating, one may help oneself with a knife (h. 21), or a spoon. Vessels of gold and silver are a luxury which Islām does not allow (h. 22). When a person is invited to a meal he should not refuse; nor should one go to a feast to which one has not been invited (h. 23). A servant may eat at the same table with his master (h. 24). Eating together is recommended (h. 25); but when doing so, one should have regard for others (hh. 26, 27). The guest must be accompanied to the door of the house (h. 28).

1. Anas said,

The Prophet, peace and blessings of Allāh be on him, sacrificed two rams of a white colour mixed with black; I saw him with his foot placed on one side of their face, uttering Bismillāh, Allāh-u-Akbar, and he slaughtered them with his own hand.[377]

(B. 73:9.)

2. Rāfi' said,

We were with the Prophet, peace and blessings of Allāh be on him, in Dhu-l-Hulaifah...... So Rāfi said, We expect or we fear the enemy tomorrow and we have no knives; may we slaughter with (the thin edge of) cane? He (the Prophet) said: "What makes the blood flow, not the teeth and the nail, and the name of Allāh is mentioned on it, eat it."[378]

(B. 47:1)

3. Nāfi' said,

Ibn 'Umar forbade (the cutting of) the spinal cord, saying, Cut what is above the bone, then leave (it) until it dies.

(B. 72:24)

4. Ibn Abbās said, Slaughtering is in the throat and in the pit above the breast between the collar bones.[379]

(B. 72:24.)

5. Mu'ādh ibn Sa'd reported,

A slave girl of Ka'b ibn Mālik was pasturing sheep in Sal', and one of the goats was afflicted, so she caught hold of it and slaughtered it with a stone. The Prophet, peace and blessings of Allāh be on him, was asked about it, and he said, "Eat it."

(B. 72:19.)

6. Zuhrī said, There is no harm in (eating) an animal slaughtered by a Christian of Arabia; if thou hearest him invoking another name than that of Allāh, do not eat it, and if thou dost not hear him, Allāh has made it lawful, and He knew their unbelief.[380]

(B. 72:22.)

7. 'Ā'ishah said, Some people said to the Prophet, peace and blessings of Allāh be on him, People[381] bring to us meat about which we do not know whether the name of Allāh was mentioned over it or not. He said, "Mention the name of Allāh over it and eat it." She said, and they had just emerged from unbelief.

(B. 72:21)

8. Abū Th'labah said,

I said, O Prophet of Allāh! We live in the land of the followers of the Book; may we eat in their vessels? And (we live) in a land where there is game,--I hunt with my bow and with my dog which is untaught and with my dog that has been taught, so what is right for me? He said: "As to what thou askest about the followers of the Book, if you can find (vessels) other than these, do not eat in them; and if you do not find (other vessels), wash them and eat in them." And what thou huntest with thy bow, and thou hast mentioned the name of Allāh, eat (it)[382]; and what thou huntest with the dog that thou hast taught, and thou hast mentioned the name of Allāh, eat (it); and what thou huntest with thy untaught dog and thou art able to slaughter it, eat it."

(B. 72:4.)

6. Washing was required because they were also used for prohibited foods.

9. 'Umar said,

'The game of the sea is that which has been hunted, and its food (ta'ām) is that which it casts forth . . . . And Ibn 'Abbās said, Eat of the game of the sea whether it is (killed) by a Christian or a Jew or a Magian.[383]

(B. 72:12.)

10. Abū Tha'labah said,

The Messenger of Allāh, peace and blessings of Allāh be on him, forbade all beasts of prey with canine teeth.[384]

(B. 72:29.)

11. Anas said,

I was giving drink to people in the abode of Abu Talhah, and their wine at that time was made of dates. Then the Messenger of Allāh, peace and blessings of Allāh be on him, ordered a crier to make it known that wine was forbidden. He said. So Abu Talhah said to me, Get out and pour it out. I poured it out, and it flowed in the streets of Madīnah.[385]

(B. 46:21.)

12. 'Ā'ishah said,

The Messenger of Allāh, peace and blessings of Allāh be on him, was asked about bit'--it is a drink made of honey and the people of Yaman used to drink it. So the Messenger of Allāh, peace and blessings of Allāh be on him, said:

"Every drink that intoxicates is prohibited."[386]

(B. 74:1)

13. Jābir said,

The Messenger of Allāh, peace and blessings of Allāh be on him, said:

"Of whatever thing a large quantity intoxicates, even a small quantity is prohibited."[387]

(AD. 25:5.)

14. Salmān reported,

The Messenger of Allāh, peace and blessings of Allāh be on him, said "The blessing of food is the washing of hands before it, and the washing of hands after it."[388]

(Tr-Msh. 20.)

15. Suwaid Ibn al-Nu'mān said:

We went forth with the Messenger of Allāh, peace and blessings of Allāh be on him, to Khaibar. When we reached Sahbā', he ordered the food to be served; and there was brought to him nothing but meal of parched barley, and we ate (of it); then he got up for the prayer and he rinsed his mouth and we rinsed our mouths.[389]

(B. 70:51.)

16. 'Umar ibn Abū Salamah said,

I was a boy being brought up in the care of the Messenger of Allāh, peace and blessings of Allāh be on him, and my hand was active in the bowl, taking from every side. So the Messenger of Allāh, peace and blessings of Allāh be on him, said to me, "Boy! Say Bismillāh and eat with thy right hand and cat from the side nearest to thee." So this was my manner of eating afterwards.

(B. 70:2.)

17. Abū Sa'īd al-Khudrī said,

When the Messenger of Allāh, peace and blessings of Allāh be on him, finished his meal, he used to say: "All praise is due to Allāh Who has given us to eat and to drink, and male us Muslims."[390]

(Tr-2 Msh. 20.)

18. Abū Qatādah said,

The Messenger of Allāh, peace and blessings of Allāh be on him, said:

"When one of you drinks, he should not blow into the vessel."[391]

(B. 4:18.)

19. Jābir said,

Abū Humaid brought a cup of milk from Naqī', and the Messenger of Allāh, peace and blessings of Allāh be on him, said to him:

"Why didst thou not cover it? Thou shouldst have placed a piece of wood on it."

(B. 74:11.)

20. Jābir reported,

The Messenger of Allāh, peace and blessings of Allāh be on him, said:

"When you go to sleep, put out the lamp and shut the doors and cover the mouths of water-skins and cover food and drink."

(B. 74:21.)

21. Ja'far ibn Amr reported,

His father informed him that he saw the Prophet, peace and blessings of Allāh be on him, cutting (meat) from the shoulder of a goat. Then he was invited to prayer, so he threw away the knife and said prayers and did not perform ablutions."[392]

(B. 4:51.)

22. Hudhaifah said, I heard the Prophet, peace and blessings of Allāh be on him, say: "Do not wear silk or silk brocade, and do not drink in vessels of gold and silver, and do not eat in bowls made of them; for they are for them in this life and for us in the next."[393]

(B. 70:29)

23. 'Abd Allāh ibn 'Umar said,

The Messenger of Allāh, peace and blessings of Allāh be on him, said: "When a person is invited (to a meal) and he does not accept (or reply), he disobeys Allāh and His Messenger; and he who goes (to a feast) without being invited enters as a thief and goes forth as a raider."

(AD. 26:I.)

24. Abū Hurairah reported on the authority of the Prophet, peace and blessings of Allāh be on him:

"When the servant brings to one of you his food, then if he does not make him sit with him (to eat at the same table), let him give him a morsel or two morsels, for he has laboured to prepare it."[394]

(B. 49:18.)

25. 'Umar said,

The Messenger of Allāh, peace and blessings of Allāh be on him, said:

"Eat together and do not eat separately, for the blessing is with the company"[395]

(IM-Msh. 20:I.)

26. Ja'far ibn Muhammad reported on the authority of his father,

When the Messenger of Allāh, peace and blessings of Allāh be on him, ate in the company of (other) people, he was the last of them (to finish) eating.[396]

(Msh. 20:1.)

27. Ibn 'Umar said,

The Messenger of Allāh, peace and blessings of Allāh be on him, said:

"When food is placed (before a company), no one should get up until the food is removed; nor should any one raise up his hand (from the food), though he may have satisfied his hunger, until the people have finished--

and he should offer an excuse--for this causes his companion to become ashamed, so he withholds his hand though he may still need food."

(IM-Msh. 20:1.)

Abū Hurairah said,

28. The Messenger of Allāh, peace and blessings of Allāh be on him, said:

"It is the sunnah that a man should accompany his guest to the door of the house."

(IM-Msh. 20:l.)

TOILET

1. "O thou who art clothed! Arise and warn, and thy Lord do magnify, and thy garments keep purified, and uncleanness do shun" (74:1-5).

2. "Say, Who has prohibited the adornment of Allāh which He has brought forth for His servants and the goodly provisions" (7: 32).

3. "O children of Adam! Attend to your embellishment at every time of prayer" (7:31).

The order to keep the garments pure and shun uncleanness of every kind is combined with the order to warn the people and magnify the Lord (v. 1). This shows the importance which is given to cleanliness in dress as well as in general habits. Adornment is not prohibited; it is, in fact, a thanksgiving for Divine blessings (v. 2). The word adornment (Ar. zinah), which is generally taken to mean apparel, includes both the dress and the make-up of a person. A good toilet is recommended even when going to prayer (v. 3). No limitations are placed upon the form or quality of clothing but extravagance and vanity must be avoided (h. 1). To be naked is forbidden (h. 2). Men are prohibited to wear silk except for a good reason, but women may wear it (hh. 3-6). Men may wear a silver ring but not a gold one, but women may wear any ornaments (hh. 7-10). The personal make-up of a man, the wearing of a moustache, beard and hair, and the use of perfumes are spoken of in hh. 11-16, while, hh. 17-20 relate to pictures or decorations.

1. The Prophet, peace and blessings of Allāh be on him, said:

"Eat and drink and wear clothes and be charitable,

not being extravagant or self- conceited."[397]

(B. 77:1.)

2. Miswar said,

I took up a heavy stone, and whilst I was going along (with it), my garment fell down. So the Messenger of Allāh, peace and blessings of Allāh be on him, said to me: "Don on thy garment, and you should not walk naked."[398]

(AD. 30:2.)

3. Abū 'Uthmān reported, A letter from 'Umar came to us that the Messenger of Allāh, peace and blessings of Allāh be on him, forbade us (wearing of) silk except this much, and he pointed with his two fingers that are next to the thumb. He said, According to our knowledge, he meant a'lām.[399]

(B. 77:25.)

4. Anas said,

The Prophet, peace and blessings of Allāh be on him, allowed the wearing of silk to Zubair and 'Abd al-Rahmān on account of itching.

(B. 77:29.)

5. Anas reported, He saw Umm Kulthūm, the daughter of the Messenger of Allāh, peace and blessings of Allāh be on him, wearing a striped garment of silk.

(B. 77:30.)

6. 'Uqbah ibn 'Āmir said,

A tunic of silk[400] was presented to the Prophet, peace and blessings of Allāh be on him, and he wore it, and said his prayers while wearing it; then he pulled it off, doffing it severely, like one hating it. and said: "This is not fit for the righteous.[401]

(B. 8:16.)

7. Abū Hurairah reported on the authority of the Prophet, of Allāh, peace and blessings of Allāh be on him,

That he forbade the wearing of a gold ring.

(B. 77:45.)

8. Anas said, When the Prophet, peace and blessings of Allāh be on him, intended to write to the Romans, it was said to him that they would not read his letter if it did not bear a seal. So he ordered a ring of silver to be made and its impress was Muhammad the Messenger of Allāh.[402]

(B. 77:52)

9. Ibn 'Abbās said, I bear witness regarding the Prophet, peace and blessings of Allāh be on him, that the Prophet, peace and blessings of Allāh be on him, went out and Bilāl was with him, and he thought that he had not made the women hear; so he exhorted them and ordered them to give in charity, and the women began to throw (their) earrings and rings, and Bilāl gathered them in a side of his garment.

(B. 3:32.)

10. Umm Salamah said,

I used to wear ornaments of gold, so I said, "Is it hoarding up, O Messenger of Allāh?" He said: "What reaches the limit of zakāt, and zakāt is paid therefrom, it is not hoarding up."[403]

(AD. 9:4.)

11. Abu Hurairah reported,

Five things are according to nature: Circumcision, and the removal of superfluous hair,[404] and the removal of hair in the armpit, and the paring of nails, and the clipping of the moustache.

(B. 77:63.)

12. Ibn 'Umar reported,

The Prophet, peace and blessings of Allāh be on him, said: "Oppose the polytheists--leave the beard to grow abundant and clip the moustaches."[405] And when Ibn 'Umar performed the pilgrimage or the 'umrah, he used to grasp his beard with his hand; what exceeded, he had it cut off.

(B. 77:64.)

13. Ibn 'Abbās reported,

The Messenger of Allāh, peace and blessings of Allāh be on him, used to let down his hair (on his forehead), the polytheists combing their hair into two parts throwing them on the two sides, while the followers of the Book used to let down their hair (on their foreheads). The Messenger of Allāh, peace and blessings of Allāh be on him, preferred agreement with the followers of the Book in matters in which he was not ordered (to follow) a particular course. Then (afterwards) the Messenger of Allāh, peace and blessings of Allāh be on him, combed his hair into two parts.'[406]

(B. 61:21)

14. 'Ā'ishah said,

I used to comb the hair of the Messenger of Allāh, peace and blessings of Allāh be on him.

(B. 6:2.)

15. 'Ā'ishah reported,

It was pleasing to the Prophet, peace and blessings of Allāh be on him, to begin on the right side, so far as he was able, in his combing (of the hair) and in his ablutions.[407]

(B. 77:77.)

16. 'Ā'ishah said, I used to perfume the Prophet, peace and blessings of Allāh be on him, with the best fragrant substance which he could find, so much so that I could discern the brightness of the fragrance in his head and in his beard.

(B. 77:74.)

17. Busr ibn Sa'id related,

Zaid ibn Khālid spoke to him, while with Busr ibn Sa'id was 'Ubaid Allāh, that Abū Talhah related to him that the Prophet, peace and blessings of Allāh be on him, said: "Angels do not enter a house in which is an image."[408] Busr said, After this Zaid ibn Khālid fell ill and we paid a visit to him, and when we were in his house we saw a curtain on which were pictures. So I said to 'Ubaid Allāh, Did he not relate to us about pictures? He said, He had said, Except figures on a cloth; didst thou not hear him? I said, No. He said, Yea! He mentioned this.

(B. 59:7.)

18. Abd Allāh Ibn 'Umar' reported,

The Messenger of Allāh, peace and blessings of Allāh be on him, said: "Those who make these images (suwar) will be punished on the day of resurrection it will be said to them,

Put life into what you made."[409]

(B. 77:89.)

19. 'Ā'ishah reported,

The Prophet, peace and blessings of Allāh be on him, did not leave in his house anything on which were figures but he broke it.[410]

(B. 77:90.)

20. Ibn 'Umar said.

The Prophet, peace and blessings of Allāh be on him, came to the house of Fātimah but did not enter it. When 'Alī came, she mentioned it to him. He spoke about it to the Prophet, peace and blessings of Allāh be on him, and he (the Prophet) said: "I saw on her door a figured curtain." And he said: "I have nothing to do with (decorations of) this world." So 'Alī came to her and mentioned this to her. She said, Let him command me about it as he likes. He (the Prophet) said: "Send it to such and such people; they are in need."

(B. 51:27.)

ETHICS (ADAB)

1. "The noblest of you in the sight of Allāh is the best of you in conduct" (49:13).

2. "And do good to your parents. If either of them or both of them reach old age with thee, say not to them, fie: nor chide them: and speak to them a generous word. And make thyself submissively gentle to them with compassion, and say, My Lord! Have mercy on them as they brought me up when I was little" (17:23, 24).

3. "And do not kill your children for fear of poverty. We give them sustenance and yourselves too" (17:31).

4. "And when about the one buried alive it is asked, For what sin was she killed?" (81:8, 9).

5. "Righteousness is this that one should believe in Allāh . . . . and give away wealth out of love for Him to the near of kin and the orphans and the needy and the wayfarer and the beggars and for the emancipation of the captives" (2:17).

6. "And they (the women) have rights similar to those (men have) over them in a just manner" (2:228).

7. "And keep them (your wives) in good fellowship" (2:229, 231).

8. "The believers are but brethren, so make peace between your brethren" (49:10).

9. "Muhammad is the Messenger of Allāh: and those with him are firm of heart against the disbelievers, merciful among themselves" (48:29).

10. "And the men who speak the truth and the women who speak the truth . . . Allāh has prepared for them forgiveness and a great reward" (33:35).

11. "Woe to every slanderer, defamer" (104:1). p. 372

12. "Let not a people deride another people nor let women deride women . . . . . Neither defame one another, nor call one another by nicknames . . . . Shun much suspicion. And spy not, nor backbite one another" (49:11, 12).

13. "And fulfil promise, for the promise shall be questioned about" (17: 34).

14. "And give full measure when you measure out, and weigh with a true balance" (17: 35).

15. "And do not kill any one whom Allāh has forbidden except for a just cause" (17: 33).

16. "And those who shun the great sins and indecencies, and whenever they are angry they forgive" (42:37).

17. "And the recompense of evil is punishment like it; but whoever forgives and amends, he shall have his reward from Allāh" (42:40).

18. "And the servants of the Beneficent are they who walk on earth in humbleness; and when the ignorant address them they say, Peace" (25:63).

19. "And go not nigh to fornication, for it is an indecency and evil is the way" (17:32).

20. "Say to the believing men that they cast down their looks and guard their private parts."

"Say to the believing women that they cast down their looks and guard their private parts, and not display their beauty except what appears thereof; and let them draw their head-coverings over their bosoms" (24:30, 31).

21. "And as for women advanced in years who do not hope for a marriage, it is no sin for them if they put off their cloaks, not displaying their beauty" (24:60).

22. "Do not enter houses other than your own houses without permission and saluting their inmates and if it is said to you, Go back. then go back" (24:27, 28).

The word adab signifies discipline of the mind, or every praiseworthy discipline by which a man is trained in any excellence. Good morals and good manners are the real test of a man's excellence (v. 1; hh. 1, 9). Goodness to one's parents occupies a very high place in the moral code of Islām, the mother coming first (v. 2: h. 2), so much so that paradise is said to be beneath the mother's feet.

3) . Kindness and love for children is inculcated (vv. 3. 4 . hh. 4, 5), and suffering on account of them is called a screen from fire (h. 6). Doing good to relatives is a source of blessings in this life and the next (v. 4; hh. 7, 8). Wives have their rights over their husbands and they must be kept in good fellowship (vv. 6, 7). The best of men is said to be one who is kindest to his wife (h. 9). and it is recommended that one should help her in her work (h. 10). Muslims are brethren--members of one body and parts of one structure-and they must help one another and he kind to one another (vv. 8. 9: hh. 11-14); their blood, property and honour being inviolable (h. 15). They are forbidden to hate and boycott one another (h. 16), to call one another kāfir or fāsiq (h. 17), and to fight with one another (h. 18). A neighbour, whether a Muslim or a non-Muslim, must be treated kindly (hh. 19. 20). One must be kind and generous to one's slaves or servants, who must in all other matters be treated on a basis of equality (hh. 21-23). Looking after widows and orphans is an act of highest merit (hh. 24. 25). Even an enemy must be treated generously (hh. 26, 27). Divine mercy is shown to him who is merciful to God's creatures (hh. 28, 29), even to dumb animals (h. 30). Man must cultivate the habit of being truthful, for truth is the basis from which virtue spring., while falsehood leads to vice (v. 10; h. 31). Special stress is laid that a man must be fair and forgiving in his dealings with other people, and must avoid everything which hurts them (vv. 11-19; h. 32) At the end are given a few verses and hadīth relating to good manners (vv. 20-22; hh. 33-41).

Many aspects of this subject have been. incidentally, dealt with in the foregoing chapters.

1. Abd Allāh ibn 'Amr said,

The Prophet, peace and blessings of Allāh be on him, used to say:

"The best of you are those who have the most excellent morals."

(B. 61:23.)

2. Abu Hurairah said, A man came to the Messenger of Allāh, peace and blessings of Allāh be on him, and said, O Messenger of Allāh! Who has the greatest right that I should keep company with him with goodness? He said, "Thy mother". He said, Who then? He said, "Thy mother." He said, Who then? He said, "Thy mother." He said, Who then? He said, "Then thy father."

(B. 78:2.)

3. Mu'āviyah Ibn Jāhimah reported,

Jāhimah came to the Prophet, peace and blessings of Allāh be on him, and said, O Messenger of Allāh! I intended that I should enlist in the fighting force and I have come to consult thee. He said: "Hast thou a mother?" He said, Yes. He said: "Then stick to her, for paradise is beneath her two feet."[411]

(Ns. 25:6.)

4. 'Ā'ishah said,

A dweller of the desert came to the Prophet, peace and blessings of Allāh be on him, and said, You kiss children but we do not kiss them. The Prophet, peace and blessings of Allāh be on him, said:

"Do I control aught for thee if Allāh has taken away mercy from thy heart?"

(B. 78:18.)

5. 'Ā'ishah reported,

The Prophet, peace and blessings of Allāh be on him, took a baby in his arms, rubbing its palate (with chewed date), and it urinated on him, so he sent for water and made it follow the urine.

(B. 78:21.)

6. 'Ā'ishah said,

'A woman came, with her being her two daughters, asking for charity but she did not find with me anything except a date. I gave it to her and she divided it between her two daughters, and did not herself eat of it. Then she got up and went out, and the Prophet, peace and blessings of Allāh be on him, entered on us and I informed him about it. So the Prophet, peace and blessings of Allāh be on him, said:

"Whoever is thrown into a trial on account of these daughters, they are a screen for him from fire."

(B. 24:10.)

7. Anas said, I heard the Messenger of Allāh, peace and blessings of Allāh be on him, say:

"Whomsoever it pleases that his sustenance should be made ample to him or that his life should be lengthened, let him be kind to his relatives."

(B. 34:11)

8. Abū Hurairah reported,

The Prophet, peace and blessings of Allāh be on him, said:

"Rahim is an offshoot of Rahmān; so Allāh said, Whoever makes his ties close with thee I will make My ties close with him, and whoever severs his ties with thee I will sever My ties with him."[412]

(B. 78:13.)

9. Abu Hurairah said, The Messenger of Allāh, peace and blessings of Allāh be on him, said:

"The most perfect of the believers in faith is the best of them in moral excellence, and the best of you are the kindest of you to their wives."

(Tr. 10:11)

10. Aswad said,

I asked 'Ā'ishah, What did the Prophet, peace and blessings of Allāh be on him, do when in his house? She said, he served his wife, meaning that he did work for his wife.

(B. 10:44.)

11. Ibn 'Umar reported,

The Messenger of Allāh, peace and blessings of Allāh be on him, said

"A Muslim is the brother of a Muslim; he does him no injustice, nor does he leave him alone (to be the victim of another's injustice); and whoever does the needful for his brother, Allāh does the needful for him; and whoever removes the distress of a Muslim, Allāh removes from him a distress out of the distresses of the day of resurrection; and whoever covers (the fault of) a Muslim, Allāh will cover his sins on the day of resurrection."

(B. 46:3.)

12. Anas said,

The Messenger of Allāh, peace and blessings of Allāh be on him, said

"Help thy brother whether he is the doer of wrong or wrong is done to him."

They (his companions) said, O Messenger of Allāh! We can help a man to whom wrong is done, but how could we help him when he is the doer of wrong? He said: "Take hold of his hands from doing wrong."

(B. 46:4)

13. Nu'mān said,

The Messenger of Allāh, peace and blessings of Allāh be on him, said:

Thou wilt see the faithful in their having mercy for one another and in their love for one another and in their kindness towards one another like the body; when one member of it ails, the entire body (ails), one part calling out the other with sleeplessness and fever."

(B. 78:27.)

14. Abū Mūsā reported,

The Prophet, peace and blessings of Allāh be on him, said:

"Believers are in relation to one another as (parts of) a structure, one part of which strengthens the other." And he inserted the fingers of one hand amid those of the other (so as to conjoin his two hands).

(B. 8:88.)

15. Ibn 'Umar reported,

The Prophet, peace and blessings of Allāh be on him, said, while at Minā: "Do you know what day is this?" They said, Allāh and His Messenger know best. He said . "This is a sacred day. Do you know what city is this?" They said, Allāh and His Messenger know best. He said, "Sacred city. Do you know what month is this?" They said, Allāh and His Messenger know best. He said: "Sacred month." Then he said: "Surely Allāh has made sacred to you your blood and your property and your honour as this day of yours is sacred in this month of yours in this city of yours."[413]

(B. 25: 132.)

16. Anas reported,

The Messenger of Allāh, peace and blessings of Allāh be on him, said:

"Do not hate one another and do not be jealous of one another and do not boycott one another, and be servants of Allāh (as) brethren; and it is not lawful for a Muslim that he should sever his relations with his brother for more than three days."

(B. 78:57.)

17. Abū Dharr reported,

He heard the Prophet, peace and blessings of Allāh be on him, say:

"A man does not accuse another of being a transgressor, nor does he accuse him of being a kāfir, but it (the epithet) comes back to him, if his companion is not such."[414]

(B. 78:44.)

18. Abū Bakrah said, I heard the Messenger of Allāh, peace and blessings of Allāh be on him, say:

"When two Muslims meet each other with their swords, both of them are in the fire."

I said, O Messenger of Allāh! This is for the murderer, but what about the one who is murdered? He said:

"He was desirous of murdering his companion."

(B. 2:21.)

19. Abū Hurairah said,

The Messenger of Allāh, peace and blessings of Allāh be on him, said:

"Whoever believes in Allāh and the latter day should not harm his neighbour, and whoever believes in Allāh and the latter day should honour his guest."[415]

(B. 78:31).

20. 'Ā'ishah reported,

'The Prophet, peace and blessings of Allāh be on him, said:

"Gabriel continued to enjoin me with good treatment towards the neighbour until I thought that he would make him heir of the property (of the deceased neighbour.)"

(B. 78:28)

21. Abū Dharr said,

.... The Prophet, peace and blessings of Allāh be on him, said to me:

"... Your slaves are your brethren, Allāh has placed them under your control; so whoever has his brother under his control should feed him from what he eats and should give him clothes to wear from what he wears, and do not impose on them a task which should overpower them, and if you impose on them such a task, then help them (in doing it)."[416]

(B. 2:21.)

22. Anas said,

I served the Prophet, peace and blessings of Allāh be on him, for ten years, and he never said to me, Fie. Nor, Why hast thou done (this)? Nor, Why hast thou not done (this)?

(B. 78: 39.)

23. Abū Hurairah said,

The Prophet, peace and blessings of Allāh be on him, said

"One who manages the affairs of the widow and the poor man is like the one who exerts himself hard in the way of Allāh, or the one who stands up for prayer in the night and fasts in the day."

(B. 69:1.)

24. Sahl ibn Sa'd reported,

The Messenger of Allāh, peace and blessings of Allāh be on him, and the man who brings up an orphan will be in paradise like this."

And he pointed with his two fingers, the forefinger and the middle finger.⁴¹⁷

(B. 78:24.)

25. Abū Hurairah reported,

Tufail ibn 'Amr al-Dausī and his companions came to the Prophet, peace and blessings of Allāh be on him, and said, O Messenger of Allāh! Daus have disobeyed and refused, so pray to Allāh for their punishment. And it was said, Daus have perished. But he said: "O Allāh! Guide Daus and bring them."⁴¹⁸ (B. 56: 100.)

26. 'Ā'ishah reported,

The Jews came to the Prophet, peace and blessings of Allāh be on him, and said, Death overtake you! 'Ā'ishah said, And you, and may Allāh curse you and may Allāh's wrath descend on you. He (the Prophet) said:

"Gently, O 'Ā'ishah! Be courteous, and keep thyself away from roughness."⁴¹⁹

(B. 78:38.)

27. Jarīr said:

The Messenger of Allāh, peace and blessings of Allāh be on him, said "Allāh has no mercy on him who is not merciful to men."⁴²⁰

(B.& M-Msh. 24:15)

28. Ibn 'Abbās said,

The Messenger of Allāh, peace and blessings of Allāh be on him, said:

"He is not of us who does not show mercy to our little ones and respect to our great ones."

(Tr-Msh. 24:15)

29. Sahl said,

The Messenger of Allāh, peace and blessings of Allāh be on him, passed by a camel that had grown extremely lean. So he said: 'Be careful of your duty to Allāh regarding these dumb animals; ride them while they are in a fit condition, and eat them while they are in a fit condition."

(AD. 15:43)

30. 'Abd Allāh reported,

The Prophet, peace and blessings of Allāh be on him, said:

"Surely truth leads to virtue, and virtue leads to paradise, and a man continues to speak the truth until he becomes thoroughly truthful; and surely falsehood leads to vice, and vice leads to the fire, and a man continues to tell lies until he is written down a great liar with Allāh"

(B. 78:60.)

31. 'Anas said,

The Prophet, peace and blessings of Allāh be on him, was not a reviler, nor foul in speech, nor a curser; to reprove one of us he would say: "What is the matter with him may his forehead abound with dust."[421]

(B. 78:38)

32. 'Alī said,

The Messenger of Allāh, peace and blessings of Allāh be on him, said:

"A Muslim owes to a Muslim six (duties) to be bestowed liberally--he should offer him salutation when he meets him,[422] and he should accept when he invites him, and he should pray for him when he sneezes, and he should visit him when he is sick, and he should follow his bier when he dies, and he should love for him what he loves for himself."

(Tr-Msh. 24:l.)

33. Abū Hurairah reported, The Prophet, peace and blessings of Allāh be on him, said "The younger one should offer salutation to the older one, and the one who is going along to the one who is sitting, and the smaller group to the larger group."

(B. 79:4)

34. 'Abd Allāh ibn 'Amr reported,

A man asked the Messenger of Allāh, peace and blessings of Allāh be on him, what Islām is the best one? He said:

"That thou feed (the poor) and offer salutation to whom thou knowest and whom thou dost not know."

(B. 2:5.)

35. Qatādah said,

I said to Anas, Did the companions of the Prophet, peace and blessings of Allāh be on him, shake hands[423] (when they met)?

He said, Yes.

(B. 79:27.)

36. 'Ā'ishah said,

Zaid ibn Hārithah[424] came to Madīnah, and the Messenger of Allāh, peace and blessings of Allāh be on him, stood up to receive him, and he embraced him[425] and kissed him.

(Tr-Msh. 24:3.)

37. 'Ubaid ibn 'Umair reported,

Abū Mūsā al-Ash'arī sought permission to see 'Umar and he was not permitted, as if he was engaged, and Abu Mūsā came back.

(B. 34:9.)

38. Sa'īd ibn Abu-l-Hasan said to Hasan,

Women, other than Arabs, keep their bosoms and their heads uncovered. He said, Turn thou away thy eyes from them."

(B. 79:2.)

39. 'Ā'ishah reported,

Saudah bint Zam'ah went out on a certain night. 'Umar saw her and recognised her and said, By Allāh, O Saudah, thou canst not hide thyself from us. So she returned to the Prophet, peace and blessings of Allāh be on him, and mentioned this to him while he was dining in my apartment . . . . . and he said: "It is permitted to you (women) that you go out for your needs."[426]

(B. 67:116.)

16. This incident relates to the time when the whole of Arabia had become Muslim. Arab women also kept their heads and bosoms uncovered before Islām. Hence the Holy Qur'ān ordered women to wear their head-coverings over their bosoms (24: 31).

40. 'Ā'ishah reported,

Asmā', daughter of Abu Bakr, came to the Messenger of Allāh, peace and blessings of Allāh be on him, and she was wearing thin clothes. The Messenger of Allāh, peace and blessings of Allāh be on him, turned away his face from her and said:

"O Asmā'! When the woman attains her majority, it is not proper that any part of her body should be seen except this and this."

And he pointed to his face and his hands."[427]

(AD. 31:30.)

THE STATE (AL-IMĀRAH)

1. "And their rule is by counsel among themselves" (42:38)

2. "Pardon them and ask protection for them, and take counsel with them in affairs of state. (3:158).

3. "Allāh commands you to make over trusts to those worthy of them, and that when you judge between people you judge with justice" (4:58).

4. "O David! We have made thee a ruler in the land, so judge between people with justice and do not follow (thy) desire" (38:26).

5. "They said: How can he hold kingship over us while we have a greater right to kingship than he, and he has not been granted abundance of wealth. He said: Surely Allāh has chosen him in preference to you, and He has increased him abundantly in knowledge and physique" (2:247).

6. "Obey Allāh and obey the Messenger and those in authority from among you, and if you quarrel about anything, refer it to Allāh and the Messenger" (4:58).

Amr means a command or an order; imārah, the possession of command or the office or authority of a commander or a ruler or a king; and amīr, the person who commands or rules, or the head of a state. The word imām (originally, a person whose example is followed or who is imitated) is also used to indicate the chief or head of a state, and so also the word khalīfah (originally, a successor or a vicegerent, or a prophet's successor).

According to the Holy Qur'ān, the Muslim State is a democracy, counsel being the foundation-stone of government (v. 1); even the Holy Prophet is ordered to consult with his followers in conducting affairs of state (v. 2). The People are required to elect as their rulers persons who are fir for this office--to make over trusts to those worthy of them--and those chosen as rulers are required to be just (vv. 3, 4). Vast knowledge and strong physique are the qualifications which should be sought for in a good ruler, not the possession of wealth (v. 5). The highest authority is that of Allāh and His Messenger, so that no law should contravene the Holy Qur'ān and the Sunnah (v. 6).

Hadīth lays it down that government is needed for the good of the people, the king or head of a state being as much responsible for the welfare of the people whom he rules, as a father or mother for the welfare of his or her children, or as a servant for the property entrusted to him (h. 1). The people's responsibility to the State is to respect its laws and obey its orders, so long as they do not require disobedience to Allāh and His Messenger (hh. 2-5). Opposition to constituted authority or rebellion against it is not allowed (h. 6), but the authority of the head of the State may be disputed in extreme cases and he may even be deposed (hh. 7, 8). The Muslim State founded by the Holy Prophet chose the fittest man as his successor after his death, and it was agreed that the State should have a single head who should carry on government with the help of his counsellors and ministers (hh. 9, 10). The Khalīfah was a paid servant of the State, like all other public servants (h. 11). No public servant could accept gifts from the public (H. xvi:18). Those entrusted with carrying on the work of government, including the head, were required to work for the good of the people (h. 12), to be gentle to them (h. 13), to lead simple lives (h. 14). to be easily accessible (h. 15), to be God-fearing (h. 16), to tax the different classes of people according to their capacity, to provide for those who could not earn and to have as much regard for the rights of their non-Muslim subjects as for those of Muslims (h. 17). In his private capacity the ruler was to be treated as any other individual Muslim (h. 18).

1. Ibn 'Umar reported,

I heard the Messenger of Allāh, peace and blessings of Allāh be on him, say:

Every one of you is a ruler and every one of you shall be questioned about those under his rule; the king is a ruler and he shall be questioned about his subjects; and the man is a ruler in his family and he shall be questioned about those under his care; and the woman is a ruler in the house of her husband, and she shall be questioned about those under her care; and the servant is a ruler so far as the property of his master is concerned, and he shall be questioned about that which is entrusted to him."[428]

(B. 11:11).

2. Anas reported,

The Prophet, peace and blessings of Allāh be on him, said:

"Hear and obey though a Negro whose head is like a raisin is appointed (to rule over you)."[429]

(B. 10:54.)

3. Ibn 'Umar reported,

The Prophet, peace and blessings of Allāh be on him, said:

"To hear and obey (the authorities) is binding, so long as one is not commanded

to disobey (God); when one is commanded to disobey (God), he shall not hear or obey."[430]

(B. 56:108.)

4. Abū Hurairah reported,

He heard the Messenger of Allāh, peace and blessings of Allāh be on him, say:

"He who obeys me obeys Allāh, and he who disobeys me disobeys Allāh and he who obeys the amīr obeys me, and he who disobeys the amīr disobeys me; and the imām is an armour for protection[431]--the battle is fought for his defence and through him protection is sought. So if he commands the doing of duty to Allāh and does justice, he has a reward for it; and if he does otherwise,' he shall suffer the evil consequences of it."

(B. 56:109.)

5. 'Alī said,

The Prophet, peace and blessings of Allāh be on him, said

"Obedience is due only in that which is good."⁴³²

(B. 64:61.)

6. Ibn 'Abbās said, peace and blessings of Allāh be on him, said:

"He who dislikes an order of his amīr should withhold himself from opposition, for he who rebels against the king by a span dies the death of jāhiliyyah."

5. The maxim that the king can do no wrong is not known to Islām. As h. 6 shows, however, constituted authority is not to be opposed simply because a person thinks that justice has not been done to him.

(B. 93:2.)

7. Abū Sa'īd said,

The Messenger of Allāh, peace and blessings of Allāh be on him, said:

The most excellent jihād is the uttering of truth in the presence of an unjust ruler."

(Tr-Msh. 17.)

8. 'Ubādah ibn Sāmit said,

'The Prophet, peace and blessings of Allāh be on him, invited us so we swore allegiance to him; and among the conditions which he laid down on us to follow was this that he had a promise from us to hear and obey, whether we liked or disliked (an order,) and whether we were in adversity or ease, even if our rights were not granted; and that we should not dispute the authority of those entrusted with it, (adding) "Unless you see (an act of) open disbelief in which you have a clear argument from Allāh."

(B. 93:2.)

9. 'Ā'ishah reported,

'The Messenger of Allāh, peace and blessings of Allāh be on him, died and the Anṣār gathered together around Sa'd ibn 'Ubādah in the porch of Banī Sā'idah and said, There shall be an amīr from among us and an amīr from among you (the Quraish). Thereupon Abu Bakr and 'Umar and Abū 'Ubaidah went to the them, and 'Umar intended to speak, but Abu Bakr asked him to remain silent ..... Then Abu Bakr spoke, and he spoke as the most eloquent of all people, and he said in his speech, We (the Quraish) are the amīrs and you (the Anṣār) are the wazīrs. Thereupon Hubāb ibn al-Mundhir said, No! By Allāh! We will not accept this; there shall be an amīr from among us and an amīr from among you. But Abu Bakr repeated, No! We are amīrs and you are the wazīrs; they (the Quraish) are the most exalted of all Arabs in position and the noblest of them as regards family: so swear allegiance to 'Umar or Abū 'Ubaidah. 'Umar said, Rather we swear allegiance to thee, for thou art' our chief and the best of us and the most beloved of us to the Messenger of Allāh, peace and blessings of Allāh be on him, So 'Umar took his hand and swore allegiance to him, and the people swore allegiance to him."[433]

(B. 69:6)

7. Kufr, as already shown (H. ii:13) means disbelief as well as an act of disbelief, or an evil deed. Kufr bawāh thus includes both open disbelief and evil deeds which are manifest to an ordinary eye. In such a case, the authority of the ruler may be contested, and he may even be deposed. It was on this ground that Imam Husain contested the authority of Yazīd, and fought against his rule.

10. Anas reported,

He heard the second sermon of 'Umar when he ascended the pulpit, and this was the day next to that on which the Prophet, peace and blessings of Allah, peace and blessings of Allāh be on him, died; ..... he said .....

But if Muhammad, peace and blessings of Allāh be on him, is dead, Allāh has given you the light[434] by which you may be guided--(with it) Allāh guided Muhammad, peace and blessings of Allāh be on him, and Abū Bakr is the companion of the Messenger of Allāh, peace and blessings of Allāh be on him, the second of the two; he is the fittest of the Muslims to control your affairs; so get up and swear allegiance to him.

Some of them had sworn allegiance to him before this in the porch of Banī Sā'idah and the masses swore allegiance to him while he was on the pulpit.

(B. 94:51.)

11. 'Ā'ishah said,

When Abū Bakr was chosen as successor (to the Prophet), he said, My people know that the profession I followed was by no means lacking in supporting my family; and now I am occupied with the affairs of the Muslims, and so the family of Abu Bakr will eat out of this (public) treasury, and he (Abu Bakr) will do work for the Muslims.[435]

(B. 34:15.)

12. Ma'qil said,

I heard the Prophet, peace and blessings of Allāh be on him, say:

"There is not a man whom Allāh grants to rule people, then he does not manage their affairs for (their) good but he will not smell the sweet odour of paradise."[436]

(B. 94:8.)

13. Abū Burdah said,

The Messenger of Allāh, peace and blessings of Allāh be on him, sent Abu Mūsā and Mu'adh ibn Jabal to Yaman, and he appointed each one of them to govern a part of Yaman, and he said, Yaman was divided into two parts; then he said "Be gentle (to the people) and be not hard (on them), and make (them) rejoice and do not incite (them) to aversion."

(B. 64:62.)

14. It is reported about 'Umar that when he appointed his governors, he laid down upon them certain conditions:

You shall not ride a horse that is not of Arabian breed; you shall not eat bread made of fine flour; you shall not wear fine clothes; and you shall not shut your doors against the needs of the people. If you do any of these things. punishment shall descend on you.

Then he went forth with them to bid them farewell.⁴³⁷

(Msh. 17:l.)

15. Hasan said,

Allāh has given orders to the rulers that they shall not follow their low desires, and shall not fear people, and shall not take a small price for Allāh's injunctions.⁴³⁸

(B. 94:16.)

16. 'Amr ibn Maimūn said,

I saw 'Umar at Madīnah a few days before he was wounded. He stopped to talk with Hudhaifah ibn al-Yaman and 'Uthmān ibn al-Hunaif. He said, How have you acted (In 'Irāq)? Do you apprehend that you may have placed a burden on the land which it cannot bear? They said, We have placed on it a burden which it can easily bear.14 Then 'Umar said, If Allāh keep me alive, I would certainly leave the widows of the people of 'Iraq so (well-provided for) that they shall not need the help of any one after me.⁴³⁹ . . . .
. . . . And he said, To him who succeeds me, I enjoin as regards the early Muhājirs that he shall respect their rights and protect their honour; and

I enjoin him to be kind to the Ansār . . . . receiving with approbation (the deeds of) those from among them who do good and pardoning those from among them who do evil; and

I enjoin him to do good to the dwellers of the towns, for they are the support of Islām and the collectors of tribute and the terror of the enemy, and that nothing shall be taken from them save what they can spare, (and that too) with their assent; and

I enjoin him to be good to the dwellers of the desert, for they are the original stock of the Arabs and the auxiliaries of Islām, so that only the less valuable of their cattle shall be taken (as zakāt), and these shall be returned to the poor among them;⁴⁴⁰

I enjoin him as regards those under the protection of Allāh and the protection of His Messenger,[441], peace and blessings of Allāh be on him, that the covenant made with them shall be fulfilled, and that battles shall be fought for their defence, and that they shall be burdened only with what they can bear.

(B. 62:8.)

ENDNOTES

[1] I have discussed this subject fully in The Religion of Islām, in the chapter on Revealed Books. (p. 6)

[2] Bukhārī opens his Jāmi' with the hadīth that follows here, and it is the first hadīth of the chapter entitled The Beginning of Revelation. But, as the subject matter of the hadīth shows, it does not really relate to this chapter; it is in fact a sort of introduction to the Collection itself. It is a very appropriate introduction indeed, for it shows not only the sincerity of purpose of the author but also warns the reader that the good and noble deeds to which he is guided by the sayings and deeds of the Prophet, will prosper only if there is sincerity of purpose beneath them. (p. 7)

[3] By a'māl (pl. of 'amal) are meant the good and noble deeds to which the Holy Prophet invited. The best of deeds would be worthless if the motives were not sincere. Sincerity thus occupies the first place in the moral development of a Muslim. (p. 7)

[4] The original word is hijrah which literally means forsaking someone or flying from a place or giving up low desires, evil tendencies or bad morals. and is specially used of the historic flight of the Holy Prophet from Makkah to Madīnah, which has become the starting-point of the Muslim era. The Muslims had to fly from Makkah because they did not enjoy freedom of conscience there and were persecuted on account of their religious convictions. Hijrah has thus become synonymous with the forsaking of worldly relations, comforts and possessions and undergoing the severest hardships for the sake of one's convictions. (p. 7)

[5] A true dream is thus a kind of Divine revelation (wahy). According to another hadīth al-ru'yā al-sahhah (the true vision) is a part of prophethood: "The Messenger of Allāh said, 'nothing has remained of prophethood except mubashshirāt' (lit. good news). (The companions) asked, 'And what is meant p. 4 by mubashshirāt?' He said, 'The true dream'" (B. 92:5). The dream of the believer is expressly called a part of prophethood in B. 92:26. In the Holy Qur'ān also al-bushrā or true visions are promised to believers (10:64). Prophethood and revelation are not therefore synonymous terms, and while prophethood has terminated, revelation of the first two kinds (42:51) will continue for ever. (p. 7)

[6] This cave (6 ft. by 2) ft. lies to the north-east of Makkah at a distance of about three miles from the city. (p. 7)

⁷ Khadījah was the Holy Prophet's wife whom he married when he was twenty-five years old while she was forty, and who remained his only wife till her death when he was fifty years of age. (p. 8)

⁸ By the Truth is meant the Spirit of Truth or the Holy Spirit, i.e., Gabriel. p. 5 He is called '"the Angel" in the words that follow. This first appearance of Gabriel which was the beginning of the highest form of revelation took place according to one report on the 25th of the month of Ramadzān. Others say it was the 17th of Ramadzān which seems to be a mistake for the 27th, for according to the Holy Qur'ān, the first revelation came on the lailat al-qadr, which occurs on one of the three nights of Ramadzān, 25th, 27th and 29th. According to a report of Ibn 'Abbās, the Holy Prophet had then attained the age of forty (B. 63:28). (p. 8)

⁹ These are the first three verses of the 96th chapter of the Holy Qur'ān, and the first five verses of this chapter are by consensus of opinion the first Quranic revelation that came to the Holy Prophet. It was after this, as appears from the hadīth that follows, that the first verses of ch. 74 were revealed. (p. 8)

¹⁰ The awe was due to his first experience of Divine revelation. (p. 8)

¹¹ The fear to which the Prophet gave expression was lest he should be unable to achieve the great task of the reformation of humanity which was imposed upon p. 7 him. Khadījah's reply clearly shows this to be the import. If any one was equal to that great task, Khadījah comforted him, it was he who had already laid down his life for the service of humanity. This also shows how well the Prophet's life was spent even before prophethood. Neither in this hadīth nor in any other is there anything to show that the Prophet feared that he would be killed by the jinn or that he had become insane. The Prophet knew for sure at the first experience that he had been raised to the dignity of prophethood and entrusted with the great task of reforming humanity. (p. 8)

¹² Pre-Islām days are called al-Jāhiliyyah (Ignorance) or ayyām al Jāhiliyyah (Time of Ignorance) as compared with the learning and light which followed in the wake of Islām. (p. 8)

¹³ Nāmūs means the angel Gabriel (Fr). Nāmūs is the person to whom the king entrusts his secrets and by it is meant (in hadīth) the angel Gabriel whom Allāh has chosen to communicate His revelations (N). This meaning has also been given by Bukhārī himself when repeating this hadīth in B. 60:22. Waraqah in fact only bore testimony to the truth of what the Holy Prophet had stated; viz., that the Holy Spirit (Gabriel) had come to him with a revelation from on high. He, p. 9 however, added that it was the very angel that had come to Moses, and this was probably a

reference to the Bible prophecy that a prophet "like unto" Moses would be raised among the Ishmaelites (Arabs). (p. 8)

[14] The temporary break of revelation was not very long; certainly not longer than six months. Ibn Ishāq's report that it lasted for three years is belied by historical facts. Persecution had begun and a large part of the Holy Qur'ān had been revealed, long before the expiry of three years. It is also an established historical fact that on account of persecution which had grown very severe the Holy Prophet was compelled, in the fourth year of the Call, to take shelter in the house of Arqam and there prayers were said in congregation, and it is a fact that the Holy Qur'ān was recited in prayers from the first. (p. 8)

[15] While the previous Hadīth relates the Holy Prophet's first experience of revelation, this one speaks of his second experience. On this occasion the first five verses of ch. 74 were revealed to him. This portion is from the Holy Prophet's own mouth, and therefore not the least doubt can be entertained as to the fact: that Gabriel's second visit to him was the occasion mentioned in this hadīth. What is, therefore, added by Zuhrī in B. 92:1 (where h. 2 is repeated) that during the break in revelation the Holy Prophet used to go to the tops of the mountains to throw himself down and Gabriel appeared to him on such occasions and comforted him that he was the true Messenger of Allāh cannot be accepted as true. This Hadīth makes it clear that Gabriel was never seen by the Holy Prophet during the break, and that when he saw him on the second occasion, he was struck with awe as on the first occasion. Zuhrī, moreover, gives no authority for his addition in B. 92:1. (p. 9)

[16] Five short verses of ch. 96 were revealed on the first occasion and five short verses of ch. 74 on the second. After that, it is stated, revelation became plentiful-- the Arabic word is hamiya which literally means became hot--and continuous, there being no break like the break between the first two revelations. (p. 9)

[17] This hadīth shows that all revelations without any exception were delivered to the Holy Prophet by the angel Gabriel and that the method of their delivery was always the same, viz., that Gabriel first recited the revelation and the Holy Prophet listened to it and then when Gabriel departed the Holy Prophet recited the same words. On the first two occasions, only five short verses were revealed and it was not difficult for the Prophet to repeat them; but after that, a shown in the last hadīth, revelation became plentiful, i.e., large portions were revealed at one time, and as Gabriel began to recite, the Holy Prophet made haste to repeat lest any word or sentence might be lost. He was, therefore, told not to make haste with it and to wait until Gabriel had delivered the whole message and then to repeat the same, being assured that it was a Divine arrangement and that nothing would be lost (75:16, 17). In another very early chapter he was Still more plainly told: "We

will make thee recite so thou shalt not forget" (87:6). There are chapters--one of these containing over a thirtieth of the Holy Qur'an--that were revealed to him in their entirety at one time, yet Gabriel recited them once only and then the Holy Prophet repeated them without omission of a word and ordered them to be written down at once.

It would further appear from this hadīth that other people saw the Holy Prophet's lips move when he received the revelation which shows that his reception of the revelation was not subjective but a real and external experience. (p. 9)

[18] The difference in the two states is one of the form the Angel assumed. In the first case it is not stated what likeness the Angel assumed--it was an angelic form beyond description--and the words came forth with the clear resonant sound of vibrating metal; in the second case the Angel assumed the likeness of a man and the words were uttered as one man talks to another. That words were spoken in both cases is clear enough from the words of the Hadīth; in both cases we are told: "I retain in memory what he says." In the first case, however, the words 'an-hu (i.e., from him) have been added to show that it was the Angel who spoke the words. In both cases the Holy Prophet saw the Angel and heard the words from the Angel and then retained them in memory; the difference was only one of the likeness of the Angel, and consequently, of the tone in which the words were uttered. (p. 9)

[19] There are many Hadīth showing that a real change came over the Holy Prophet when revelation came down upon him. Here it is stated that perspiration ran down his brow on a severely cold day; according to h. 6, Zaid felt his thigh being crushed under the Holy Prophet's thigh when revelation came on: h. 7 says that Ya'lā saw the Holy Prophet when revelation descended on him and "his face was red"; according to h. 8, when revelation descended on the Holy Prophet, "he appeared distressed and a change came over his face." All these hadīth show that whenever revelation came down upon the Holy Prophet, whether he was in public or in private, there was a real change which could not be assumed. It is clear from this that though revelation came to the Holy Prophet in a state of wakefulness, yet there was a transition from the physical environment to the spiritual sphere, the effect of which was witnessed on the body. The new senses which were required to receive the revelation necessitated the coming of a kind of death over the body. The story that "froth appeared before his mouth" is a pure invention and no trace of it is to be met with in any hadīth. (p. 10)

[20] A place between Makkah and Tā'if. (p. 10)

[21] The change was so perfect that it resembled a state of sleep, though as the p. 15 hadīth makes it clear, he was not asleep and was just at that moment talking to his companions. (p. 10)

²² The companions hung down their heads out of respect. (p. 10)

²³ This hadīth shows what the Islamic conception of religion is. Religion does not consist in performing too many devotional exercises; these are in fact discouraged as they ultimately overpower the man who indulges in them. Religion is the name of acting aright and keeping to the mean course; this would keep a man in good heart. The truly religious man will smile in the face of everyone, as did the Holy Prophet. What is generally considered to be Divine worship is really the seeking of Divine help for acting aright and keeping to the mean. Thus is every Muslim taught to pray daily and hourly: "Guide us on the right path: the path of those to whom Thou hast been gracious" (1,5,6). (p. 13)

²⁴ 'Ā'ishah admired the devotional exercises of a certain woman but the Holy Prophet warned her of excess of these because, he said, people indulge in these and then get tired of them. The chief aim of religion is, as made clear in the concluding words, to bring about perseverance in the character of a man, He is, therefore, told to adopt that course in religious devotion in which he can keep constant. (p. 13)

²⁵ There are many versions of this hadīth and in all of them it is made clear by the Holy Prophet that a man has several duties to perform and he must keep all of them in mind in devoting himself to religious exercise. No religious exercise, whether it is keeping the fast or standing up in prayer, will do him good if he neglects his worldly duties. In fact, religious devotion is meant to make a man fitter for the performance of his duties which he owes to others. In the development of the spiritual, the physical side and worldly duties are not to be neglected. (p. 14)

²⁶ The man who is imbued with a truly religious spirit avoids not only what is manifestly unlawful but even the doubtful things which might lead him into the unlawful. The concluding portion of the hadīth shows that religion does not consist in the devotional exercises which a man may perform but in the presence in him of a right mentality--the mentality to act aright and avoid the wrong. A sound mind is of the essence of religion, as the Holy Qur'ān says: "Except him who comes to Allāh with a sound mind" (26:89). (p. 14)

²⁷ At the end of this hadīth it is added that the Holy Prophet said that it was Gabriel who had come to teach people their religion. The hadīth is related with slight variations by 'Umar, but Bukhārī does not accept it. In 'Umar's version, describing īmān (faith) the Holy Prophet is reported to have said instead of "in meeting with Him," "that thou believe in qadar, in the good of it and the evil of it." The belief in qadar is evidently a doctrine of later growth and it is perhaps on account of this flaw that Bukhārī does not accept the version attributed to 'Umar. Another

variation in 'Umar's version is that in describing what Islām is, the pilgrimage to Makkah is also spoken of; this is evidently an omission in Abū Hurairah's version. And further, instead of "that thou shalt worship Allāh and not associate aught with Him" in Abū Hurairah's version, we have in 'Umar's, "That thou bear witness that there is no god but Allāh and that Muhammad is the Messenger of Allāh."
This hadīth makes a distinction between Īmān (faith) and Islām, showing that the former relates to matters of conviction and the latter to matters of practice. The third term ihsān is not a technical term and indicates the state of sincerity in one's conviction or practice--to feel oneself in Divine presence. Īmān and Islām are often used interchangeably but, as distinguished from each other, īmān means a belief in Allāh, the angels, the messengers (which includes the Books or the messages). liqā'-Allāh (which means meeting with Allāh), and in a life after death; while Islām means the worshipping ('ibādah) of Allāh, keeping up prayer, fasting in the month of Ramadzān. paying zakāt (a fixed portion of one's savings) and the pilgrimage to Makkah.
The man who accepts these principles is a Muslim, and a member of the Muslim brotherhood. (p. 15)

[28] This hadīth corroborates the definition of Islām as given in the previous one. In fact, the first requisite of Islām--the bearing of witness that there is no god but Allāh and that Muhammad is the Messenger of Allāh--includes all the other four, because they are a part of the teachings of the Holy Prophet. They are mentioned along with the basic principle on account of their importance. (p. 15)

[29] The word seventy is used in Arabic as a perfect number and signifies a large number. This hadīth shows that Īmān (Faith) carries a much wider significance than that which may generally be attached to it. It is not limited to certain matters relating to belief, to the conviction that certain principles are true, but extends to the carrying out of those principles into action; nor is it limited to certain religious acts or devotions but covers all good qualities and actions that benefit humanity, Īmān is represented as a big tree with branches extending in all directions. The confession of Divine Unity which is the basic principle of Islām is the highest branch of this tree, while even the removal from the way of what may cause harm to a passer-by is a branch of the tree of faith. The making of roads for the convenience of the public is therefore an act of faith. Thus all acts which aim at doing good to humanity are branches of the tree of faith, and faith thus signifies the proper development of all human faculties. Hayā' translated here as modesty, is specially mentioned because it originally signifies that quality which makes one shun all evil things (R). (p. 15)

[30] Though here only love for the Prophet is spoken of, yet what is meant is love for Allāh and His Prophet, as h. 10 shows. Love for a person springs from the good which he does to us or from the benefit which we may derive from him. As the

Holy Prophet is the greatest benefactor of humanity, and of his ummah in particular, every Muslim is required to have greater love for him than to any other human being. Highest love for the Holy Prophet is made a test of faith, because the stronger the ties which bind a man to him the greater the strength with which he will be able to walk in his footsteps and the larger his capacity to do good to humanity.

Practically, the Muslim world to-day has provided an entire failure under this test. The Holy Prophet and his teachings are misrepresented throughout the world and he is abused as no other religious leader has been abused; but Muslims do not stir a single finger to remove the misrepresentations and carry the true teachings of Islām to a world which is groping in the dark. (p. 15)

[31] Here is another test of real faith. It is not simply doing to others as one would like them to do to oneself; it is much more--to love for others what one loves for oneself. Such a state of mind can arise only from the highest disinterestedness. Muslims judge each other by the repetition of certain formulae and by belief in certain doctrines; the Holy Prophet required them to be judged by their love for Allāh and His Prophet and by their love for humanity. (p. 16)

[32] Here is another definition of Islām. A man is called a Muslim when he declares his faith in Unity, but he becomes a Muslim actually when he begins to lead his life as a Muslim, as a man of peace from whose tongue and hand all Muslims are safe. It is one thing to enter Islām and quite another to live it. Such life of peace not only raises the individual's character to a high level; it p. 27 also lays down the basis of a perfect brotherhood. It is not meant that a Muslim is at liberty to do harm to non-Muslims by his tongue or his hand; Muslims are mentioned in the hadīth because it is with one's own community that one has largely to deal. The aim is to lay the foundations of a world-wide brotherhood in which every one should feel himself safe, and that brotherhood can draw others into it only if they find themselves safe from the tongue and hand of a Muslim. There is another version of this hadīth in which the word "people" is used instead of "Muslims": "A Muslim is he from whose tongue and hand people are safe" (Ibn Habān). (p. 16)

[33] This is how Islām introduced spiritual meaning into physical words--Hijrah or flying from home becomes flying from evil. (p. 16)

[34] Here the act of abusing a Muslim (i.e., offending him with one's tongue) is called transgression, and the act of fighting him (or, offending him with one's hand) is called Kufr. It is not meant that such a man becomes a disbeliever or is outside the pale of Islām, for in the Holy Qur'ān itself two parties of believers are spoken of as fighting with each other (49:9). The act itself may amount to kufr, but the doer of it does not thereby become a kāfir, so long as he professes faith in the kalimah, the

Unity of Allāh and the messengership of Muhammad, which is the basic principle of Islām. (p. 16)

[35] I have omitted here the portion of the Hadīth which speaks of according an equal treatment to slaves, and have quoted only the words of the Holy Prophet which show that abusing another man is an act of ignorance which word in Muslim terminology is equivalent to unbelief. Abū Dharr had used the words Ibn al-saudā', or son of a Negro woman, regarding another; and as these words were used contemptuously, they were considered an abuse of one Muslim by another, which was an act of ignorance or unbelief. In fact, every evil deed is an act of kufr according to the Holy Prophet, just as every good deed is an act of faith. Neither does a disbeliever become a believer if he does a good deed nor a believer a disbeliever if he does an evil deed. The line of demarcation between the believer and the disbeliever, the Muslim and the kāfir is the confession that God is one and that Muhammad is His Messenger--Lā ilāha illallāh Muhammad-un Rassūl Allāh. (p. 17)

[36] That is to say, a person who tells lies, breaks promises and is unfaithful to trusts has no faith in him--nothing of the teachings of Islām, and his profession of faith is simply hypocrisy. (p. 17)

[37] Here a more practical test is given. If you see a man saying his prayers in the Islamic mode and with his face to the Qiblah, that is a sure test that he is a Muslim--for him is the covenant of Allāh and the covenant of His Messenger--and to call him a kāfir is violation of the covenant of Allāh. The Holy Qur'ān lays down a still more practical and a broader test: "And say not to any one who offers you (Islamic) salutation, Thou art not a believer" (4:94). When a person says to another al-salāmu 'alaikum to show thereby that he is a Muslim, he cannot be called a disbeliever or kāfir. The author of the Mawāqif says: generality of the theologians and the jurists are agreed that none of the Ahl Qiblah (persons facing the Qiblah in their prayers) can be called a kāfir (Mf. P. 600). (p. 17)

[38] This hadīth and the one previous to it show that when a person professes that God is one and that Muhammad is His Messenger with a sincere heart, i.e., trying to the best of his knowledge to follow the Divine commandments and walk in the footsteps of the Holy Prophet, he is saved from the fire and shall enter paradise. (p. 18)

[39] Faithfulness to Allāh consists in submitting to Divine commandments; faithfulness to His Messenger means following in his footsteps; faithfulness to Muslim leaders consists in obeying their orders so long as they do not go against Allāh and His Messenger; and faithfulness to Muslims in general consists in doing one's utmost for their good. This is the quintessence of the religion of Islām.

This saying of the Holy Prophet is quoted by Bukhārī in the heading of this chapter. (p. 18)

[40] The words in Arabic are lā ḥasada illā fi-thnataini, which may be rendered as meaning "there shall be no ḥasad but in two cases." But as ḥasad or the desire that another person shall be deprived of the advantages which he has, is totally prohibited by the moral code of Islām; the word illā is here used as an istithnā' munqaṭī'. Ḥasad (envy) and ghibṭah (emulation) have one thing in common, viz., a desire regarding advantages or excellence which another man possesses; but in ḥasad the desire is that he shall be deprived of them, while in ghibṭah it is that the desirer may be favoured with similar advantages. By using the word ghibṭah in the heading of this chapter, Bukhārī shows that while ḥasad is prohibited here, ghibṭah is recommended in two cases. (p. 20)

[41] The word in the original is ḥikmah which may be rendered wisdom or knowledge. According to R. it means "the knowledge of things and the doing of good." (p. 20)

[42] The desire to have knowledge is here made akin to the desire to possess wealth which is a natural desire in every human heart, and thus it is made clear that the acquisition of knowledge is as important as that of wealth, and every human being should acquire both. The desire to possess either, however, is made subject to a further condition: the possessor of wealth spends it in the cause of Truth, and the possessor of knowledge teaches it to others, so that the benefit of humanity is the real end in view. In the Holy Qur'ān, knowledge is spoken of as the greatest wealth: "And whoever is given knowledge (ḥikmah), he indeed is given abundant wealth" (2:269) (p. 20).

[43] It was the case of a deputation of the Rabī'ah tribe that came to the Holy Prophet from Bahrain on (the Persian Gulf). They were told to remember all that they had learned in their residence at Madīnah and to teach it to their people. The duty to teach others is laid on all Muslims in h. 3. (p. 20)

[44] Here we are told that, so far as education was concerned, even slave-girls were not to be neglected. They had to be trained well and educated in the best manner. This was what Islām aimed at, and this was to be the Muslims' highest ideal; not only were free citizens to be trained and educated but even slaves, who were considered by the Arabs to have a very low status--not so low, however, as the unfortunate untouchables in India--were to he brought up to the level of the free citizen by proper education and training, and not only boys but girl, as well. The questions of mass education, female education and emancipation of slaves were thus forestalled by the Holy Prophet thirteen hundred years before modern civilization. (p. 20)

[45] Bukhârî mentions this hadîth under the heading, "Should a separate day be fixed for the education of woman?" It shows that from the Islamic point of view it is desirable that there should be separate arrangements for the education of men and women. (p. 21)

[46] Although the Holy Prophet himself did not know reading or writing, be encouraged both. There is a misunderstanding as to the prohibition of writing down hadîth. As this hadîth shows, the Holy Prophet himself ordered the writing down of hadîth when it was needed. Generally, however, writing of hadîth was not considered desirable as it was feared that persons who were not cautions enough might confuse the verses of the Holy Qur'ân with hadîth. As the next hadîth, however, shows there were some people who regularly resorted to writing hadîth. (p. 21)

[47] The words "in Syriac" are not in Bukhârî but they are added here on the authority of AD. and Tr. This hadîth shows that the Holy Prophet ordered the learning of other languages as well. (p. 21)

[48] He was told to learn the art of writing and then write down hadîth. (p. 22)

[49] The superiority of race over race and family over family is recognised--people are mines like mines of gold and silver--among Muslims as well as non-Muslims, but it is added that this superiority is maintained through attainment of knowledge. If persons belonging to a superior race discard knowledge, they lose their superiority. Racial or family superiority is thus subject to the acquisition of knowledge. (p. 22)

[50] This Hadîth lays down upon every Muslim the obligation of acquiring knowledge. Hikmah means wisdom or knowledge, and dzâllah means a lost animal or an object of persevering quest (LL.), so that the believer should set out in search of knowledge as perseveringly as the owner of a lost animal would search for it. (p. 22)

[51] These two sayings of the Holy Prophet are related by Bukhârî in the heading of the tenth chapter of his "Book of Knowledge." The latter part shows that stress was laid not only on the acquisition of knowledge but also on conveying it to others or on teaching it. (p. 23)

[52] This is also a saying of the Holy Prophet and forms part of the heading of B. 3:10. It is related as a separate hadîth in Tr. Knowledge is here described as the inheritance of the prophets and is called a great fortune. (p. 23)

[53] The words every Muslim include both men and women, while another version adds and every Muslim woman. Its authorities are said to be weak. It should, however, be noted that the more authentic hadîth quoted above also make obligatory upon all Muslims, men as well as women, to acquire knowledge. (p. 23)

[54] "The Hour" in the language of Islâm indicates as regards an individual, his death; as regards a nation, the hour of its doom; and as regards the whole of humanity, the destruction of all. Evidently, what is meant here is the doom of a particular nation, just as knowledge brings life to a nation, ignorance seals its doom. Thus have Muslims fallen on evil days; instead of that thirst for knowledge which characterized their ancestors, ignorance is now rampant. (p. 23)

[55] A pure mind in a pure body is the watchword of Islâm. Here cleanliness is not next to godliness but it is half of godliness or faith. (p. 26)

[56] This hadîth and the previous one lay down in general terms that purification is a necessary condition of prayer, which in fact means that a man should always keep himself free from impurities, since prayer is said five times a day. The habit of outward purification is thus developed through an institution which is meant to purify the soul, and a Muslim is required to keep his body, his clothes, in fact, the whole of his environment, clean. Charity like prayer purifies the mind, and as what is acquired by unlawful means is impure, the pure and the impure cannot go together. (p. 26)

[57] Khubuth is the plural of khabîth (an evil person) and khabâ'ith is the plural of khabîthah (an evil person of feminine gender), and the words are generally understood as meaning the devils, but according to the Nihâyah, the first word may also be read as khubth which means impure deeds and the second word may also mean evil habits. Thus from outward defilement attention is directed to inward impurities. (p. 26)

[58] Other hadîth speak of stones for cleaning purposes, but water was used when available even after cleaning with earth or stones. These may appear to be minor details, but the minutest details are necessary to develop habits of cleanliness. Water or earth was also used after urinating. (p. 26)

[59] This with and the one following speak of pebbles or balls of dry earth for cleaning purposes. Toilet paper would serve the same purpose. (p. 27)

[60] For evacuating himself a man must not, therefore, sit in a place where he can be seen by others; i.e., when he goes out into fields. Latrines must be made on the same principle. (p. 27)

⁶¹ So there must be either urinals or a man must retire to some other proper place of retirement. (p. 27)

⁶² This shows a high degree of care for public convenience and the protection of public places and water-sources from contamination. (p. 28)

⁶³ To urinate in a standing posture is therefore not prohibited. (p. 28)

⁶⁴ This was done to remove any vestige of uncleanness which might remain on the hand after the simple flow of water. Soap may be used for the same purpose. (p. 28)

⁶⁵ Evidently it was a public place where other people were present and by spitting in his handkerchief he showed that it was not proper to spit on the ground in public places. Besides being indecent, it is insanitary. (p. 29)

⁶⁶ The spittle should be taken in a handkerchief if one is overcome in prayer. (p. 29)

⁶⁷ The Holy Prophet thus taught that outward cleanness was also a means of pleasing the Lord and that uncleanness was therefore hateful to God. (p. 29)

⁶⁸ The use of the tooth-brush after sleep is essential because there is no access of light or air into the mouth during sleep, and the dirt that has there accumulated must be cleaned at once. (p. 30)

⁶⁹ Ablution, which means washing of certain parts of the body that are generally exposed and where dust or dirt is likely to settle, is a preparation for going into Divine presence. The object is undoubtedly twofold, that a man should be clean and that he should feel that he stands in need of the purification of the soul as he stands in need of the cleaning of the body. The remembrance of Allāh is needed to direct attention to this. The beginning should be made with Bismillāh as in the case of all important affairs, while h. 42. speaks of the prayer when the ablution ends. (p. 31)

⁷⁰ The various reports show that there was great latitude in these matters. The cleaning might be effected in some cases by washing once only while in others it might require repetition. Maqā'id, according to Ibn Hajar, is the name of a place in Madīnah. According to others, it means a place where people sit together. (p. 32)

⁷¹ In performing ablution the right hand should be washed first and then the left. The same rule is to be followed in washing the feet. (p. 32)

⁷² The complete Mash (wiping) of the head thus includes the ears, their inner side as well as the outer. (p. 32)

⁷³ The word tāhiratain (both being clean) in the hadīth refers to the two feet, but the meaning is generally taken to be that the boots were put on after performing ablution. The next hadīth shows that socks are treated similarly, i.e., it is sufficient to pass wet hands over them when they are worn after performing ablution. This may be done for one day and night, i.e., the socks or boots must bc taken off and the feet washed once in every twenty-four hours, but in the case of one who is journeying the time-limit is three days and nights. See h. (p. 33)

⁷⁴ The Arabic word is ahdatha which means originally he caused or occasioned a thing, and is technically applied to the voiding of ordure. When Abū Hurairah was asked, what hadath was, he simply said, breaking wind but it includes the passing of urine, stools and wind. To this must be added sound sleep as stated in h. 39 and vomiting (h.40), though there is a difference of opinion in the latter case. The reason for a fresh ablution after sound sleep seems to be that one does not know if one has passed wind in that condition. Bukhārī makes it clear that ablution is only necessary when something passes out through the makhrajain, the two ways of natural evacuation. The flowing of blood from wounds or the spitting of blood does not necessitate ablution. If a man performs ablution by wiping his boots or socks, and then takes them off, fresh ablution is not necessary (hh, 32, 34). Taking food or milk does not call for fresh ablution. but the mouth should be rinsed in both cases. (B. 4:50, 51, 52.)
There are certain hadīth speaking of the necessity of ablution in certain other cases. For instance, there is a hadīth which says that ablution should be performed if one has kissed one's wife, but this is contradicted by other hadīth. The clear rule laid down by Bukhārī that ablution is necessitated only by what passes out of the two outlets of natural evacuation is the safest rule. Sound sleep and vomiting are the only exceptions. (p. 33)

⁷⁵ There is no harm if there is a little interval in washing the different parts so long as ablution is a continuous act. (p. 34)

⁷⁶ Taking a bath once a week, on Fridays, is made incumbent irrespective of other needs. It does not mean that a Muslim should take a bath only once a week; it is the minimum requirement, and the whole body as well as the head must be washed by both men and women, rich and poor, at least once a week. To keep oneself clean has already been stated to be half the faith, and in the hot and even temperate seasons nothing less than a daily bath can serve that purpose, but in the cold season and in the case of generality of people who cannot afford a daily bath, the washing of the whole body once a week is an absolute necessity. (p. 35)

⁷⁷ This was a kind of disinfectant; soap would serve the same purpose. A man who is initiated into Islām must clean himself outwardly also by having a bath, and this was further meant to serve as a hint that he should henceforward aim at both purity of body and purity of mind. (p. 36)

⁷⁸ Janābah (from janb meaning a side) is literally the putting of a thing aside or making a person avoid a thing. In the religious terminology of Islām, the state of Janābah arises from nocturnal pollution (ihtilām) and coitus (sexual intercourse) for both men and women. There are contradictory hadīth as to whether bath is necessary in case of sexual intercourse when there is no emission, and Bukhārī favours the view that wudzū' or ablution is sufficient in such a case, but that bath is better. The person who is in a state of janābah, is called junub. Such a man must take a bath before he can say his prayers. (p. 36)

⁷⁹ A bath is necessary for women after menses (haidz) and puerpurium (nifās), i.e., the flow of blood after childbirth. During the period of menses and puerpurium, a woman is exempted from prayer. Menstruation generally lasts from three to ten days, and a bath is needed when the flow stops, after a minimum period of three days. Bath must necessarily be taken after the maximum period of ten days, and if the flow continues after that, it is called istihādzah, and the rules relating to menses do not apply to this state. (p. 36)

⁸⁰ This hadīth shows that the state of janābah is not a state of defilement. The junub can do everything; he is simply required to take a bath before saying his prayers. (p. 36)

⁸¹ This Hadīth removes another great misconception. The woman, who has her menses on, is not impure. There is a large number of hadīth showing that her social relation with her husband or other members of society remain unchanged. (p. 37)

⁸² That is to say, he should either be in a closed bath-room where he cannot be seen by others, or if he is in an open place, he should cover himself from waist to knees. (p. 37)

⁸³ Tayammum from am ma (he repaired to a thing) means resorting to earth when one is unable to find water in sufficient quantity for ablution or bath, or when one is unable to use it on account of illness or for fear of contracting disease. If water is available in such quantity as can barely suffice for drinking or preparing food, it is permissible to resort to tayammum instead of ablution or bath. (p. 38)

⁸⁴ This hadīth shows that tayammum takes the place not only of ablution but also of bath. It also shows the manner in which tayammum is performed. The hands

should be struck on clean earth, then the dust should be shaken. or blown off, then the back of each hand should be wiped with the other and then the face should be wiped with both hands. There are other hadīth which give a slightly different process. but as the object is simply to remind a man that he is going to a Higher Presence. this simple process serves the purpose well enough. Bukhārī relates that Yahyā ibn Sa'īd said that there was no harm in performing tayammum on sabkhah, i.e., on ground on the surface of which salt had appeared (B. 7:6) And generally anything would do, or, the surface of which dust might have settled. (p. 38)

[85] It is related in one hadīth that the night was severely cold, and the Holy Prophet considered the excuse to be valid. In this case 'Amr led the prayers. (p. 38)

[86] This hadīth shows that when it is harmful to apply water to a particular part of the body, it is sufficient to wipe that part. In this case the wounded man had a bath on the advice of his friends, and the wound got septic and he died. The Prophet upbraided his companions for giving an advice which was not based on knowledge. (p. 38)

[87] According to the Holy Qur'ān and the Hadīth, a Muslim does not stand in need of a consecrated place to say his Prayers, Here the whole earth is called a mosque. (p. 42)

[88] This hadīth shows that a mosque should be built facing towards the Ka'bah, which., according to the Holy Qur'ān, is the first mosque built on the earth. Before the revelation referred to in this hadīth (v. 2), Muslims used to face towards Jerusalem which was the qiblah of the Israelite prophets. It was about sixteen or seventeen months after the Hijra that the Holy Prophet received the revelation to make the Ka'bah his qiblah. The idea underlying the Qiblah is to bring about unity of purpose. As in a large country the direction of the Ka'bah would be different in the north from that in the south, it is stated in a hadīth (Ah. 1, 223) that "it is not fit for one country to have two qiblahs," for different qiblahs in one country would destroy the very purpose of the Qiblah. (p. 42)

[89] It shows not only that arrangements were made for cleaning the mosque, but also that the person who did this service was specially honoured by the Holy Prophet, Another hadīth shows that it was a woman (p. 43).

[90] The pulpit was needed only for the Friday sermon. The pulpit and the mats formed the only furniture of the mosque. (p. 44)

[91] This shows that prayers had sometimes to be said on bare ground. (p. 44)

⁹² It shows that a man may have a private mosque of his own in his house. It can serve the purpose of a mosque for saying prayers in congregation, but it does not thereby acquire the character of a mosque and remains a private place. (p. 44)

⁹³ It shows that prayers are really meant to be said in congregation in the mosque, but a part of them, such as tahajjud or sunnah prayers, are recommended to be said in houses. A house in which Allāh's name is not remembered is likened to a grave, because it is devoid of spiritual life. (p. 44)

⁹⁴ The Suffah was situated in the northern part of the Mosque, covered with a p. 78 roof but with open sides. Here resided those whose object was to study the Qur'ān and the Hadīth and their number is said to have at one time reached four hundred. Among them were well-to-do people, such as Sa'd ibn Abī Waqqās, but mostly poor people, such as Abū Hurairah. (p. 44)

⁹⁵ The mosque was thus a place where everything which related to the good of the individual or the community was to be learned or taught, and hence it became the cultural centre of Islām. (p. 45)

⁹⁶ The Prophet's Mosque had a very wide open yard where people gathered together, and where, as many hadīth show, tents were pitched sometimes, and on one side of which a large number of students were accommodated. It was in this open court that the Abyssinians were giving a display of their skill with spears. 'Ā'ishah's chamber opened into this yard. (p. 45)

⁹⁷ It is an incident of the time of 'Umar. Hassān was reciting a poem in the mosque when 'Umar prohibited him. On this he called Abu Hurairah to bear witness that he used to recite poems in the mosque in the presence of the Holy Prophet. According to a report in Tr., the Holy Prophet used to ask Hassān to refute in verse the scurrilous attacks made on the Holy Prophet by his enemies in their poems, and this was done in the mosque. (p. 45)

⁹⁸ A woman could not only enter the mosque but she could also, if necessary, take up her residence in the mosque. The putting up of a tent for a slave-girl in the mosque shows that she must have resided there for a sufficiently long time. (p. 46)

⁹⁹ Evidently this prisoner was an idolater, yet he was kept under restraint in the mosque. (p. 46)

¹⁰⁰ This hadīth shows that in the Holy Prophet's time the mosque served many purposes besides that of saying prayers. On the present occasion it served the purpose of the treasury, because there was at the time no separate treasury. The hadīth further shows how little attraction wealth had for the Holy Prophet. The

money was there, a hundred thousand dirhams, but he did not even took at it. Neither did he take one pie of it into his house, nor did he reserve any portion of it for future needs. (p. 47)

[101] Spitting in the mosque is prohibited, both because of the sacredness of the place and because it is a gathering-place for the people. Elsewhere it is stated that the Holy Prophet was offended when he saw spittle on the wall of the mosque (IV:17). Burying is spoken of here because the floor of the mosque was of loose gravel. (p. 47)

[102] Being a desert Arab, the man was not aware of the sacred character of the mosque. (p. 48)

[103] As h. 20 shows, the Holy Prophet allowed Hassān to recite his verses in the mosque, because they were religious in character. The carrying on of trade in the mosque is forbidden because it would change the atmosphere of the mosque into that of a market. The last prohibition aims at maintaining the serenity of the prayers. People sitting in groups would usually indulge in talk which would disturb the calm and quiet necessary to a prayerful attitude. And that is the reason why Muslims so strongly resent noise or music before mosques at the time of prayers. (p. 48)

[104] The doors of the Holy Prophet's apartments opened into the mosque, and so did those of some other houses. But later on, all these doors were closed so that the mosque should not be used as a thoroughfare. (p. 49)

[105] So that their noxious stink may not offend others. (p. 49)

[106] This Hadīth shows that prayers may be said with shoes on. Hence a man can also go into the mosque without removing his shoes, but that they must be clean is a necessary condition. It must further be remembered that the floor of the mosque was of gravel. and shoes were needed as a protection from heat or cold. The practice now is that shoes are left outside the mosque. But if needed as a protection from severe heat or severe cold or for some other reason, a man may go into the mosque with shoes on if they are clean. The case of a non-Muslim is different. He can enter the mosque only on sufferance, and he must, therefore, be required to remove his shoes as a mark of respect. (p. 49)

[107] It appears from other hadīth that the portion that follows relates to another occasion. A consultation was held but nothing was decided then, though 'Umar seems to have made a suggestion that, instead of ringing a bell or blowing a horn, a man should be appointed to give a call for prayers. According to one hadīth 'Abd Allāh ibn Zaid was shown in a vision how to give a call for prayer. So when the

Messenger of Allāh came the next day, he informed him: O Messenger of Allāh! I was half asleep and half awake when there came to me one who showed me how to deliver the adhān. The narrator of the Hadīth added, 'Umar had been shown it twenty days previously but concealed it, then he informed the Holy Prophet (AD. 2:27). Bukhārī refers to this by quoting 'Umar as saying, Would you not appoint a man who should give a call for prayer. It was, however, the Holy Prophet's order-- or maybe, he himself had received a revelation, similar to the visions of 'Abd Allāh and 'Umar as some reports show--which gave the sanction to the adhān. (p. 52)

[108] The repetition of the shahādah a second time as stated in this hadīth is known as tarjī' (lit. returning to a thing again and again). As the previous hadīth and the one that follows show, the general practice in the Holy Prophet's time was that the adhān consisted of fifteen sentences, Allāhu-Akbar four times, ashhadu an lā ilāha illa-llāh twice, ashhadu anna Muhammadan Rasūlu-llāh twice (both sentences beginning with ashhadu are known as the shahādah) hayya 'ala-l-salā (pronounced 'ala-s-salā) twice (turning the face to the right), hayya 'ala-l-falāh twice (turning the face to the left), Allāhu Akbar twice and lā ilāha illa-llāh once. The tarji' or repeating the two shahādah sentences twice again in a still louder voice seems to have been resorted to only occasionally. In the adhān for the morning prayer the sentence al-salātu (pronounced as-salāt) khair-un mina-l-naum (pronounced minan-naum) was added after hayya 'ala-l-falāh, and repeated twice. (p. 53)

[109] As compared with the adhān, the sentences were uttered only once in the iqāmah, according to this Hadīth. the significance being that sentences that were uttered twice in the adhān were uttered once in the iqāmah. The iqāmah thus consists of Allāhu Akbar being uttered twice--in the adhān it is uttered four times-- each of the shahādah sentences once, hayya 'ala-l-salā and hayy'ala-l-falāh each once (without turning to right or left), qad qāmati-l-salā twice, Allāhu Akbar and lā ilāha illa-llāh once.
But the iqāmah may also consist of all the sentences of the adhān with the addition in its proper place of qad qāmati-l-salā uttered twice. Between the delivery of the adhān and the iqāmah there is another difference. The sentences of the adhān are delivered leisurely and in as loud a voice as possible, while the delivery of the iqāmah is marked by quickness. (p. 53)

[110] Fore-fingers are not put into ears in the iqāmah. (p. 54)

[111] With hayya 'ala-l-salā, the mu'adhdhin turns his face to the right side and with hayya 'ala-l-falāh to the left. (p. 54)

[112] A high place, the top of a house or a minaret, would carry the voice farthest. (p. 54)

[113] The voice in delivering the adhān should be raised as high as possible. (p. 55)

[114] The hadīth speaks of the imām as dzāmin, being as it were a surety that prayers are observed in the right manner; and it speaks of the mu'adhdhin (one p. 98 who delivers the adhān) as mu'taman, i.e., one in whom trust is placed, which indicates on the one hand that he is the keeper of the time of prayer and on the other that he must be a man who is respected on account of his high qualities. (p. 55)

[115] The imām should have regard for the weakest and make his prayer so light that the weakest man may not feel it a burden. (p. 55)

[116] Islām thus requires that a duty which relates to the prayers should be performed out of love. (p. 55)

[117] Hayya 'ala-l-salā being an order, the proper response to it is that given in this hadīth, When the adhān is being delivered, the hearer should repeat its sentences and when it is finished, be should offer the prayer mentioned in the next hadīth. (p. 56)

[118] "Breakfast" here means the meal taken before dawn when a man intends to fast. The hadīth thus allows the calling out of the adhān before the time of prayer. By prayer in the concluding portion is meant the tahajjud prayer. (p. 56)

[119] By the two adhāns are meant the adhān and the iqāmah. The interval between the two should be at least such that a man may be- able to say two rak'ahs of optional prayer. Another hadīth says that there should be an interval such that a man taking his food may finish it, say, about a quarter of an hour. (p. 57)

[120] There may be exceptions to this general rule. Sudā' is the name of a tribe in Yaman and Ziyād was a member of this tribe. (p. 57)

[121] The words are meant simply to lay stress on the point that Muslims should try their best to join the congregational prayer. (p. 59)

[122] Though prayer in congregation is of an obligatory nature, yet, on certain occasions when attendance would be hard on people, they are allowed to say prayers in their abodes. (p. 61)

[123] Even women must join the congregation if they are otherwise free. Mothers sometimes took their babies along with them when going to attend the congregation. (p. 61)

[124] In such a case, the man is required to take hold of a man from the last row and make him stand along with himself behind the row so that the two together may form a row. (p. 62)

[125] In congregational prayers the women formed a row by themselves behind the male rows: and even if there was a single woman, she formed a row by herself, Women were not allowed to mix with the men in their rows, as such a course would have led to the evil which is witnessed in church gatherings. (p. 62)

[126] While alive, the Holy Prophet himself acted as imām and led the prayers. During his last illness he became too weak to leave his bed and to go out to pray in congregation; so he directed that Abū Bakr should lead the prayers. This Hadīth, along with the Holy Prophet's practice, is conclusive proof that the man who held the highest place of honour in the community on account of his righteousness acted as imām, for after the Holy Prophet Abū Bakr was admittedly the most excellent of his followers. (p. 64)

[127] Evidently what is meant is excellence in knowledge of the Holy Qur'ān. not merely its recitation. (p. 64)

[128] Precedence in hijrah was an indication of precedence in sacrifices for Islām. (p. 64)

[129] Thus the master of the house or the imām of a particular mosque has a greater right to lead the prayers there than a mere visitor. (p. 64)

[130] The mu'adhdhin and the imām, the two office-bearers of the mosque, are thus to be chosen for their moral excellence and knowledge of the Qur'ān. (p. 64)

[131] A slave became the imām because he excelled others in knowledge. (p. 64)

[132] No one can be chosen as imām for carrying on jihād or for leading prayers unless he possesses the requisite qualifications. and, therefore, a man who is guilty of heinous sins cannot be chosen for either purpose. But if such a p. 115 man is chosen by mistake or if he commits such a sin after he has been chosen, he must be followed so long as he is not removed from that office, as no organization can be maintained otherwise. (p. 65)

[133] This shows that a woman may act as imām. There is nothing to show that there were no males among the people of her house; on the other hand. it is clearly stated that she had a mu'adhdhin who was evidently a male. (p. 65)

¹³⁴ If a man joins the congregational service in sajdah, it should not be counted as a rak'ah, from which it follows that if he joins it in ruku', it shall be counted as a rak'ah. (p. 66)

¹³⁵ Hh. 12, 13 give the position of the imām. He should stand in the front, forming a row by himself, and he should also be in the middle, so that the rows behind him should have an equal number of men on his right and left. (p. 66)

¹³⁶ If there are only two men in a congregational service, they should stand in the same row. the imām standing on the left. If, however, a third man joins later, either the imām should go forward and stand in front, or the first follower should step behind, forming with the new-comer a row behind the imām. (p. 67)

¹³⁷ This was the Holy Prophet's tahajjud prayer in the mosque during Ramadzān. The enclosure was made of mats. The hadīth shows that there is harm if anything intervenes between the imām and the congregation. (p. 67)

¹³⁸ This is a comprehensive hadīth relating to the times of prayer. It further shows that the mode of prayer, the rak'ahs and the time thereof were taught to the Holy Prophet by Divine revelation, as it was Gabriel who led the prayers and the Holy Prophet followed him. Gabriel pointed out the time-limits within which different prayers could be said. The different times thus are: :Zuhr--when the sun begins to decline till 'Asr; 'Asr--when the sun is about midway on its course to setting till it begins to set; Maghrib--after the sun sets till the disappearance of the red glow in the west; 'Ishā'-after the disappearance of the red glow till midnight (as other hadīth show); Fajr--after dawn till sunrise. Where the days are too shot;. he Zuhr and the 'Asr prayers may be combined, and where the nights are too short, the Maghrib and the 'Ishā' may be combined (h. 6). Where the days or nights extend over 24 hours, the times of prayer may be fixed in accordance with the times of work and rest. Thus the morning prayer may be said on rising from sleep, the Maghrib and the 'Ishā' when going to bed, and the Zuhr and the 'Asr in the middle of the day's work. (p. 70)

¹³⁹ What is forbidden is the commencing of prayer purposely when the sun is setting or when it is rising. If, however, a man begins his prayer before the setting of the sun, and it begins to set when he is still praying. he should finish his prayer. Similarly in the case of the rising of the sun. The prohibition aims at avoiding resemblance with sun-worshippers. (p. 71)

¹⁴⁰This Hadīth allows the combining of; Zuhr with 'Asr prayer and that of Maghrib with 'Ishā'. According to another hadīth (Ah. I. 223), the Holy Prophet did this when there was "neither danger nor rain," and he did this so that "his ummah may not be in difficulty." This shows that the prayers spoken of may be combined in case of

danger or rain. and even when there is no such reason. The combined prayers may be said at either prayer time. In combining prayers the sunnah that fall between the two prayers are dropped. (p. 71)

[141] The hadīth does not mean that only two prayers are sufficient. It only lays stress on their special importance. Or, perhaps, the man found it difficult to attend the congregational prayer five times daily, and he was told to be mindful specially of these two prayers and not to miss them in congregation. (p. 71)

[142] Also known as the battle of Ahzāb or Confederates, which took place in 5 A.H. (p. 71)

[143] When the prayer-time is missed unavoidably, it may be said even after the time for it has passed. (p. 71)

[144] A long hadīth is narrated by Bukhārī, showing that when sleep overcomes a person, and he misses the prayer at the right time, he should say it when he gets up (B. 9:35). (p. 72)

[145] He disliked it, because one who went to sleep before he said the prayer might miss the prayer altogether: and because he wanted prayer to be the last act before going to bed, so that he should go to bed with a prayerful mind. (p. 72)

[146] In order to apply the mind fully to prayer, it was necessary that there should be nothing, even in the environment, which should lead the mind away from it. That is also the reason why the mosque should be a simple structure. (p. 72)

[147] Casting side glances would undoubtedly divert the attention from prayer, and this is not desirable. This is called a snatching away by the devil. (p. 72)

[148] This order is also meant as a precaution against distraction. But scent was recommended on Fridays on account of the larger gatherings. (p. 73)

[149] Everything which disturbs the clam of mind, should be avoided, as this would be inconsistent with a prayerful attitude. Muslims need a calm atmosphere within and without the mosque, and this is the reason why they resent music before mosques. (p. 73)

[150] This could be done in the case of a camel or a horse. A man who is in a boat or in a railway carriage should turn his face to the nearest direction to Qiblah in the first instance, but he is not required to continue changing the direction as the boat or the railway changes its direction. (p. 73)

¹⁵¹ A man must be decently dressed according to his means. Any dress, that is regarded as decent in society, is looked upon as decent for prayers. (p. 74)

¹⁵² This is forbidden, because by so doing a man would distract the attention of the person who is praying. The Holy Prophet set up a sutrah--a spear or a staff, etc.--in front of him when praying in an open place (B. 8:90). (p. 74)

¹⁵³ Dhikr means literally remembrance, and in relation to prayer it includes all utterances regarding the praise and glorification of God, recitations from the Holy Qur'ān and supplications to God. (p. 76)

¹⁵⁴ Rak'ah (from raka'a, he bent or bowed down), taken as meaning a single act of standing in prayer, is really a unit in the Islamic institution of prayer. It consists really of all the four possible worshipful positions. viz., standing, bowing down, prostration and sitting. Its full description is given in h. 4. A man first stands in prayer, then bows down, then stands upright again. then falls down in prostration. then raises himself up and sits down. then falls down in prostration again and then raises himself up again. This is called one rak'ah, After every two rak'ahs the sitting position is assumed for a longer time. The standing position is called qiyām, the bowing down rukū', the prostration sajdah and the sitting position jalsah when it is a short sitting between the two sajdahs, and qa'dah when it is a longer sitting for reciting tashahhud after two rak'ahs or at the end of prayer. This hadīth contains full details of the number of rak'ahs for the different prayers with the exception of Fajr, which consists of two rak'ahs, but the statement made here that nafl or sunnah rak'ahs were said during journeys is contradicted by Bukhārī (h. 32). (p. 77)

¹⁵⁵ From the hadīth that have gone before it appears that he said two rak'ahs before Zuhr. It, is therefore, reasonable to conclude that sometimes he said two rak'ahs sunnah and sometimes four. (p. 77)

¹⁵⁶ This applies when two rak'ahs have been said. (p. 77)

¹⁵⁷ This is called takbīr tahrīmah, the first takbīr with which a person enters the state of prayer. (p. 78)

¹⁵⁸ In this state the left foot was brought forward to make himself more at ease, as the sitting after the last rak'ah lasted longer. According to B. 10: 145. where a person is unable to take a particular position he may take any other in which he finds himself comfortable. (p. 78)

¹⁵⁹ This is the position of the hands in qiyām, whether the hands are placed on the breast or below the navel. (p. 78)

¹⁶⁰ Including the tip of the nose (B. 10:135). (p. 78)

¹⁶¹ Tashahhud is the dhikr referred to in h 23. It is so called because it ends with the Kalimah Shahādah. (p. 79)

¹⁶² The same is the position of the hands when one sits between the two sajdahs. (p. 79)

¹⁶³ This direction shows that the Holy Prophet wanted the people to know the significance of what they recited in their prayers. Mere repetition of words without understanding their meaning does not serve the real purpose of prayer. The recitations, which are essential in prayer-service, are so few that a child, as well as an adult, can learn their significance within three months. It may, however, be noted that some of the phrases, which are more frequently repeated in prayer, are understood by Muslims generally, whether they are educated or not. such as Allāhu Akbar, Subhāna Rabbiya-l-'Azīm, etc. Moreover, the different postures are a great help in creating a prayerful mood. (p. 79)

¹⁶⁴ This hadīth mentions the different adhkār to be uttered in the change from one posture to another. It will be noted that except for what is uttered in rising from rukū', Allāhu Akbar (Allāh is the Greatest) is uttered in all other changes including the one when a person enters the state of prayer. (p. 79)

¹⁶⁵ The dhikr mentioned in this hadīth and the next goes by the name of istiftāh which means the desiring to open, the real opening of prayer being the chapter Fātihah as noted in h. 12. (p. 79)

¹⁶⁶ The opening of the Holy Qur'ān is thus also the opening of prayer, Prayer is said to open with al hamdu li-llāhi (the Fātihah), because it is with this prayer that the imām opens the prayer in a loud voice, the dhikr called istiftāh being uttered individually in a voice audible to oneself only. (p. 80)

¹⁶⁷ The Fātihah is thus an essential part of every rak'ah of every prayer. Abu Hurairah is reported to have said that the Fātihah should be recited in a low voice even when following the imām (M-Msh. 4:12). (p. 80)

¹⁶⁸ Āmīna (from the root amn meaning security) occurs always with fatihah over the final letter, and it means O Allāh! Listen to or Answer my prayer or May it be so! (N). It is generally uttered at the end of prayers: when the imām utters a prayer, those who follow say āmīna, The Fātihah being a prayer is generally followed by āmīna and when the imām recites the Fatihah in a loud voice, those who follow should say āmīna in a loud voice. Bukhārī has a chapter (10:111) with the heading "The saying of the imām āmīna in a loud voice", and under this head

he says: "Ibn al-Zubair and those behind him said āmīna until there was an echo in the mosque". (p. 80)

[169] In the first two rak'ahs of all prayers, some portion of the Holy Qur'ān is added to the Fātihah, but in the third and fourth rak'ahs only the Fātihah is recited. There are many hadīth in which it is related that the Holy Prophet recited such and such a sūrah in the Maghrib, 'Ishā' or Fajr prayer, the recitation in these three prayers being in a loud voice, as against the Zuhr and 'Asr prayers in which the recitation was in a voice audible to oneself. (p. 81)

[170] There are several verses in the Holy Qur'ān, fourteen in all, the recital of which is followed by an actual prostration. One such verse occurs in ch. 84. The practice of the Holy Prophet was that he performed a sajdah on the recital of such a verse even when he recited it in prayer-service. (p. 81)

[171] This shows that the whole prayer should be made a supplication to God, so that even when reciting the Qur'ān in prayer one should make supplications to the Divine Being for His mercy and seek refuge in Him.
The dhikr in rukū' and sajdah, as mentioned in this hadīth, should be repeated thrice at least, as other hadīth show. (p. 81)

[172] From this it appears that those who prayed were not bound by uttering only prescribed words but were free to give vent to their feelings as best they could. The dhikr mentioned here is now generally adopted, as it was approved by the Holy Prophet. (p. 82)

[173] The prayer after rising from rukū' is known as qunūt, the name given to the p. 149 special prayer of witr. This hadīth further shows that any petition whatsoever may be made in any posture during the prescribed prayers. The Holy Prophet spoke the Arabic language and he therefore made all supplications to God in Arabic. Following this practice everyone is at liberty to ask for anything from God in his own language. (p. 82)

[174] The state of sajdah or prostration is a state of utmost humility. and the humbler a man feels before the Great Maker, the nearer he is to Him. He is told to make most of his petitions in this state. These petitions may be made in any language. Undoubtedly those made in the language which a man generally speaks would give the best expression to his deep feelings and are most fitted to lay open his mind before God. (p. 82)

[175] As other hadīth show, this prayer is offered in the sitting position, called qa'dah, which is necessarily adopted after every two rak'ahs and after the final rak'ah. It is

known as tashahhud on account of the shahādah (bearing of witness) in the concluding sentence. (p. 83)

[176] This is meant to lay stress on the fact that the observance of prayer does not mean the utterance of certain stated formulæ only; it is really an occasion of opening one's mind before the Maker to its fullest extent. (p. 83)

[177] The salā on the Holy Prophet, as the words show, is really a prayer for the exaltation and spread of the Holy Prophet's cause; in other words, for the exaltation and spread of truth in the world. (p. 83)

[178] The grave really stands for the condition after death till the day of Resurrection. (p. 84)

[179] Al-Masīh is the Arabic word for the Messiah or the Christ, and al-Dajjāl (from dajl meaning covering or covering of truth with falsehood) is the Anti-Christ, so called "because he will cover the earth with his adherents," or "because of his lying in arrogating to himself godship." or "because he will traverse most of the regions of earth", or "because he will cover mankind with his infidelity", or "because he will cover the truth with falsehood," or "because he will involve men in confusion or doubt by falsehood or will manifest the contrary of what he conceals," or from dajjāl, signifying gold or gold-wash for gilding, "because treasures will follow him wherever he goes," or from dajjāla, signifying a great company of men journeying together covering the ground by their multitude or carrying goods for traffic. (LL.) The tribulation of the Anti-Christ is spoken of as the greatest tribulation that has appeared in the world, and it is stated in hadīth that the first and the last ten verses of the chapter entitled Kahf (ch. 18) afford a protection from it: "He who remembers the first ten verses of the chapter entitled the Cave is protected from the tribulation of the Dajjāl" (A.D. 36:14; Tr. 31:59; IM. 36:33; Ah. VI, 446). Now the verses referred to speak of the Christian doctrine, and therefore there is not the least doubt that the tribulation of the Dajjāl means the tribulation of the Christian or materialistic civilization with which we are faced in these days, and the name Anti-Christ given to it is due to the fact that it is opposed to the true teaching of Christ, who never taught the doctrines of Sonship and Atonement. (p. 84)

[180] The Taslīm is the final act of prayer, and its words are the same as the words of the greetings of Muslims to each other. It may be noted that the prayer of the Muslim begins with the greatness of Allāh (in Allāhu Akbar) and ends with the mercy of Allāh (in rahmatu-llāh). (p. 84)

[181] The Holy Prophet forgot to sit after the second rak'ah and performed two sajdahs before taslīm. This is called sajdah al sahw, sahw meaning forgetting. Another hadīth shows that the Holy Prophet said two rak'ahs instead of four, and

when he was informed of it, he first completed the number and then performed two sajdahs (B. 22:3). According to another hadīth (B. 8:31; 22:2) when five rak'ahs were said instead of four, and the Holy Prophet was informed of this after finishing the prayer, he performed only two sajdahs which were followed by taslīm. In all cases the sajdahs were followed by taslīm. only. In 22: 4, Bukhārī quotes Qatādah that there is no additional tashahhud in cases of forgetfulness. When the imām makes a mistake, any one of those following him may point it out to him simply by saying Subhān Allāh, the implication being that every human being is liable to error. (p. 85)

[182] The Holy Prophet. however, said the witr prayer in journey (B. 14:6), and his tahajjud prayer as well (B. 18:6). The sunnah before the Fajr prayer are an exception, as one hadīth shows that he never dropped them (B. 19:22). (p. 85)

[183] According to this hadīth. ə person who has to stay at one place even for nineteen days in the course of a journey may continue to shorten the prayer. But as nineteen days is nowhere spoken of as the limit, the prayer may be shortened even for a longer period in such a case. When a person settles down at a place, the case is different, and he must complete the prayer. So also in touring when that is part of the duty of a person. (p. 86)

[184] Juwāthā was a village in Bahrain, and Bukhārī's heading of the chapter in which this hadīth is mentioned is "Friday service in towns and villages." (p. 87)

[185] In this case, it was not even a village where Friday service was held. There were only some workers on the field, and the manager of the land was required to look after their spiritual needs and hold a Friday service for them. Ruzaiq was governor of Ailah under Umar ibn 'Abd al-'Azīz. (p. 88)

[186] The additional adhān is called the third adhān--actually it is the first--, the ordinary adhān and the iqāmah being the other two. As the hadīth shows, this adhān, delivered some time before the imām ascended the pulpit. was meant to inform the people that they should get ready for the prayer, and it was, therefore, delivered at Zaurā', a place in the market of Madīnah. (p. 89)

[187] Two rak'ahs of prayer must be said before the service is held. Two rak'ahs are also said after the service is over, as in the Zuhr prayer. (p. 89)

[188] The imām sits on the pulpit and a call for prayer is then sounded. He then stands up and delivers the sermon, as the next hadīth shows. (p. 90)

[189] The Friday sermon is thus divided into two parts, the imām sitting down to take a little rest in the middle. The Holy Prophet used to take some verse of the Holy

Qur'ān as his text, which he explained to the audience. The object of the sermon is to give true guidance to the congregation on the various questions of life; and it is, therefore, quite meaningless to deliver the sermon in Arabic to people who do not understand that language. (p. 90)

190 This shows that the Holy Qur'ān was recited in a loud voice in the Friday service. (p. 91)

191 The interval between one new moon and the next is sometimes twenty-nine days and sometimes thirty. If there is cloud or mist, and the new moon cannot p. 167 be seen, there are two ways suggested to determine its appearance; either thirty days may be completed (h. 2), or the appearance of the new moon may be determined by calculation based on the course of the moon (h. 1). According to another hadīth (B. 30:13), the Arabs did not keep an account of the course of the moon, and therefore the easier way for them was to complete the interval of thirty days. It follows, therefore. that it is not forbidden for a people who keep the account to determine the appearance of the moon from its course. This would bring about more uniformity in the observance of the 'Īd in one country. Wireless, however, has made uniformity possible even if the actual appearance of the moon is depended upon. (p. 93)

192 The Musallā (lit. the place of prayer) means here the place where the 'Īd service was generally held. In the 'Īd service, the prayers were said first and the sermon delivered afterwards. The sermon not only contained general injunctions but also dealt with measures relating to the welfare of the community. (p. 94)

193 In the sermon the men were asked to join the army if the raising of an army was necessary, and the women were asked to contribute to the expenses. Charity in the Holy Prophet's day was directed as much towards the defence of the community as towards the help of the poor. (p. 94)

194 All women, even young girls, were commanded to go forth for the 'Īd service. Menstruating women took part in all functions: only they did not join the prayer-service (B. 13:15). (p. 94)

195 Being the festival of breaking fasts, it is necessary that something should be eaten before prayer, According to another hadīth, food should be taken on the 'Īd al-Adzhā after prayers have been said, but this perhaps refers to partaking of the meat of the animal sacrificed. (p. 95)

196 The time of the 'Īd prayer is the breakfast time. (p. 95)

[197] This relates to the 'Īd al-Adzḥā. Sacrifice was not allowed before prayers, for such procedure would have given precedence to the physical enjoyment of partaking of meat over the spiritual bliss of bowing before God. (p. 96)

[198] Musinnah means full-grown, "and is applied to an animal of the ox-kind and to the sheep or goat, at the least in the third year." Jadhā'ah "as applied to a sheep, a year old: and sometime less than a year...; or eight months old or nine... or from six months old to seven........and applied to a goat a year old.......; applied to a bull, in his second year or in his third year: and applied to a camel in his fifth year" (LL). (p. 96)

[199] This shows that the animal to be sacrificed should be healthy and sound, without any manifest disfigurement. (p. 97)

[200] One goat or one sheep for one man or one household is the rule, but a cow or a camel would suffice for seven, the latter even for ten according to another Hadīth (Tr-Msh. 4:48). (p. 97)

[201] The animal to be sacrificed may be slaughtered on the day of the 'Īd after the prayers have been said or at any time during the two following days, these being the days of the pilgrims' stay in Minā. (p. 97)

[202] In the Holy Prophet's time, the Fitr charity was collected at a centre and then distributed. The present practice in the Muslim world to leave it to individual choice is against the Holy Prophet's Sunnah. Worked out as an institution as it was in the Holy Prophet's time, it can prove a source of immense benefit to the Muslim community. (p. 97)

[203] By two 'Īds are meant the 'Īd and Friday. (p. 98)

[204] Discussing the meaning of this hadīth under the word nazala, Ibn Athīr says: "descending and ascending, motion and state of rest, are the properties of matter, while Allāh is supremely exalted above this and hallowed; and the meaning is the descending of Divine mercy and grace and their nearness to servants". The statement is, therefore, metaphorical, and the significance is that the man who seeks communion with the Divine Being at such a time, when the whole of nature is in a state of quiet and the mind of man himself free generally from all anxieties and worries, will find Him nearest to his heart. Such a time is, therefore, fittest for communion with the Divine Being, and that is the time of Tahajjud prayer. (p. 100)

[205] The Tahajjud prayer consists, according to this hadīth of eleven rak'ahs, but this number may, as explained in the next two, be reduced to nine or seven rak'ahs, or

even less, when the time at hand before the break of the dawn does not suffice to complete the total. (p. 100)

[206] This is the practice now generally followed. The Holy Prophet himself made the witr a part of the Tahajjud prayer. (p. 101)

[207] Qunūt means the being constantly obedient, and is technically applied to the prayer offered in a standing posture in the last rak'ah of any prayer, before or after the performance of the rukū'; in the congregational service it was offered by the imām after rising from the rukū' (B. 10: 126). There are other forms of the qunūt, prayer--in fact, any prayer may be offered as qunūt. (p. 101)

[208] The prayer spoken of in this hadīth is the Tarāwīh prayer said in Ramadzān. The Holy Qur'ān is recited in this prayer, from the beginning, in such portions that the whole is finished by the end of the month. It is apparent from this hadīth that no such prayer was said by the Holy Prophet. A reference to H. viii:15 would show that when the Holy Prophet was in a state of i'tikāf in the month of Ramadzān, some people joined him when they saw him saying the tahajjud prayer, and thus, tahajjud was on that occasion said in congregation, though the Holy Prophet never meant it. This continued for three days, after which the Holy Prophet intentionally discontinued it. (p. 102)

[209] The best time for istikhārah is after the 'Ishā' prayer. (p. 103)

[210] Istikhārah is an individual prayer. and it may be continued for several days until the mind through Divine help is settled on an affair. It is not necessary that a man should be informed in a vision as to the course which he should adopt. (p. 103)

[211] The eclipse prayer is a congregational service in which both men and women take part (B. 16:10). The particular eclipse which is spoken of in this hadīth occurred on the very day on which Ibrāhīm, the Holy Prophet's eighteen months old son, died (B. 16:17). (p. 104)

[212] This was a special service for rain held in an open place. Prayer may also be offered for rain without holding a special service (H xi. 13, B. 11:35). (p. 104)

[213] This chapter is full of expressions of Divine greatness and glory. (p. 106)

[214] 'Uthmān ibn Maz'ūn was the first person to die from among those who had fled from Makkah to Madīnah for the sake of their faith in Allāh. (p. 107)

[215] Ibrāhīm was the Holy Prophet's son by his Coptic wife, Mary. He died when he was eighteen months old. The words uttered by the Holy Prophet on this occasion

will serve as a beacon to the world in its tragedies. Abu Saif's wife was wet-nurse to the Holy Prophet's son. (p. 107)

²¹⁶ A Muslim must bear the calamity of the death of a friend or a relative patiently. Weeping is but a sign of tenderness and compassion in the human heart, but wailing and other manifestations which are not consistent with patience are forbidden. (p. 108)

²¹⁷ Sahūliyyah were so called in relation to Sahūl, a place in Yaman, where they were woven or whence they were brought; or they were garments beaten and washed and whitened, so called in relation to sahūl meaning one who beats and washes and whitens clothes. (LL). (p. 108)

²¹⁸ Only the first two commandments relate to this chapter, following a bier and visiting a sick person. (p. 109)

²¹⁹ Equal respect must be shown to a bier whether it is that of a Muslim or a non-Muslim. (p. 109)

²²⁰ The Negus was the ruler of Abyssinia. He had become a Muslim. The hadīth shows that a burial service may be held over a dead body in its absence. It further shows that the funeral service consisted of four takbīrs. (p. 110)

²²¹ Women were advised not to go perhaps, because, in the first place they could not help in carrying the bier, but more so because they might break down under grief. (p. 110)

²²² A fuller account is given in B. 23:5. The burial service over the deceased had been held during the night. and the Holy Prophet was not informed. So he held a burial service over again on the grave. The hadīth further shows that the people arranged themselves into ranks behind the imām. The general practice is to have at least three ranks (AD-Msh. 5:5), but there is no harm if there are two (B. 23:54). (p. 110)

²²³ Ibn 'Abbās recited the Fātihah in a voice which others could hear, so that they might know that it was the Holy Prophet's practice. This shows that it was ordinarily recited in a low voice not audible, and further that it was meant to be so recited by the imām as well as the congregation. The same is the case with the prayers after other takbīrs. The Fatihāh is recited after the first takbīr; al-salāt 'ala-l-Nabī, as in the sitting position in prayer, after the second and an intercessory prayer for the deceased (hh. 22, 23) after the third while the taslīm is uttered after the fourth. (p. 111)

[224] The burial service is thus an intercessory prayer for the deceased one, and any prayer may be offered. Hadīth contains several such prayers. The one generally adopted is given in the next hadīth. (p. 111)

[225] According to one report, the word dhukhr-an (a treasure) is added before the final word ajr-an. No burial service is held over a still-born child (B. 23:80). (p. 112)

[226] According to one hadīth, the Holy Prophet did not lead the burial service of a man who committed suicide, but his companions held such a service. (p. 112)

[227] The Arabic word is musannam which means raised from the ground like the sanām (hump) of the camel. (p. 113)

[228] The prohibition to plaster, and build on a grave may have been due to the waste of money which it would involve. Sitting on the grave is prohibited because it is disrespectful. (p. 113)

[229] Talbīnah (from laban meaning milk) is food made of bran, milk and honey, or simply of bran and honey, so called because it is white like milk; and tharīd is bread crumbled into small pieces with fingers over which broth is poured, sometimes prepared with marrow and with eggs, considered to be most delicious. It shows that there was a gathering when a person died, the object no doubt being to console the bereaved family. When they dispersed, food was sent by some near relative to the family itself and very nearly related friends. The whole gathering did not partake of food. (p. 114)

[230] To sit in some place so that people may come and express their sympathy with and console the bereaved family is, therefore, according to the Holy Prophet's practice. Praying for the deceased one is not forbidden, but there is no authority for the present practice to offer prayers by the raising up of hands with every newcomer. The only prayer was the burial service and a prayer on the grave. (p. 114)

[231] Abuse is forbidden not only in regard to the dead from among Muslims but the dead in general. But criticism is not forbidden in any case; it sometimes becomes a necessity, as in the case of the reporters of hadīth. (p. 114)

[232] This Hadīth and the one that follows show that charity on behalf of the dead is a source of benefit to them: and it appears that charity on behalf of the dead was generally practised in early Islām. Recital of the Holy Qur'ān to the dying ones is recommended (h. 1), but the practice of reciting the Holy p. 207 Qur'ān over the dead body or on a grave is not traceable to the Holy Prophet and is an innovation. Recital of the Holy Qur'ān is a good deed in itself, but to do it for remuneration does not bring any good to the reciter and certainly none to the dead. There is no

authority of the Holy Prophet for the Qul ceremony on the third day, or for the ceremonies connected with the tenth and fortieth days after death. Nor can they be considered as acts of charity, for they are not for the benefit of the poor. (p. 114)

[233] Doing good to beasts is, like the doing of good to human beings, a deed of charity: while cruelty to animals is forbidden just like cruelty to human beings (B. & M-Msh. 6:7). (p. 119)

[234] See v. 4 quoted above. There charity is first enjoined-wealth must be given away out of love for God-and after it is mentioned the giving of zakāt. It is thus shown that these are two separate duties, the voluntary duty of giving away to others as much as one likes, and the obligatory duty of giving away 2½ p.c. out of one's savings after every twelve months. (p. 120)

[235] The minimum on which zakāt is payable is called nisāb. In the case of cereals and fruits, the nisāb was five wasaq, which comes to between 20 and 30 maunds, according to different calculations. In the case of camels, the nisāb was five, in that of goats and sheep, 40. In the case of silver it was five auqiyah or 200 dirhams which comes to a little over Rs. 50. According to one hadīth (AD. 9:5), the nisāb in case of gold was twenty dīnārs, about 3 oz. Under present conditions a uniform nisāb would lead to greater facility, and as money is the standard in all payments, it would be quite in conformity with the spirit of the shari'ah if a money value of Rs. 50 is fixed as the minimum on which zakāt is payable in the case of all possessions. No zakāt is payable in things which are required for daily use (Tr-Msh 6:2). Jewels and precious stones are also excepted. (p. 120)

[236] Zakāt is paid annually after calculating the savings of that year. (p. 121)

[237] Umm Salamah was the Holy Prophet's wife. The Hadīth shows that zakāt must be paid on gold and silver ornaments, whether they are actually worn or not. The reference in the word kanz used in this hadīth is to the following verse:
"Those who hoard up gold and silver and do not spend it in Allāh's way, announce to them a painful chastisement" (9:39).
Thus gold and silver may be hoarded only if zakāt is regularly paid thereon. (p. 121)

[238] Zakāt was paid on camels and sheep which were kept for trade purposes, and therefore there is no reason for excepting trade goods. But while there is a natural increase in the case of animals, out of which zakāt is paid, the capital involved in goods for trade may sometimes lie dormant. There is no reliable hadīth to show how zakāt was calculated on merchandise; a reasonable course would be to take as the basis of calculation the profit which is gained by trading. (p. 121)

²³⁹ Zakāt being a tax on hoardings or possessions must be paid by every owner of property even though he happens to be an orphan. The guardian of the orphan is, therefore, enjoined to carry on trade with the capital, so that the capital itself may not be consumed. (p. 121)

²⁴⁰ Zakāt was the most important source of revenue of the Muslim state, and during the Holy Prophet's lifetime zakāt was collected in the government treasury. When the Holy Prophet died, many of the Arabian tribes which had just entered Islām rebelled against the Caliph and apostatized. There were others whose rebellion consisted only in refusing the payment of zakāt into the public treasury. It is these tribes that are spoken of in this hadīth, as the words of Abū Bakr show: "If they withhold from me even a she-kid." Making a difference between prayer and zakāt also meant the same. They did not apostatize but they refused to pay the zakāt, and this was a refusal to admit the authority of the central government. Abū Bakr's action on this occasion shows that zakāt cannot be distributed according to the will of the individual who pays the zakāt, but it must be collected and distributed by a central organization. (p. 122)

²⁴¹ This collector withheld a part of what he had brought, saying that that part of his collections was presented to him. The Holy Prophet decided that no one who was appointed as a collector could receive personal presents. This is mentioned in detail in B. 51:17. (p. 122)

²⁴² One-third or one-fourth of the zakāt may be left with the owner for distribution according to his choice. (p. 122)

²⁴³ Agricultural produce was taxed on a different basis. This was the land revenue of the Muslim state, and it is only a fraction of the land revenue under the British rule in India. Under non-Muslim rule, when land revenue goes to the state, zakāt should be calculated only on the savings of the year. (p. 123)

²⁴⁴ The one-fifth taken from treasure-trove is not zakāt in the proper sense, as it is taken only once. (p. 123)

²⁴⁵ 'Umar took one-fifth from amber, and Hasan's view is generally upheld. (p. 123)

²⁴⁶ Abu-l-Qāsim is the kunyah of the Holy Prophet. (p. 126)

²⁴⁷ Khait literally means a cord. (p. 126)

²⁴⁸ Lailat al-Qadr means the grand night or the night of majesty. It is the night on which the revelation of the Holy Qur'ān began (97:1). As stated in other hadīth, it must be particularly sought on the 25th, 27th and 29th of Ramadzān (B. 2 35).

Confining oneself to the mosque during the lost ten days of Ramadzān is known as i'tikāf. See next hadīth. (p. 129)

[249] Ihrām, (from haram, a forbidden thing) signifies entering upon a state that causes what is avowed before to be forbidden or unlawful, and it is technically used to indicate the condition in which the pilgrim is required to put himself. What acts or things become forbidden in the state of ihrām is explained here and in the three hadīth that follow. (p. 132)

[250] This hadīth explains what the pilgrim should not wear when he enters upon a state of ihrām. Men wore only two seamless sheets, a sheet reaching from the navel to below the knees. (izār) and a sheet which covers the upper part of the body (ridā'), while women wore their ordinary simple garments. Wars is a plant with which clothes are dyed. Clothes dyed red or yellow are thus forbidden. (p. 132)

[251] Bukhārī explains that 'Ā'ishah allowed knickerbockers only for those who drove her riding camel. Trousers are allowed when an izār cannot be had (B. & M-Msh. 11:11). (p. 133)

[252] The veil was worn in Arabia as a mark of rank: and it was, therefore, disallowed when a woman was in a state of ihrām, as pilgrimage required the obliteration of all differences of rank. Forbidding a veil in pilgrimage is further a conclusive proof that the Holy Qur'ān did not enjoin the wearing of veil, as in that case the prohibition here stated would be a contradiction of the Holy Qur'ān. Gloves are not allowed because like the veil they are a mark of rank. Ornaments are allowed because they are not a mark of rank. and are worn by even ordinary people and labouring classes. (p. 133)

[253] Talbīd is the putting upon one's head gum or something glutinous, in order that the hair might become compact. This is allowed in the state of ihrām, lest the hair should become dishevelled or dusty. (p. 133)

[254] When the pilgrims reach the places mentioned or places opposite them in the sea, they enter into the state of ihrām. Such a place is called miqāt, an appointed place, or muhill, the place of raising voices with labbaika. (p. 133)

[255] Labbaika (from labb-un, obeying or serving) means, I am at thy service or wait intent upon obedience to thee, or I am in attendance upon thee, or I am in thy presence, time after time (LL.) These are the oft-repeated words of the pilgrim when he enters upon a state of ihrām. (p. 134)

[256] This is called tawāf al-qudūm. Tawāf (from tafa, he went round) is technically going round the Ka'bah. The tawāf Consists of seven circuits (h. 18). (p. 134)

[257] This hadīth shows that men and women performed the different acts of devotion together; only the women did not mix with men, just as in prayer in mosques they formed separate ranks. It further shows that a change was already coming over the simplicity of the Holy Prophet's time, and already men were thinking of enforcing stricter measures for the seclusion of women. and restraining their freedom. In fact, this was a necessary outcome of the ease which Muslims began to enjoy on account of their conquests. (p. 134)

[258] The Ka'bah has four comers (arkān, sing. rukn): the Black Stone called here al-Rukn, the Corner, but generally known as al-hajar al-aswad or the Black Stone, and the corners on the Yaman side are known as the Yamānī corners; the other two being the Shāmī (on the side of Syria) and the 'Irāqī (on the side of Mesopotamia). The circuit is commenced at the Black Stone which is the corner stone of the Ka'bah--it is often called al-Rukn or the Corner. The other corners may also be kissed, but the kissing of the Black Stone, the cornerstone of the Ka'bah, is one of the chief features of pilgrimage. Jesus Christ was referring to this very stone when he said, "The stone which the builders rejected, the same is become the head of the corner" (Matt. 21:42). It is, in fact, an emblem, a token, that part of the progeny of Abraham, Ishmael and p. 243 his descendants, which was rejected by the Israelites. was to become the cornerstone of the Kingdom of God. That there is no idea at all of Divine honour being paid to the Black Stone in kissing it, is shown by the next two hadīth. See also B. 25: 58. (p. 135)

[259] The Shāmī and the 'Irāqī corners. This shows that all four corners were kissed. (p. 135)

[260] Tawāf is compared to prayer to show that the mind must be entirely engrossed with the idea of Divine presence. This comparison further draws attention to the fact that outward purity is as necessary in tawāf as in prayer. (p. 135)

[261] Safā and Marwah are two little hills near Makkah. This devotional act of Hajj is called sa'y. The running between Safā and Marwah, is performed seven times (B. 25:79.) The limits are indicated by two minarets. In the case of 'umrah, the pilgrim gets out of the state of ihrām with the sa'y. (p. 136)

[262] Tarwiyah means watering or satisfying the thirst, and the 8th of Dhu-l-Hijjah is so called because on that day the pilgrims provide themselves with water for the following days which are to be spent in Minā and 'Arafāt. The hajj proper p. 246 thus begins on the 8th Dhu-l-Hijjah and pilgrims who get out of the state of ihrām on performing the 'umrah, enter into ihrām for hajj on this date. (p. 136)

²⁶³ The 'Arafah is the ninth day of Dhu-l-Hijjah. The pilgrims remain in Minā on the 8th, and on the ninth they proceed to 'Arafāt about nine miles from Makkah. 'Arafah is derived from 'arf which means knowledge. The halting at 'Arafāt is called wuqūf. It lasts only for a few hours, from afternoon till sunset, but it is the most important of the devotional acts of hajj so much so that there is no hajj without it. A sermon is here delivered by the imām on the mount known as the Jabal al-Rahmah (The Mountain of Mercy). In the pre-Islām days, the Quraish did not go to 'Arafāt, as they considered themselves superior to the other tribes. Islām obliterated this distinction. (2:197; B. 25:91). (p. 136)

²⁶⁴ Minā is left at noon on the 9th, and the Zuhr and 'Asr prayers are combined in 'Arafāt where the pilgrims stay till sunset. (p. 136)

²⁶⁵ After returning from 'Arafāt, the night is passed at Muzdalifah which is also called Jam'. Here the Maghrib and 'Ishā' prayers are combined, and then the morning prayer is said at a very early hour. The sunnah or supererogatory part is dropped when the prayers arc combined. (p. 137)

²⁶⁶ The day of Sacrifice is the 10th Dhu-l-Hijjah. Animals are sacrificed at about breakfast time. (p. 137)

²⁶⁷ This is called the tawāf al-ifādzah, i.e., the tawāf after returning from 'Arafāt. (p. 137)

²⁶⁸ The same rule should be followed in relation to the 'Īd sacrifices. Organized properly, the institution would be a source of immense strength financially. (p. 137)

²⁶⁹ Thus the flesh of the sacrificed animals may even be dried and kept for use when one likes. (p. 138)

²⁷⁰ The shaving of heads or the clipping of hair is a sign that the state of ihrām is over. (p. 138)

²⁷¹ The days of Minā are the tenth of Dhu-l-Hijjah and the following two or three days, the latter being called ayyām al-tashriq. (p. 138)

²⁷² The throwing of stones is described in detail in B. 25:142. It was a reminder of the spiritual fight which a man must be prepared to wage against evil. The throwing of stones teaches the lesson that man must learn to hate evil, and that he should try to keep the Devil at a stone's throw. (p. 138)

[273] Muhassab is in Minā. The tawāf spoken of here is called the tawāf al-wadā' or the tawāf of departure from Makkah. (p. 139)

[274] Material advantages may thus be combined with the great spiritual lesson learned in hajj. (p. 139)

[275] In the heading of 97:10. this hadīth is related with a slight variation: "A party of my umma shall remain in the ascendant, propagating the Truth, and these are the learned ones (ahl al-'ilm)." This shows that Bukhārī took the word jihād in the wider sense. (p. 142)

[276] The following explanation of this hadīth is given in the 'Aun al-Ma'būd, a commentary of Adū Dawūd, on the authority of Nawavī: "This party consists of different classes of the faithful, of them being the brave fighters, the faqīhs (jurists), the muhaddithīn (collectors of Hadīth), the zāhids (those who devote themselves to the worship of God), those who command the doing of good and prohibit evil, and a variety of other people who do other good deeds." Fighting in the way of Allāh thus includes the service of Islām in any form. (p. 143)

[277] The preceding two Hadīth contain a prophecy that among the Muslim community there shall always be learned people who shall help the cause of Islām to become ascendant in the world; this goes a step further and contains a further prophecy that generally at intervals of a century divinely inspired people shall be raised among Muslims and they shall revive the faith of the Muslim community.
A person thus raised by God is called a mujaddid (one who revives) in the terminology of Islām. The mujaddid is a muhaddath (one to whom God speaks though he is not a prophet), and he is raised up by God to remove errors that have crept in among Muslims and to shed new light on the great religious truths of Islām in the new circumstances which Muslims may have to face in every new age. The most famous names falling under this category in this country are those of Sayyid Ahmad of Sirhind, popularly known as Mujaddid Alf Thāni, Shāh Walī Allāh of Delhi, Sayyid Ahmad of Bareily, and Mirzā Ghulām Ahmad of Qādiān, the founder of the Ahmadiyyah movement, who was accepted generally as the Mujaddid of the fourteenth century of Hijrah, but who was later opposed owing to his claim to be the Messiah, whose advent is spoken of in Hadīth prophecies. (p. 143)

[278] These instructions were given to 'Ali by the Holy Prophet in the expedition of Khaibar, which shows that invitation to Islām was the greatest jihād of Muslims. (p. 144)

[279] This Hadīth which speaks of the Holy Prophet inviting the Cæsar to Islām forms part of the chapter on Jihad in the Bukhārī, which again shows the wide sense in

which jihād was interpreted by Muslims. The subject-matter of the letter written is produced in the next hadīth, which should be treated as a supplement to this hadīth. (p. 144)

[280] This happened at Hudaibiyah where the famous truce of that name was concluded. Swearing allegiance for death meant that a man would defend Islām and stand by the Holy Prophet even though he had to face death. (p. 145)

[281] The word zilāl used in the hadīth is plural of zill which generally means shadow, but it really means that which serves to protect a thing. The Hadīth emphasizes a Muslim's duty to be always ready to fight for the defence of the Truth. Muslims could not use the sword otherwise than in defence (v. 5). (p. 145)

[282] The Arabic word for martyr is shahīd which means a witness of truth. One who is killed in defence of the Faith is called a shahīd because he as it were sees the truth with his own eyes and lays down his life for it. This hadīth shows further that every one who devotes his life to the service of the Truth is a shahīd, whether he is killed in a battle for the defence of Faith or dies a natural death or dies of plague or cholera. (p. 146)

[283] This shows that in the Holy Prophet's time women did the duty of nursing the wounded and helping the armies of Islām in all other possible ways. As the next hadīth shows, they did the duty of carrying the slain to Madīnah. In B. 56: 63, it is related that a woman, named Bint Milhān, requested the Holy Prophet to pray for her to be among those who sailed on the seas to fight in the way of Allāh. (p. 146)

[284] Thus in the exigency of battles Islām did not allow the killing of non combatants. "Do not kill a woman, nor a labourer." "Do not kill an old man, nor a child, nor a woman", are the words of other hadīth, (AD-Msh. 18:4). (p. 147)

[285] The hadīth begins with the words, I have been commanded, and the command to fight is contained in the Holy Qur'ān in the following words: "And fight in the way of Allāh with those who fight with you and do not exceed this limit" (v. 5). Muslims, therefore, could not resort to fighting unless an enemy was the first to assume hostilities. What the hadīth means is that fighting begun under these conditions is to cease when the enemy people accept Islām. Bukhārī himself hints at this when he quotes this hadīth under the heading if they repent and keep up prayer and pay the poor-rate, then leave their way free," i.e., cease fighting with them. (p. 147)

[286] Marriage is here recognised as a means of moral elevation and spiritual exaltation. Fasting has a castrating effect inasmuch as the carnal passions are thereby subdued. According to another hadīth, marriage is recognised as the

Sunnah of the Holy Prophet, and it is added; "He who abstains from my Sunnah is not of me." (B. 67:l.) (p. 150)

[287] So in Islām there are no eunuchs for the kingdom of heaven. On the other hand, marrying and keeping oneself chaste is a means of attaining the kingdom of heaven. (p. 150)

[288] The technical word for temporary marriage is mut'ah. It is derived from matā' meaning profiting for a long time. Mut'ah is considered to be a legal form of marriage by the Shī'ahs, but the vast majority of the Muslim community p. 269 rejects it on the basis of the hadīth quoted here. The Holy Qur'ān uses the word ihsān (lit. being inaccessible) for marriage, and thus looks upon marriage as a permanent relation which can be cutoff only by divorce. For all other kinds of sexual relationship it uses the word safāh, which signifies fornication According to some hadīth, mut'ah was allowed by the Holy Prophet in a war. Even if this be true, it may have been allowed at an earlier stage, reform having been brought about gradually, but there is not the least doubt that it was finally disallowed. (p. 151)

[289] Khitbah or asking a woman in marriage is a preliminary stage. The dowry to be settled on the woman must then be agreed upon. There is no limitation p. 272 to this amount; it may be a heap of gold (v. 11), or it may be a ring of iron, or even service rendered to the woman in teaching her (B. 67:51). In fact, the amount of the dowry depends on the circumstances of the contracting parties. (p. 151)

[290] Hh. 8 and 9 show that a woman must be given in marriage by her guardian; but the guardian, whether father or anyone else must obtain the woman's consent. As many hadīth show, a woman is at liberty to offer her hand to anyone, and Bukhārī heads one of his chapters as follows: "A woman offering herself for marriage to a virtuous man" (B. 67:33). In such a case, the state is considered to be the guardian (B. 67:41). (p. 152)

[291] Thus the woman has the choice of repudiating a marriage to which she is not a consenting party. The word thayyib includes both a woman whose husband has died and a woman who has been divorced. (p. 152)

[292] Marriage must be contracted so far as possible between equals. This is technically known as marriage in kuf' or kufu' (pl. akfā'). Bukhārī explains this by heading his chapter as "Al-Akfa fi-l-dīn" (67:16), or Equals in religion; making it clear that all Muslims are equal in one sense. There are examples recorded in Hadīth in which a woman of the high family of Quraish was married to a slave or a freed slave (B. 64: 12). (p. 152)

²⁹³ Religion. in contrast with the other three, builds character, and hence the word din carries the significance of character here. (p. 152)

²⁹⁴ Any conditions which the parties agree upon may be laid down in the marriage contract, so long as they are not against the law. For instance, it is stated that a woman shall not impose a condition requiring the divorce of her sister (B. 67:54). (p. 153)

²⁹⁵ The dowry must be made over to the woman, and her father or guardian has no right to it. Hence shighār is forbidden. (p. 153)

²⁹⁶ Duff or daff is the tambourine, and the object of beating with daff at marriage is to make it publicly known. It also furnishes a kind of music. (p. 153)

²⁹⁷ The khutbah or sermon at marriage helps the publicity of the marriage, and serves the double purpose of sanctifying the marriage contract and informing the parties of their responsibilities. The three verses of the Holy Qur'ān quoted in the sermon are 4:1 (a part), 3:101, and 33:70, 71. V. 4: 1 runs thus: p. 275
"O people! Be careful of your duty to your Lord. Who created you from a single being and created its mate of the same kind, and spread from these two many men and women; and be careful of your duty to Allāh by Whom you demand one of another your rights and to the ties of relationship; surely Allāh ever watches over you."
The whole of this verse may be recited instead of the part given in the Hadīth. They all lay stress on carefulness to duty. and the person who delivers the sermon must expatiate on them to make the audience realize their import. The khutbah is followed by ījāb and qubūl, i.e.. the acceptance of the parties to the contract, and the amount of dowry is made publicly known. This is followed by a prayer by the whole gathering that the union may be blessed. (p. 153)

²⁹⁸ The nikāh was followed by a ceremony of conducting the bride to the bridegroom, called 'urs or 'urus, at which people gathered together, and thus it received additional publicity. The hadīth further shows the Holy Prophet's deep love for women and children. As these women and children were from among the Ansār, the Hadīth is narrated by Bukhārī in a chapter dealing with "the love of the Ansār." (p. 154)

²⁹⁹ The word used in the hadīth is lahw, which means a thing in which a man delights himself and which occupies him so as to divert him, and includes every diversion, pastime, sport or play. Here it means music. (p. 154)

³⁰⁰ Giving of presents at marriage is therefore in accordance with the Sunnah. (p. 154)

[301] This feast is called walimah and it is given by the bridegroom when the bride has been conducted to him. It is said to be derived from iltiyām which means gathering together of two people. (p. 155)

[302] 'Azl was a birth-control device. It originally means putting a thing aside or away, and with reference to sexual relations, paulo ante emissionem (penem suum) extraxit, et extra vulvam semen emisit. It is allowed when conception is likely to endanger the woman's life or impair her health. (p. 155)

[303] This is the first act with regard to a Muslim baby. The words of the adhān are repeated opposite the right ear, and the words of iqāmah opposite the left. The latter is based on a report in the Sharh al-Sunnah showing that 'Umar ibn 'Abd al-'Azīz followed this practice. The practice is traced back to the Holy Prophet in the Musnad of Abū Ya'lā. The utterance of words relating to the unity and greatness of Allāh in the ears of a new-born baby shows that the Holy Prophet was aware of the existence of the sub-conscious mind. (p. 156)

[304] The Arabic word is hannaka-hū. The word tahnīk is derived from hanak which means the interior of the upper part of the inside of the mouth, or the palate. The new-born baby is made to taste either a chewed date as in this case, or honey, by some elderly member of the family. The naming of the baby, the tahnīk and a prayer for him are thus the sunnah of the Holy Prophet. (p. 156)

[305] The word 'aqīqah is derived from 'aqqa meaning he clave, split or cut; and 'aqqa an waladi-hī signifies he slaughtered as a sacrifice for his child a sheep or a goat (on the seventh day after the birth). This is called 'aqīqah, but the word is also applied to the hair, of a young one recently born, that comes forth on his head in his mother's belly, the hair being shaved on the seventh day. It is in reference to this that the Hadīth speaks of removing of uncleanness. (p. 156)

[306] This is the general practice, but as the next hadīth shows, one goat suffices in the case of the boy as well. It is only for those who can afford. (p. 156)

[307] This hadīth shows that divorce should be resorted to only in cases of extreme hardship, A Muslim is required to face the difficulties of the married life, and to avoid disruption of family relations, so long as possible, turning to divorce only as a last resort. (p. 160)

[308] This hadīth recognises the right of the wife to demand a divorce, so much so that she may demand it even without any harm being caused to her, though she is told that in such a case she will displease God. (p. 160)

[309] In this case, the wife had no specific complaint against her husband, and there was neither desertion, nor ill-treatment. She said that she could not pull on with him. and her right to have a divorce was not refused. But she was required to return the orchard which the husband had given to her as dowry. This is technically called khul', lit., undoing of a knot. The words I hate disbelief in Islām mean that she could not pull on with him as a faithful Muslim wife should; according to another version the words are lā utīqu-hū, i.e., I cannot bear him. (p. 160)

[310] This hadīth relates to procedure in the matter of divorce. It shows that divorce is not effective unless it is pronounced when the wife is clean 'Iddah, or the period during which a woman must wait before remarrying, is stated in v. 4 (2:228) to be three qurū'. The word qurū' is plural of qar' which signifies the entering from the state of cleanness into a state of menstruation, and is in normal cases about four weeks. (p. 161)

[311] See note on h. 7. (p. 161)

[312] This hadīth and h. 5 show that divorce uttered on one occasion, whether uttered once or thrice--in fact. any number of times,--counts only as one divorce, and this was made clear by the Holy Prophet himself: while h. 6 shows that pronouncing divorce thrice on a single occasion is un-Islamic. Even the jurists call it talāq bid'ī (an innovation), but they consider it irrevocable in the terms of 2 230: as these Hadīth show, the Holy Prophet did nor consider it such. The procedure of talāq according to Islām is laid down clearly in the Holy Qur'ān. It is to be pronounced once while the woman is in a clean condition, and it is followed by a period of waiting, called the 'iddah (65:1), during which the parties may be reconciled to each other, or after which the parties may marry each other again (2:228, 232). Such a divorce, called a revocable divorce, may be pronounced twice (2:229). the option for reconciliation or remarriage being with the parties: but if it is uttered a third time, it becomes irrevocable as laid down in 2:230. 'Umar's object in making effective three divorces pronounced on one occasion (h. 5) was to warn the people that they would have to take the evil consequences of following an un-Islamic practice, but the result is just the contrary of what he intended. This hadīth shows that whenever a woman was divorced, whether the divorce was on that occasion pronounced once or thrice, it was a single act of divorce and revocable. Divorce became irrevocable only when two revocable divorces were first pronounced, hence the occasion for the third divorce spoken of it., 2:230 was a rare event. (p. 162)

[313] As marriage is a public act, so is divorce; it must be pronounced in the presence of witnesses. (p. 162)

[314] The wives of the Holy Prophet demanded certain comforts which in the later days of the Holy Prophet's life fell to the lot of Muslim women generally. Just then the Holy Prophet received a revelation telling him to give his wives the option of remaining with him without these comforts, or to have the material benefits and get themselves divorced. They chose the first alternative. This was not a divorce. (p. 163)

[315] So that if no news of the husband is received within this period, the wife can marry. Imām Mālik holds the view that in all cases where the husband is mafqūd al-khabar, the wife should wait for four years and may marry after this. (p. 163)

[316] The procedure of li'ān, when a husband accuses the wife of adultery and there is no evidence. is laid down in the Holy Qur'ān (24:6-9). The marital relation is in this case cut off. The dowry remains the wife's. (B. 68:51). (p. 163)

[317] Ilā' is spoken of in the Holy Qur'an in the following words: "Those who swear that they will not go in to their wives should wait four months" (2:225). (p. 163)

[318] The humblest work thus carries with it a dignity. Bukhārī mentions a number of professions in the headings of his chapters, such as that of meat-seller and butcher (B. 34:21), goldsmith (B. 34:28), blacksmith (B, 34:29), tailor (B. 34:30), weaver (B. 34:31), carpenter (B. 34:32); and mentions hadīth showing that they were looked upon as honourable by the Holy Prophet, those who followed them being treated on a basis of perfect equality with other members of Muslim society. (p. 165)

[319] Duty to God is thus placed higher than duty to self or duty to others. (p. 165)

[320] The truthful, honest merchant works for the benefit of humanity, and thus finds a place with those righteous servants of God whose lives are devoted to the benefit of humanity. (p. 165)

[321] Any defect in the thing sold must be made manifest. In the case of a barter, both parties must do it. (p. 166)

[322] In pre-Islamic days Munābadhah (from nabdh, to throw away) and mulāmasah (from lams, to touch) were two kinds of sale in which the purchaser had no occasion to examine the thing purchased. (p. 166)

[323] This is technically known as ihtikār, and it is resorted to by grain merchants to enhance the price of grain when it comes into their possession. (p. 167)

[324] Najsh (from najasha, he roused or pursued the game) means augmenting the price of an article of merchandise, not desiring to purchase it but in order that

another might hear and augment in the same manner or outbidding in a sale in order that another might fall into a snare, the bidder himself not wanting the thing, or praising an article of merchandise simply to deceive another person (LL). Perfect honesty is thus enjoined in all business transactions. The first part of the hadīth aims at eliminating the commission agent who on account of his cleverness generally proves a curse to the simple villager or agriculturist, for whose protection the direction is particularly meant. (p. 168)

[325] To sell a thing by auction is thus allowed. (p. 168)

[326] This was a device by which the purchaser of a milch animal was deceived and induced to pay a higher price. Such a sale may he repudiated. (p. 168)

[327] This was a kind of speculation, not trade in the proper sense, because the thing purchased did not exist. (p. 168)

[328] It is due to neglect of this useful advice that immovable property is passing out of the hands of the Muslim community in India at a very fast pace. A Muslim is enjoined to meet his ordinary or extraordinary expenses out of his earnings or savings, and he must not sell his immovable property unless he intends to invest the price of it in acquiring similar property. (p. 169)

[329] Islām came to exterminate idolatry, and hence it could not allow trade in idols. As regards things forbidden as food, evidently a Muslim has nothing p. 301 to do with them, and he cannot be allowed to carry them to other people. So far the words of the hadīth are quite in consonance with the spirit of Islām. which looks upon every profession as a service to humanity, besides being the means of earning a livelihood for a man. But here follow the words:
It was said, O Messenger of Allāh! Inform us about the fat of the dead (animal); for, with it boots are rubbed and skins are greased and people light their lamps with it. He said: 'No! it is forbidden' (B. 34: 112).
If this part of the hadīth is accepted as authentic, the question arises, Did the Holy Prophet mean to say that it was forbidden to Muslims that they should make use of the fat of the dead animal to light lamps or grease skins? This would mean that not only was the eating of the dead animal forbidden, but anything which formed part of it could not he used in any other way. This is nowhere stated in the Holy Qur'ān. where only the eating of certain things is forbidden, Moreover, the hadīth that follows, riot only makes such use lawful but clearly makes it necessary (b. 18). When the Holy Prophet saw a dead goat with its skin on it, he said :"Why did you not benefit by its skin?" If it was necessary to benefit by the skin, why not by the bones or the fat, so long as they were not used for eating purposes? The Holy Prophet could not, therefore, say that it was unlawful to use any part of a dead animal whose flesh was forbidden and this part of the hadīth cannot be accepted.

Imām Sh'āfi'ī and others have interpreted this part as meaning that it was the trading in such things as fats that was forbidden, not their use. There is no reason in this. If the use of a certain thing is allowed for a certain purpose, trading in it cannot be forbidden if limited to that purpose. The Holy Prophet made it necessary that the skins of the animals whose flesh was forbidden should be made use of, but how could that be done if trading in it was prohibited? Evidently there has been some misconception relating to the latter portion of the hadīth. (p. 169)

[330] The words of the Holy Prophet make it clear that a thing which may not be eaten may be put to any other use. (p. 169)

[331] Bukhārī's heading of the chapter is "Warning against the consequences of engrossment with the implements of agriculture or going beyond the limit ordained." The hadīth, therefore, implies that a nation which gives itself up entirely to agriculture neglecting other lines of its development cannot rise to a position of glory. (p. 171)

[332] This is technically called mukhābrah, from khabr meaning information see h. 7. (p. 171)

[333] Evidently this was advice given to people who had vast tracts of land, which they could not manage to cultivate for themselves. It did not mean that land could not be let to a tenant. (p. 172)

[334] Without water there would be no herbage; hence owners of land situated on watercourses were required to allow the flow of excess water to other people's land or even to barren tracts which would thus become grass fields for cattle. Matters relating to irrigation are technically known as musāqāt which literally means giving to drink. (p. 172)

[335] The digging of a well is regarded as an act of the greatest merit. When the Holy Prophet came to Madīnah, the only well of sweet water there was the property of a Jew, and Muslims had to purchase drinking water from him. 'Uthmān thereupon bought the Rūma well, and made it waqf. (p. 172)

[336] Muslims were thus required to be very scrupulous in the matter of other people's rights to land. (p. 173)

[337] Qarat is the same as carat, but its weight is said to be four grains, a carat being 3 1/5 gr. It is in some parts a twenty-fourth. and in others a twentieth, part of a dīnār. The word ra'ā signifies both he pastured the cattle and he ruled. Looking after the welfare of animals is thus connected with devotion to the welfare of humanity. (p. 175)

³³⁸ The direction contained in this hadīth is of a general nature and relates to all contracts, subject to the basic rule that no condition opposed to the law of Islām is valid. Bukhārī mentions this hadīth in the book entitled "Services" to show that the relation between master and servant is a contract in reality. (p. 176)

³³⁹ The hadīth relates to the Holy Prophet's flight to Madīnah, and shows, along with h. 7, that either of the contracting parties in the relation of master and servant may be a non-Muslim. (p. 176)

³⁴⁰ Service rendered, of whatever kind it might be, brought a remuneration, and it made no difference that the service was rendered in connection with the Book of Allāh. For instance, a person who taught the Holy Qur'ān was entitled to remuneration; so was a person who wrote the Holy Qur'ān or did any other service in relation to the Holy Book. (p. 176)

³⁴¹ This is part of a long hadīth, according to which three men were overtaken with a severe affliction from which God delivered them because of some good which each had done. The good in this case was that the man did nor allow the due of a labourer to lie idle, and made over to him immense wealth instead of the paltry remuneration which he demanded. (p. 177)

³⁴² This simply shows that the Holy Prophet made the best selection from among those whom he deemed to be fit for service. and would not take a man simply because he approached him while another did not. As v. 4 shows, it is not forbidden to ask for a certain service. (p. 177)

³⁴³ A public servant cannot take anything as a gift. He is entitled only to his wages. (p. 178)

³⁴⁴ The mention of a horse is followed in the hadīth by the mention of a camel and that of gold and silver and billets in similar words. The condition described here relates to the resurrection, and hence it speaks of spiritual experience in physical terms, the significance being that every dishonesty, great or small, shall ultimately be brought to light and punished. (p. 178)

³⁴⁵ The Holy Prophet did not forbid the saying of funeral prayers over the bier of a person who was in debt. By refusing to say prayers himself, he wanted only to discourage the habit of contracting debts when one had not the means to pay. According to another version of the same hadīth (B. 38:3), the Holy Prophet said funeral prayers over a person who was in debt but who had left property from which the debt could be paid. As shown further on (h. 8). the Holy Prophet himself

undertook the payment of the debts of those who died in debt later on, when the state treasury had the means to pay them. (p. 180)

[346] The significance is that Allāh grants him the means to pay it. (p. 181)

[347] To get more and more wealth becomes a passion with wealthy people, and this passion deprives them of the noblest human sentiments. Hence they are said to be the poorer. The narrator, while saying thus and thus, moved his hands right and left, to show that wealth must be given away liberally if one has the good fortune to possess it. (p. 181)

[348] Thus, if the debtor of his own free will gives more than what is due, it is not usury or interest. (p. 181)

[349] The legalization of 'irdz (honour) is the using of harsh words, and that of 'uqūbah (punishment) is imprisonment (B. 43:13). Thus it is only the rich man who can be sent to prison for refusing to pay his debt; regarding the man in straitened circumstances, the law of Islām is that recommended in H. xxii:5--the debt should be remitted. (p. 182)

[350] Kall (burden) includes both a family to maintain and debts to be paid. It is thus the Muslim state that is required to undertake both the maintenance of uncared-for families and the payment of unpaid debts. (p. 182)

[351] Hh. 9 and 10 show that the law relating to mortgage as laid down in the Holy Qur'ān (v. 2) is not limited to cases when one is journeying or when there is no scribe. The law is a general one, the only limitation being chat the property mortgaged shall be in the possession of the mortgagee. This hadīth shows that when a person has to spend money on the. thing mortgaged, he is entitled to derive benefit from it. Hence a house or land can be mortgaged subject to the condition that the possession shall be made over to the mortgagee who is entitled to live in the house or let it on hire, if he carries out the repairs, and to till the land and have the produce of it if he spends on it. (p. 182)

[352] The rules laid down in hh. 11, 12 are subject to the condition that there is no collusion. (p. 183)

[353] Parts of the verses referred to here are quoted in the heading of this chapter (vv. 3, 4). In v, 3. it is stated that Allāh has allowed trade and forbidden usury, but as intoxicants were prohibited to Muslims, the Holy Prophet made it clear, when reciting this verse, that trade in intoxicants was also prohibited. (p. 183)

354 The Arabic word which is here translated as usury is ribā (an excess or addition), and means an addition over and above the principal sum that is lent (LL), and thus includes both usury and interest. The Holy Qur'ān compares the devourers of usury to those whom the Devil has prostrated by his touch (2:275), p. 324 indicating that usury leads to selfishness of the worst type. Islām aims at a co-operative system of trade and banking so that the capitalist should share the profit as well as the loss of the borrower. The underlying idea in the prohibition of interest on money is that labour is a higher asset than money.
The hadīth quoted here condemns the payer of the usury and the scribe and the witnesses along with the usurer, because they abet the crime. (p. 183)

355 This is a prophecy relating to the present time. Material civilization has at its culmination brought about a state of things when no transaction can be carried on without payment of interest. (p. 183)

356 Barīrah was a freed slave-girl. She sent a gift to the Holy Prophet out of the charity she had received. and the Holy Prophet accepted it. (p. 185)

357 It shows that the Holy Prophet taught the exchanging of gifts. (p. 185)

358 Bukhārī relates this hadīth to show that having a witness when making a gift was a good practice. 'Amrah was the mother, and it was her son who received the gift. The Prophet disallowed this gift, making it clear that all children should be treated alike. (p. 185)

359 Asmā' was Zubair's wife. (p. 186)

360 This is the case of a gift to two (or more) persons jointly. (p. 186)

361 A gift may thus be given out of one share in undivided property. (p. 186)

362 This was a gift from a non-Muslim. (p. 186)

363 This was the case of a gift being given to a non-Muslim. (p. 187)

364 'Umrā (from 'amara, he lived) was a pre-Islamic transaction, a man's assigning to another a house for the life of the latter, so that when he died, the property reverted to the heirs of the assignor.
A similar transaction was ruqbā (from raqaba, he waited), by which a man assigned to another a house on condition that if the assignor died first, the house became the property of the assignee, and if the assignee died first, the house reverted to the assignor, as if each waited for the death of the other. Bukhārī does not speak of ruqbā which, according to the best opinion, is not allowed in Islām. With regard

to 'umrā, it is agreed that when it is expressly stated that the property shall pass to the heirs of the assignee or when no condition is laid down, it shall be a gift in all respects and shall not revert to the assignor; but when an express condition is laid down that on the death of the. assignee it shall revert to the assignor or his heirs, there are two opinions; firstly, that the transaction shall take effect in accordance with the condition laid down, as if it were a loan; and secondly, that it shall be looked upon as a gift, the condition being dealt with as illegal and unenforceable. (p. 187)

[365] The case cited in this hadīth is known as waqf (from waqafa, he stood still or stopped). The property, generally immovable, is in this case not allowed to be sold or otherwise disposed of, only the profits accruing therefrom are dedicated to charitable purposes. But as in this case the relatives are included among those who share in the profits though they may not be needy, it has become the basis for what is more particularly known as waqf 'ala-l-aulād, i.e., a waqf for the benefit of a man's children. The property is made inalienable and cannot be divided among the heirs, and the profit from it are spent for the benefit of the children, though a part must necessarily be for charitable objects. (p. 188)

[366] Jazāka-llāh (may Allāh reward thee) is the best form of thanking a man for any benefit or gift received from him, It is both an expression of thankfulness to him and a pravor for him, and it is the common form which a Muslim thanks another. (p. 188)

[367] Sa'd later rose to prominence under 'Umar as the conqueror of Persia. The incident related here took place in the 10th year of Hijrah as the mention of the Farewell pilgrimage shows. This shows conclusively that the order to make a bequest, as laid down in 2:180, was never abrogated. The hadīth further shows that the will was prescribed especially for charitable objects, and therefore only one-third of the property could be disposed of by will, so that the heirs may not be deprived altogether. (p. 191)

[368] As the shares or the heirs are fixed by the Holy Qur'ān, a will in favour of the heirs would practically be an annulment of that injunction. If, however, the heir, agreed, there would be no objection to a testator dispensing of his property in a particular manner. (p. 191)

[369] Abū Talhah had property which he wanted to devote to charitable objects. The Holy Prophet advised him to give it to his own needy relatives who were not entitled to receive anything as heirs. (p. 191)

[370] The debts take precedence because the property to which the will relates can only be ascertained after the debts are paid. (p. 191)

371 For eight years at Madīnah the Muslims and the disbelievers were divided into two camps at war with each other, and this order was probably given under these circumstances. (p. 191)

372 This is considered to be the basic rule in inheritance. The appointed portions are given in v. 3. If anything remains after that, it goes to the nearest male relative. (p. 192)

373 The application of the rule given in the first part fails in some cases. A person leaves both parents who would take one-third, two or more daughters who would take two-thirds, and a husband or wife for whom nothing remains. If all the children are treated alike, whether there are only sons or only daughters or sons and daughters, the difficulty would not arise. In the latter part of the hadīth it is stated that if there are sons and daughters, beginning p. 339 should be made with the person who inherits with them. If this rule is applied in all cases, the difficulty does not arise. Thus. if there are parents and husband or wife along with children, they will receive their shares first, one-sixth each in the case of parents and one-fourth or one-eighth in the case of husband or wife, and the remainder would go to sons or sons and daughters; but if there are daughters only, they would take one-half or two-thirds of the remainder, as the case may be. (p. 192)

374 The son's children are thus deprived if there is a son living. There is nothing related from the Holy Prophet in this respect and the companions had different opinions in matters relating to inheritance (h. 11), The opinion given by Zaid is, therefore, not final. In B. 85: 7 , it is stated that Ibn Mas'ūd gave a certain portion to the daughter of a deceased son, treating her as a second daughter. Taking this case into consideration, a deceased son's children should take the place of their father. (p. 192)

375 In this case the inheritance was given to a very remote ancestor's descendants. According to the hadīth that follows, when no other heirs could be found it was given to a freed slave. Only in extreme cases was the property made over to the State treasury (bait-al-māl), as stated in h. 14. But then the State was also made responsible for paying justly contracted unpaid debts of deceased persons. (p. 193)

376 If there is a Muslim state, it would take the place of the Holy Prophet; if not, the Muslim community would inherit from the man who has no other heir, near or distant. (p. 193)

377 The concluding portion of this hadīth relates the exact words that must be uttered when an animal is slaughtered. The condition that Allāh's name must p. 345 be mentioned over the slaughtered animal is laid down to make man realize that the taking of a life, even though it be an animal, is a serious matter, and that it is by Divine permission that man does it, not by his superior might. If a man forgets to mention the name of Allāh, the meat is still allowed (B. 72:15). (p. 196)

378 This hadīth shows that an animal may be slaughtered with any sharp instrument that makes the blood flow out. The object is that blood which contains poisons should not form part of human food. (p. 197)

379 There are two ways of slaughtering; dhabh in which the throat is cut from beneath at the part next to the head. while the animal is made to lie down under one's foot, and nahr, in which the animal is stabbed, while in a standing posture, in the nahr (the place where the wind-pipe commences in the uppermost part of the breast). The latter practice is resorted to in the case of bigger animals. such as camels and cows, on account of the difficulty of making them lie down. But an animal that may be stabbed may also be slaughtered. In both cases, it is a necessary condition that the spinal cord is not cut. If, however. the head is cut off by mistake, it does not make the meat unlawful (B. 72:24). (p. 197)

380 The view expressed here by Zuhrī is supported by Ibn 'Abbās (Ah, I, 302), who explains the word food in 5:5--The food of those who have been given the Book is lawful for you--"as meaning the animal slaughtered by them. Only if it is known for certain that a name other than that of Allāh has been invoked, would it be unlawful. (p. 198)

381 These people, as 'Ā'ishah explains, were recent converts to Islām, and therefore it was doubtful whether they observed the details of the Law. (p. 198)

382 The same rule would apply to game shot with a gun. The Bismillāh should be uttered at the time of loading the gun or when firing it. If a Muslim p. 348 forgets to mention the name of Allāh, the same rule would apply as in slaughtering. i.e., the game is allowed as food. (p. 198)

383 The reference here is to v. 6 quoted above. The ta'ām (lit. food) of the sea is distinguished from its game, and means what is found, the sea having thrown it on dry land, or what is left by the water having receded from it, for the catching of which no struggle is needed. Fish, even it caught alive, is not required to be slaughtered. Eel, frog or tortoise may be eaten, according to some. (p. 198)

384 Muslim adds, birds of prey with claw 19:2). (p. 199)

385 The Arabic word for wine is khamr, from khamara meaning he covered or veiled a thing; and wine is so called because it veils (obscures) the intellect (LL). It is not only the expressed juice of grapes when it has fermented but the intoxicating

expressed juice of anything (LL). In Arabia, at that time, wine was generally made of grapes, dates, wheat, barley and honey (B. 74: 4). Fresh juice of grapes or dates is not prohibited (B. 67:72). (p. 199)

386 Everything which intoxicates is prohibited, whether it is a drink or any other drug cannot, therefore, be used even in small quantities (p. 199)

387 An intoxicant unless, of course, it is used as a medicine to save life, for which purpose the Holy Qur'ān expressly allows the use of prohibited foods: "Whoever is driven to necessity, not desiring nor exceeding the limit, no sin shall be upon him" (2:173, 6:146). (p. 199)

388 The word used here is wudzū', but it means only the washing of hands. (p. 200)

389 Rinsing of the mouth after taking food is necessary, so that particles of food may not be left in the mouth to rot. (p. 200)

390 A Muslim is taught to start food with the mention of the name of Allāh, and to give thanks to God after having finished it. He thus feels the Divine presence when satisfying his physical desires. (p. 200)

391 The words of another hadīth (Ah, I. 309) are that the Holy Prophet forbade blowing on food and drink. (p. 200)

392 It is not forbidden to help oneself in eating with a spoon or a fork, as the Holy Prophet helped himself with a knife in this case. (p. 201)

393 These are luxuries which can be enjoyed by the rich at the expense of the poor; hence they are forbidden to a Muslim. (p. 201)

394 To make the servant sit at the same table with his master shows the extent to which the Islamic brotherhood minimizes differences of rank and wealth. (p. 202)

395 Islām thus requires even the people of a household to take their food together. (p. 202)

396 This hadīth and the one that follows relate to good manners in eating. p. 358The man who eats less than his companion should eat slowly, so that he finishes along with his companions. (p. 202)

397 Those who wear long garments, or trail the train of the garment, in order to be looked at or for vanity are censured (B. 77:4, 5), but the mere wearing of a long garment is not forbidden (B. 77:2). (p. 204)

³⁹⁸ The parts of the body which must be covered are called the 'aurah, which is thus defined: The part or parts of the body which it is indecent to expose; in a man what is between the navel and the knee, and in a free woman all the person except the face and the hands as far as the wrist" (LL).
To be naked even in private (except in case of necessity) is forbidden, as the Holy Prophet is reported to have said in answer to such a question "Allāh has a greater right than men that one should be ashamed of Him" (AD. 30: 2). (p. 205)

³⁹⁹ 'A'lām is the plural of 'alam which means an impression or a trace, and the a'lām of a garment is the ornamental or variegated border thereof (LL). The wearing of silk is prohibited for men, except for special reasons, but not for women, because men must be accustomed to lead a hard life. The wearing of khazz (a cloth woven of wool and silk) is allowed (Ah. iv, 233) (p. 205)

⁴⁰⁰ Farrūj is a garment of the kind called qabā' (a kind of tunic), having a slit in its hinder part (LL). (p. 205)

⁴⁰¹ Only the righteous among males are meant, as women are allowed to wear silk, as the above hadīth shows. (p. 205)

⁴⁰² The Holy Prophet had a ring made for him when letters were written to the neighbouring potentates in the year 6 A.H., and upon the signet of it were engraved the words Muhammad Rasūl Allāh. These three words were written as another hadīth shows, in three lines, Allāh being at the top, Rasūl in the middle and Muhammad at the bottom. (p. 206)

⁴⁰³ These hadīth show that ornaments of all kinds are allowed for women. Umm Salamah was the Holy Prophet's wife. (p. 206)

⁴⁰⁴ Superfluous hair below the navel is meant. Istihdād means shaving with a razor. (p. 206)

⁴⁰⁵ It shows that the polytheists generally shaved the beard. (p. 207)

⁴⁰⁶ This hadīth shows that the Holy Prophet wore his hair in different ways at different times, and he never forbade a particular way of wearing one's hair. Sadl (or the Christian way of wearing one's hair) was leaving a lock of hair on the forehead, while farq (or the Arab way) was letting down of the hair on the two sides with a line between them. The Holy Prophet did it in both ways at different times. Another hadīth speaks of the dhawā'ib (tuft of hair on the forehead) of Ibn 'Abbās (B. 77: 71.) (p. 207)

⁴⁰⁷ These hadīth show that the Holy Prophet was careful about his toilet. (p. 207)

⁴⁰⁸ 'Sūrah means an image or a picture. According to another version (B. 59: 7), the Holy Prophet is reported to have said that "Angels do not enter a house in which is a dog or a sūrah." But the Holy Qur'ān allows the keeping of dogs for hunting (5: 4), and so does Hadīth (H. xxviii:8); and the keeping of watchdogs is also allowed. Similarly, the Holy Qur'ān speaks of tamāthīl (images) being made for Solomon, and it would not be right to say that angels did not on this account come into the house of Solomon, a prophet of God. The hadīth, therefore, which speaks of angels not visiting a place where images (or pictures) and dogs are to be found cannot be accepted in a literal sense. It is for this reason that an authority like Rāghib interprets the word bait (house) occurring p. 368 in this Hadīth as meaning the heart, the significance being that the man in whose heart images or idols have a place, and who bows before them, does not receive the angels of Divine mercy. The concluding words of this hadīth, making an exception in favour of raqm fi-l-thaub--(figures on a cloth)--and the same would be the case with regard to figures on a paper--confirm the conclusion arrived at above. What is forbidden is the keeping of images or pictures for paying them Divine honours. (p. 208)

⁴⁰⁹ As made clear in the previous note, only such people could be threatened with punishment as made images for worship. (p. 208)

⁴¹⁰ It may be due simply to his love for simplicity and hatred of decorations, This is made clear in the next hadīth which states that the Holy Prophet disliked a figured curtain on the door of his daughter Fātimah, and asked her to send the same to people who stood in need of it. It did not mean that he prohibited the use of decorated or figured cloth; otherwise he would not have sent the same to others. Perhaps he only wanted his daughter to live a simple life like himself. (p. 208)

⁴¹¹ This hadīth gives the highest place of honour to woman. (p. 213)

⁴¹² The word rahim means the womb, hence relationship by the female side; but it also carries the wider significance of relationship in general; and Rahmān means the God of mercy or the Beneficent God. The hadīth signifies that relationship is deeply connected with mercy in its very nature. So whoever makes close ties of relationship by kindness to relatives God is kind to him, and whoever severs the ties of relationship by ill-treatment towards relatives God is displeased with him. One must be kind to relatives though they be non-Muslims (B. 11:7). (p. 214)

⁴¹³ These memorable words, making inviolable the blood, property and honour of one Muslim to another, wore uttered on the sacred day of Sacrifices, in the sacred month of Dhu-l-Hijjah, in the sacred city of Makkah. (p. 216)

⁴¹⁴ The Holy Prophet thus emphasized that one member of the Muslim brotherhood should not call another fāsiq (transgressor), or kāfir (disbeliever). The man who did this deserved to have the very epithet applied to him by way of punishment. (p. 217)

⁴¹⁵ The sending of gifts to neighbours is recommended (H xxvi:1). Ihrām al dzaif (honouring the guest) is specially enjoined on Muslims In another hadīth, p. 383 it is stated that special food should be prepared for the guest for one day and night-- this is called his ja'izah, while entertainment of the guest, his dziyāfah, lasts for three days. What is spent on the guest after that is termed sadaqah or charity. (p. 217)

⁴¹⁶ The hadīth speaks of slaves, but the words are equally applicable to servants, specially the concluding portion. (p. 218)

⁴¹⁷ The Holy Prophet pointed with his two fingers which are close to each other, meaning that the man who brings up an orphan will be with him in paradise. (p. 219)

⁴¹⁸ The Holy Prophet thus refused to pray for the punishment of even those who disobeyed and he prayed for their guidance. (p. 219)

⁴¹⁹ The Muslim salutation al-salāmu 'alai kum means peace be to you. The Jews mischievously corrupted it into as-sāmu 'alai-kum which means death overtake you. The Holy Prophet did not allow discourtesy even to such enemies. (p. 219)

⁴²⁰ Thus a Muslim is required to be merciful to all men, whether they are Muslims or non-Muslims. (p. 219)

⁴²¹ The meaning is, may he be frequent in prostrating himself. (p. 220)

⁴²² The words of the Muslim salutation are al-salāmu 'alai-kum and the salutation is generally returned by saying wa 'alai-kum-us-salām (peace be with you). To this are sometimes added the words wa rahmat-ullāhi wa barakātuh (and the mercy of Allāh and His blessings). Salutation is offered by men to women and vice versa (B. 79:16). (p. 220)

⁴²³ This is called musāfahah (from safh meaning side), the two men joining their hands as a mark of love. (p. 221)

⁴²⁴ 'Zaid was a slave whom the Holy Prophet had set free, and on account of his deep attachment to the Holy Prophet, he was called his son. (p. 221)

⁴²⁵ This is called mu'ānaqah (from 'unuq meaning neck). Some ḥadīth show that the Holy Prophet disallowed it, but he may have done this simply to show that it should not be generally resorted to. (p. 221)

⁴²⁶ We find women in the Holy Prophet's time repairing unveiled to mosques to join the congregational prayers (B. 10:162), carrying provisions for soldiers (B. 56:66), taking care of the sick and the wounded (B. 56:67), taking part in actual fighting when necessary (B. 56:62), helping their husbands in the labour of the field (B. 67:108), serving the male guests at a feast (B. 67:78), carrying on business (B. 1154) carrying on trade with men (B. 34:67), and so on. (p. 222)

⁴²⁷ A woman is not required to cover her face or wear a veil. In fact, in pilgrimage she is required to keep herself unveiled (B. 25:23), because the veil was worn as a mark of rank, and was not required by the law of Islām. (p. 222)

⁴²⁸ The Arabic word rā' (from ra'y, pasturing cattle) means a keeper, guarder, ruler or governor. Imām means a leader, and the king is also called an imām. The king or ruler is here placed in the same category as a servant. Just as a servant is entrusted with certain property for which he is responsible to the master, the king or the ruler is entrusted with the care of the people and the guarding of their rights; and for the proper discharge of his duties. He is responsible in the first place to God Who is the real Master, and then to the people in relation to whom he occupies the position of a servant. Hereditary kingship is therefore foreign to the Islamic conception of the State. (p. 224)

⁴²⁹ Thus even a Negro, if he is fit for the job, may be placed in authority over people of a white race; considerations of race and colour carry no weight Islām. According to another version, the words are a Negro slave (M. 17), so that even a slave may be entrusted with command. (p. 225)

⁴³⁰ Law is above all, even above the king or supreme authority; an order against the Holy Qur'ān and authoritative ḥadīth cannot therefore be accepted. (p. 225)

⁴³¹ Amīr literally means one who holds command, and the word is applied to any person who is entrusted with any kind of authority over others. The highest ruling authority in Islām was called Amīr al-Mu'minīn (Commander of the Faithful). The amīr or the imām is here called junnah, or an armour for protection, because without the institution of imārah, or subjection to authority, a people cannot protect themselves either from an enemy or from one another's injustice. (p. 225)

⁴³² These are the concluding words of the ḥadīth, according to which the amīr appointed over a small force required those under him to enter fire. but they refused to obey him. The Holy Prophet approved of their action, and added the

words quoted here. According to another hadīth (B. 64: 60), when Khālid, who was appointed commander of a small force, ordered certain prisoners of war to be put to death, Ibn 'Umar and others refused to kill as the order was against the clear teachings of the Holy Qur'ān; and the Holy Prophet approved of their action. So an order should be disobeyed when it is against the clear precepts of the Law. (p. 226)

[433] Conclusive evidence is afforded by this hadīth that the Islamic State was a democracy in which the head was chosen by the people themselves. Abū Bakr was admittedly the best among the companions and the fittest man to be the head of the State and to control its affairs. as this hadīth and the one that follows show. The Ansār were at first under the impression that there could be two amīrs or two heads of the State, but they were ultimately convinced that this position was untenable, and there was an agreement on the point that the State must have a single head, with ministers and counsellors to help him. Wazīr (from wizr, burden) means an aider or helper, and hence a king's minister. 'Umar's election as the head of the State after Abū Bakr was made in a different way. Before his death Abū Bakr consulted the leading men of the Muslims community, and nominated as his successor 'Umar, who during his own caliphate had acted as his right-hand man, and who was, admittedly the most outstanding personality in Islām after Abū Bakr. 'Umar. on his death-bed, adopted yet a third course by appointing an elective council. There were then six eminent men, every one of whom was fit to hold the reins of government, and 'Umar decided that these six should choose one from among themselves as the amīr, and the mantle fell upon 'Uthmān. There were some differences when 'Uthmān died, but the majority favoured 'Ali who was the fourth head of the Islamic State after the Holy Prophet. In all four cases, election was the basic principle in appointing the head of the State, though different methods were adopted to avoid dissensions. (p. 227)

[434] By Light is meant the Holy Qur'ān, the basis of the Islamic law, to which even the head of the State was subject. Abū Bakr is called the "Second of the two" because during the Flight he was in the cave with the Holy Prophet. (p. 227)

[435] The head of the State was thus paid a fixed salary from the public treasury, like all other public servants. (p. 228)

[436] Officers of government are, thus required to manage the affairs of the public for the good of the public. (p. 228)

[437] A governor was thus required to lead the life of an ordinary Muslim citizen. That there is a direction not to ride any but a horse of Arabian breed shows that governors were required to be good horsemen as well. The ruling authorities were further required to be easily accessible to the public. The Holy Prophet himself set

an example in this respect as he had no door-keepers even after he became ruler of Arabia (B. 23:31). (p. 229)

[438] Selflessness was thus the first requisite of those who were entrusted with rule. (p. 229)

[439] 'Umar apparently was thinking of making the State responsible for the maintenance of widows He had already introduced old-age pensions and made arrangements for the grant of allowances to the weak and the disabled. (p. 229)

[440] The conditions under which the urban and the rural populations lived were different, and 'Umar was therefore anxious that the Muslim State should have regard for the welfare of both. People were to be taxed with their assent, which shows that the State worked on purely democratic principles. (p. 229)

[441] The non-Muslims living in a Muslim state were known as ahl al dhimmah or dhimmīs, dhimmah meaning a covenant. Here they are spoken of as being under the protection of Allāh and the protection of Allāh's Messenger, and the sacredness of their right is thus enhanced. They enjoyed freedom to the same extent as the Muslim subjects of a Muslim state, and had the additional advantage of being free from military service on payment of a small tax. which was by all means a smaller burden than zakāt which Muslims were required to my in addition to their liability to military service, being required to fight in the defence of Islām as well as non-Muslims. (p. 230)

www.ingramcontent.com/pod-product-compliance
Lightning Source LLC
Chambersburg PA
CBHW071659160426
43195CB00012B/1513